AGRICULTURAL IMPLEMENTS
OF THE ROMAN WORLD

FOR

JOHN CROOK

AGRICULTURAL IMPLEMENTS OF THE ROMAN WORLD

BY

K.D.WHITE

Reader in Classics, University of Reading

CAMBRIDGE

AT THE UNIVERSITY PRESS

1967

Published by the Syndics of the Cambridge University Press
Bentley House, 200 Euston Road, London, N.W. 1
American Branch: 32 East 57th Street, New York, N.Y. 10022

Library of Congress Catalogue Card Number: 67–10350

Printed in Great Britain
at the University Printing House, Cambridge
(Brooke Crutchley, University Printer)

CONTENTS

CONTENTS

CATALOGUE RAISONNÉ OF ALL IMPLEMENTS ILLUSTRATED IN THE TEXT

The plates will be found between pp. 192 and 193

NOTES ON THE PLATES

1. Miniature from a French manuscript of the fourteenth century, now in the British Museum, London. The work is entitled *Libre des propriétés des choses*, and is a French translation of Bartolomeo de Granville, *De Proprietatibus Rerum*.

Centre background, a walled medieval town with a twin-towered entrance gate. To left, an orchard with fruit pickers. To right, a workman chopping, stacking and bundling wood. Right foreground, a stand of ripe grain, and a reaper about to commence operations. In his left hand, a hook with a long straight shaft for gathering in the sheaves before cutting (the hook is obscured by a tree). In his right hand, a short-handled scythe (see p. 102). In the extreme right foreground another labourer, kneeling, sharpens a heavy sickle of semicircular shape with a hammer.

2(*a*) Large square digging-spade from Campania, now in the National Museum, Naples (inv. no. 71749). The type is very rare, and was probably used for trenching operations in heavy wet ground. Unlike its northern counterpart, it is oversquare, the width of the blade exceeding the depth by 7 cm.

Dimensions: 31 cm deep (47 cm including the iron socket); 38 cm wide.

(*b*) Iron single-bladed digging-hoe (*sarculum simplex*) from the villa of Herennius Florus at Boscoreale, near Pompeii, Central Italy. Now in the Museum of Natural History, Chicago, U.S.A. (cat. no. 26151). For operations performed with this implement see pp. 45 f.

Dimensions: depth of blade 18·5 cm; breadth at top 18·5–19 cm.

(*c*) Iron single-bladed digging-hoe (*sarculum simplex*) from Etruria, now in the Archaeological Museum, Florence (inv. no. 10752). Almost identical in design with the Italian 'zappetta da cavatore' (Fig. 25, p. 47). For cultivating in vineyards and orchards.

Dimensions: depth of blade, 18·5 cm; width at bottom, 8·5 cm; maximum width, 12 cm.

(*d*) Iron single-bladed digging-hoe (*sarculum simplex*), with pear-shaped blade, from Boscoreale, now in the Natural History Museum, Chicago (inv. no. 26154). Much worn on the right side of the blade.

Dimensions: depth of blade, 13 cm; width, 9·9 cm.

3. *Digging with the bidens.* Part of a mosaic pavement from the north-east portico of the Great Palace of the Emperors, Istanbul, Turkey. From *The Great Palace of the Emperors*, 2nd report, ed. by D. Talbot Rice (Edinburgh, 1958), pl. 47.

Two labourers digging with heavy, long-handled *bidentes*. They are digging in échelon, as is still customary practice in breaking ground with the spade or the hoe. The nearer of the two diggers leans forward as he completes the stroke, while his companion has swung his hoe above his head and is bending forward to make the downstroke. Only the lower part of the handle of his implement is preserved. Both labourers are wearing leggings to protect them from thorns. For the design of the *bidens* see pp. 49 ff.

4. Winter operations in the vineyard: *ablaqueatio* (échausselage) and *sarritio* (sarclage).

Part of a large mosaic pavement discovered at Cherchel, Algeria, in April 1925. J. Bérard, 'Mosaïques inédites de Cherchel', *MEFR*, LII (1935), pl. III and pp. 113 ff. The largest surviving panel is 3·60 × 5·50 m. and consists of four superimposed layers, the third and fourth of which depict work in the vineyard.

Ablaqueatio (échausselage). The scene is a trellised vineyard (*pergula*—Palladius 3. 13. 5) in winter (the vines are quite bare). In the third register three labourers, armed with two-pronged drag-hoes (*bidentes*) are breaking up the soil around the vines. Each is shown in a different phase of the stroke, the first has just struck the clod, the second has almost finished his stroke, while the third is at the top of his swing (his *bidens* can be seen close to the top of the trellis). The vines are trained on strong multiple stakes with single cross-members.

Sarritio (sarclage). In the centre, two large vines with spiralling branches which, unlike those of 8 (*a*), are self-supporting (Columella, *De Arb.* 4. 1). There are two similar vines to the right, much mutilated. In front a labourer plies his *bidens* vigorously under the eye of a supervisor. The latter, stick in hand, is propped against a vinestock, and seems from his attitude to be reprimanding the labourer for poor work done on the left-hand vine. To the right, another labourer at the same task, his body turned away from the scene in the centre.

5(*a*) Heavy iron drag-hoe (*rastrum*) with five tines closely spaced, from Etruria, now in the Archaeological Museum, Florence (inv. no. 10779). For the various uses of these implements see p. 55.

Dimensions: width at top, 15 cm; length of centre tine, 12 cm; maximum depth of bar, 5 cm; gap between tines, 2·4 cm; approximate width of socket, 4 cm.

(*b*) Six-pronged iron drag-hoe (*rastrum*) from Boscoreale, now in the Natural History Museum, Chicago (inv. no. 26159). The teeth are much more widely spaced than those of 5 (*a*), and the bar is much lighter. On the uses of the implement see p. 55.

Dimensions: 30 cm at top; length of longest tine, 17·4 cm; gap between tines, 4 cm.

6(*a*) Heavy plain woodman's axe (*securis simplex*) used for tree felling; from Campania, now in the National Museum, Naples (not inventoried). The design has remained virtually unchanged down to the present day. On the uses of the implement see pp. 60 f.

Dimensions: length, 23·5 cm; maximum width, 16 cm; width at socket, 5·4 cm.

(*b*) Plain woodman's axe (lighter than 6 (*a*)) from Boscoreale, now in the Natural History Museum, Chicago (inv. no. 26157).

Dimensions: length, 19 cm; maximum width, 9·6 cm; width at socket, 2 cm.

(*c*) Iron hatchet (*dolabra*) with plain hammer back, from Campania, now in the National Museum, Naples (not inventoried). On the uses of the implement see pp. 60 f.

Dimensions: length of blade, 21·5 cm; width of cutting edge, 5·4 cm; width at socket, 2·7 cm.

(*d*) Iron adze-axe (*securis dolabrata*) from Boscoreale, now in the Museum of Natural History, Chicago (inv. no. 26156).

Dimensions: overall length, 32·8 cm; width of axe-blade, 7 cm. On the uses of these double implements see p. 61.

7(*a*) Bronze tanged sickle (*falx messoria*), of typical open shape, from Campania, now in the National Museum, Naples (inv. no. 21659).

Dimensions: length of arc, 50 cm; average width of blade, 5 cm.

(*b*) Iron tanged sickle (*falx messoria*), of open shape, from Boscoreale, now in the Museum of Natural History, Chicago (inv. no. 26164).

Dimensions: length of arc, 48 cm; average width of blade, 5 cm.

8(*a*) Iron gardening fork (*furca ferrea*) from Boscoreale, now in the Natural History Museum, Chicago (inv. no. 26160). On the identification of this implement see pp. 107 f.

Dimensions: length (including socket), 41 cm; length of tines, 14·2 cm; gap between tines, 4·5 cm.

(*b*) Heavy iron tree-pruning billhook (*falx arboraria*) with right-angled hook, from Boscoreale, now in the Natural History Museum, Chicago (inv. no. 26162).

Dimensions: length, 23 cm; width across angle, 7 cm; length of hook, 9·5 cm.

(*c*) Tanged billhook, broad-bladed, with short hook, found at Villa de la Semois, Étalle, South Belgium. Now in the Musée gaumais, Virton.

Dimensions: length, 38 cm; length of tang, 18 cm; maximum width of blade, 7 cm. On the uses of this implement see p. 87.

(*d*) Iron gardening fork with rounded tines and heavy socket, perhaps fitted with a short handle for working in seed-beds (see p. 107). From Boscoreale, now in the Museum of Natural History, Chicago (inv. no. 26160).

Dimensions: length to end of socket, 28·8 cm; gap between tines, 5 cm; length of tines, 18 cm; width of tines, 3·6 cm.

9(*a*) Scythe-blade of unusually great length, with heavy flange, and sharp backward curvature towards the heel. One of thirteen identical specimens from a large hoard of Romano-British implements found at Great Chesterford, near Cambridge, England, in 1854. R. C. Neville, *Arch. Journ.* XIII, 1 (March 1856), 7–13. On the problems connected with these implements see Appendix E(3).

Dimensions: length of span, 151 cm; length of chord, 120·5 cm; length of tang, 21·5 cm; length of spike, 1·2 cm.

(*b*) Long-handled bronze brush-hook (*falcastrum*=*runco*), with open crescent-shaped blade and long socket, from Campania. Now in the National Museum, Naples (inv. no. 112242). On the design and use of this implement see pp. 91 ff.

Dimensions: chord, 27 cm; average width, 4·5 cm; length of tang, 22 cm.

(*c*) Heel of an exact reconstruction of the scythe shown in Plate 9(*a*).

10(*a*) Large votive model of a body-ard from Telamon, Etruria, now in the Archaeological Museum, Florence (inv. no. 70940). A. S. F. Gow, 'The ancient plough', *JHS*, XXXIV (1914), pl. XX (*c*); Haudricourt–Delamarre, pl. III, 10, and pp. 82, 270. See p. 142.

(*b*) Bronze votive model of a beam-ard with 'arrow-head' foreshare and ground-wrests, from Cologne, now in the Römisch-Germanisches Zentralmuseum, Mainz, West Germany (inv. no. 29898). W. Haberey in *Bonn. Jahrb.* CLIX (1949), 94 ff.; W. H. Manning, 'The plough in Roman Britain', *JRS*, LIV (1964), pl. VIII, 1; Haudricourt–Delamarre, p. 81, fig. 16, and p. 82. See p. 143.

11(*a*) Bronze votive model of a keeled beam-ard with ground-wrests from Sussex, now in the British Museum (inv. no. 54.12.27.76). W. H. Manning, 'The plough in Roman Britain', *JRS*, LIV (1964), p. 56, fig. 4 (A).

(*b*) Bronze model of a ploughing team and ploughman, from Pierce-bridge, Co. Durham, England, now in the British Museum, London. W. H. Manning, *art. cit.* p. 56, fig. 4 (B). See p. 143.

12. Ploughing operations in an olive-grove. The topmost layer of the large mosaic pavement from Cherchel, Algeria (see Plate 4 above).

Ploughing and clod-breaking. In the foreground to right, a plough drawn by a pair of high-spirited bulls; behind, the ploughman leans

forward over the plough, pressing down with his full weight on the handle; in front of the bulls, a second labourer armed with a stout stick is engaged in smashing the clods thrown up in the previous furrow. In the background, a row of olive trees. On the design of the plough see p. 138.

Sowing and ploughing in the seed. To the left, against a similar background to that above, another plough-team, preceded by a sower; the operation depicted is evidently that of ploughing in the seed. Note the size and depth of the seed-basket.

13. Seasonal operations. Two of the sculptured panels from the central soffit of the arch known as the Porte de Mars at Reims, north-east France.

Haymaking. Of the seven surviving panels representing seven of the twelve seasons of the year, that for July represents a harvesting scene, almost certainly the operation of cutting hay with implements mid-way in design between the sickle and the scythe. Three labourers are represented in the tableau; to the left, a labourer resting on the handle of his implement; centre, another labourer sharpening his implement with a honing-stone; to his right, a third labourer in the act of cutting, employing both hands, and using a sweeping action. For a full discussion on the implement see Appendix E (4), pp. 209 f.

Reaping with the *vallus*. The tableau for August, in spite of inaccuracies in the drawing (see p. 162), evidently represents a *vallus* or heading-machine for grain. Bence's drawing shows, to left, a man walking to the left, but turning round towards the frame of the machine, which he is cleaning with a stick; behind the toothed frame may be seen the left-hand wheel of the machine, incorrectly angled in the drawing, and the head, neck and forequarters of a mule or donkey, walking to the left.

A. de Laborde, *Les monuments de la France* (Paris, 1816), pl. CXIII (reproducing the drawings made earlier by H. Bence).

14. The Arlon *vallus*. Right-hand portion of a mutilated relief panel, depicting a *vallus* or heading-machine in motion. In spite of the damaged surface, the narrow shafts, the steersman, and part of the hindquarters of the animal are clearly visible. Found at Arlon (*Orolaunum vicus*), South Belgium, in 1854. Now in Museum, Arlon. E. Espérandieu, *Gaule*, t. v, no. 4037.

15. The Buzenol *vallus*. Part of a scene from farming life, depicted on the face of a sculptured slab found embedded in a terrace wall constructed in the late imperial period as additional fortification to the Gallo-Roman stronghold of Montauban-Buzenol, in the Luxemburg province of Belgium, close to the border.

Size of slab, 38 × 52 cm; depth of field, 3 cm.

For a full account of the scene see pp. 162 ff. J. Mertens, 'Sculptures romaines de Buzenol', *Le pays gaumais*, XIX (1958), pls. XIV, XV, and pp. 31–2.

16. The Trier *vallus*. Central portion of a mutilated relief panel depicting a *vallus* or heading-machine. Only the right-hand wheel, part of the container, and the head and forequarters of the animal have survived. Found at Trier, West Germany, in 1890. First identified as part of a *vallus* by H. Cüppers, *Trierer Zeitschr.* XXVII (1964), 151 ff.

We should like to thank the following for permission to reproduce illustrations:

The Trustees of the British Museum: Plates 1, 11 (*a*), 11 (*b*), 13.

Soprintendenza alle Antichità delle Province di Napoli e Caserta: Plates 2(*a*), 6(*a*), 6(*c*), 7(*a*), 9(*b*).

The Natural History Museum, Chicago, U.S.A.: Plates 2 (*b*), 2 (*d*), 5 (*b*), 6(*b*), 6(*d*), 7(*b*), 8(*a*), 8(*c*), 8(*d*).

Soprintendenza alle Antichità d'Etruria: Plates 2 (*c*), 5 (*a*), 10 (*a*).

Edinburgh University Press: Plate 3.

The Museum of Archaeology and Ethnology, Cambridge: Plate 9(*a*).

Römisch-Germanisches Zentralmuseum, Mainz: Plate 10 (*a*).

A.C.L. Bruxelles: Plates 14 and 15.

Rheinisches Landesmuseum, Trier: Plate 16.

PREFACE

My obligations to colleagues and former colleagues, as well as to scholars, scientists and technical experts in many different fields, are very great. In particular, I wish to acknowledge with a deep sense of gratitude the assistance of the following: Professor L. A. Thompson, of the University of Ibadan, who undertook the major task of drawing the implements from which, with one or two exceptions, the text-figures have been made; Mr H. J. Hopfen, of the Agricultural Engineering Branch of the Food and Agricultural Organization of the United Nations in Rome, who placed at my disposal his knowledge of agricultural implements and techniques in many parts of the world; Mr John Beckwith, Keeper in the Department of Architecture and Sculpture at the Victoria and Albert Museum, London, who helped me greatly in the task of tracking down archaeological material; Dr Joseph Mertens, of the University of Louvain, who not only supplied me with numerous photographs and offprints, but personally conducted me to the site of the Buzenol discoveries; Professor Gianfranco Tibiletti and the staff of the Istituto di Storia Antica at Pavia, for much bibliographical help; the Director and Staff of the Institute of Classical Studies, London, for generous help, especially in moments of crisis; Mr Andrew Jewell and his colleagues at the Museum of English Rural Life at Reading, for initiating me into the mechanics of ploughing and other complex agricultural operations; Mr Harry Caswell, of the Institute of Agricultural Research at Samaru, Northern Nigeria, for much assistance on technical problems; and Professor Sir Roger Mynors, Merton Professor of Latin at Oxford, who has been a constant source of encouragement. Dr Mary Smallwood, Reader in Classics at the University of Belfast, read the whole work in typescript, and did much to regularize and clarify the text; and Mr Nicholas Montagu, of the Department of Philosophy at the University of Reading, read the first proofs. To all these, and to the Syndics of the Cambridge University Press for undertaking the publication of a complicated and difficult text, I wish to express my sincere gratitude. Part of my debt to my friend Mr John Crook, Fellow of St John's College, Cambridge, is acknowledged on another page.

K.D.W.

LIST OF ABBREVIATIONS

The abbreviation of references to Greek and Roman authorities follows the usual conventions. The list that follows includes those that will be, and some that may be, unfamiliar to readers.

Arch. Journ.	*Archaeological Journal*
Billiard, *L'Agriculture*	R. Billiard, *L'Agriculture dans l'antiquité d'après les Géorgiques de Virgile*, Paris, 1928
Billiard, *La Vigne*	R. Billiard, *La Vigne dans l'antiquité*, Lyon, 1913
Blümlein, *Bilder*	C. Blümlein, *Bilder aus dem Römisch-Germanischen Kulturleben*, München–Berlin, 1926
Bonn. Jahrb.	*Bonner Jahrbücher*
Bruno, *Apporti*	M. G. Bruno, *Apporti delle Glosse alla conoscenza del lessico agricolo latino, Rend. Ist. Lomb.* XCIII (1959), 115–54
Bruno, *Lessico*	M. G. Bruno, *Il lessico agricolo latino e le sue continuazioni romanze, Rend. Ist. Lomb.* XCI (1957), 381–406, 921–1035
Cichorius, *Traianssäule*	C. Cichorius, *Die Reliefs der Traianssäule*, Berlin, 1896–1900
CIL	*Corpus Inscriptionum Latinarum*
Corp. Gloss.	*Corpus Glossariorum Latinorum*, ed. G. Goetz, Leipzig, 1888–1923
Daremberg–Saglio	Ch. Daremberg and E. Saglio, *Dictionnaire des antiquités grecques et romaines*, Paris, 1877–1919
Del Pelo Pardi, *Attrezzi*	G. del Pelo Pardi, *Gli attrezzi da taglio per uso agricolo in Italia*, Nuovi Annali dell'Agricoltura, Roma, 1933
Ernout–Meillet	A. Ernout and A. Meillet, *Dictionnaire étymologique de la langue latine*, 4th ed. Paris, 1959
ESAR	*Economic Survey of Ancient Rome*, ed. T. Frank, Baltimore, 1933–40
Espérandieu, *Gaule*	E. Espérandieu, *Recueil général des bas-reliefs, statues et bustes de la Gaule romaine*, Paris, 1907–29
Field Mus. Nat. Hist. Anthr.	Field Museum of Natural History and Anthropology (now the Museum of Natural History), Chicago, Ill., U.S.A.
Gaz. Arch.	*Gazette Archéologique*
HT	*A History of Technology*, ed. C. Singer and others, Oxford, 1957
Hanfmann, *Season Sarcophagus*	G. M. A. Hanfmann, *The Season Sarcophagus in Dumbarton Oaks*, Dumbarton Oaks Studies II, vol. II, Cambridge, Mass.
Haudricourt–Delamarre	A. G. Haudricourt and M. J.-B. Delamarre, *L'Homme et la charrue à travers le monde*, 3rd ed. Paris, 1955

Hopfen, *FIATR*	H. J. Hopfen, *Farm Implements for Arid and Tropical Regions*, Rome, 1960
Jaberg–Jud	C. Jaberg and J. Jud, *Sprach- und Sachatlas Italiens und der Südschweiz*, Zürich, 1928–40
Jope, *HT*	E. M. Jope, 'Agricultural Implements' in *A History of Technology*, ed. C. Singer and others, Oxford, 1957
JHS	*Journal of Hellenic Studies*
JRS	*Journal of Roman Studies*
Kolendo	J. Kolendo, 'La moissonneuse antique en Gaule romaine', *Annales: économies, sociétés, civilisations*, xv (1960), 1099–114
Le Gall	J. le Gall, 'Les "falces" et la "faux"', Ét. d'arch. class. II à la mém. de M. Launey, *Annales de l'Est*, mém. 22 (1959), 4, 44–72
Leser, *Entstehung*	P. Leser, *Die Entstehung und Verbreitung des Pfluges*, Münster i. Westphal., 1951
LS	C. T. Lewis and C. Short, *A Latin Dictionary*, Oxford, 1880
LSJ	H. G. Liddell and R. Scott, *A Greek–English Lexicon*, 9th ed., ed. by H. Stuart Jones, Oxford, 1940
MEFR	*École française de Rome, mélanges d'archéologie et d'histoire*
Meyer-Lübke	W. Meyer-Lübke, *Romanisches etymologisches Wörterbuch*, 3rd edition, Heidelberg, 1935
Not. degli Scavi	*Notizie degli scavi di antichità*
OED	*Oxford English Dictionary*
Petrie, *TW*	Sir W. M. Flinders Petrie, *Tools and Weapons*, London, 1917
Prêcheur-Canonge	Th. Prêcheur-Canonge, 'Inventaire des mosaïques romaines d'Afrique du nord' in *La vie rurale de l'Afrique romaine*, Publ. de l'Univ. de Tunis, Paris, n.d. (1962)
Proc. Soc. Ant. Scot.	*Proceedings of the Society of Antiquaries of Scotland*
R-E	A. Pauly, C. Wissowa and W. Kroll, *Realencyclopädie der classischen Altertumswissenschaft*, Stuttgart, 1894–
REA	*Revue des études anciennes*
REL	*Revue des études latines*
Reinach, *Cat. Ill.*	S. Reinach, *Catalogue illustré du musée des antiquités nationales de St-Germain-en-Laye*, Paris, 1923
Renard	M. Renard, 'Technique et agriculture en pays trévire et rémois, *Latomus*, XVIII (1959), 77–109, 307–33
Rend. Ist. Lomb.	*Rendiconti dell'Istituto Lombardo*
Rich, *Dict. Ant.*	A. Rich, *A Dictionary of Greek and Roman Antiquities*, 4th ed., London, 1874
Rostovtzeff, *SEHRE*[2]	M. Rostovtzeff, *A Social and Economic History of the Roman Empire*, 2nd ed., ed. by P. M. Fraser, Oxford, 1957
Savastano, *Arboricoltura*	A. Savastano, *Arboricoltura*, Napoli, 1914
Steensberg	A. Steensberg, *Ancient Harvesting Implements*, transl. by W. E. Calvert, Copenhagen, 1943

Stern, *Calendrier*	H. Stern, *Le Calendrier de 354: étude sur son texte et ses illustrations*, Paris, 1953
Thielscher, *Belehrung*	H. Thielscher, *Des Marcus Catos Belehrung über die Landwirtschaft*, Berlin, 1963
Trierer Zeitschr.	*Trierer Zeitschrift*
Walde–Hofmann	A. Walde, *Lateinisches etymologisches Wörterbuch*, 3rd ed., revised by J. B. Hofmann, Heidelberg, 1938

INTRODUCTION

A liberated slave named Gaius Furius Chresimus was very unpopular because he obtained much more bountiful crops from a rather modest farm than his neighbours did from their very large estates, and it was thought that he was using magic spells to entice away other people's crops. He was therefore indicted by the curule aedile Spurius Albinus; and, fearing that he would be found guilty when the time came for the tribes to return their verdict, he brought into court all his agricultural implements, and led in his farm servants, sturdy people, all well-clad and well cared-for. He brought in iron tools of excellent workmanship, heavy mattocks, ponderous ploughshares, and well-fed oxen. 'These, citizens,' he said, 'are my magic spells; I cannot show you or produce to you in court my midnight toil, my early risings and my sweat.' This caused him to be acquitted by a unanimous verdict. (Pliny, *NH* 18. 41–3)

1. SCOPE OF THE ENQUIRY

Throughout Roman history, a very large percentage of the population was engaged in some branch of agriculture. The earliest evidence we have concerning early settlement in and around Rome points to a fairly large population, most of whom were engaged in subsistence farming on small plots of ground. The predominant features of soil and climate in this region, and the size of farm units, tended to promote the growth of an intensive smallholding farm economy, such as may still be found in many parts of Italy today. The variety of crops, the limited size of farm units, and the need to maximize productivity have combined to spur on the husbandman to conserve the precious topsoil, to replenish its fertility, and to work with speed and ingenuity in face of a climate that is more than ordinarily capricious. The careful tillage required by this type of farming has resulted in the development of a range of digging and cultivating tools, each adapted to meet regional or local requirements. In many spheres of ancient economic activity, for example in mining and metallurgy, in engineering and in industry, we are hampered in our enquiries by lack of adequate technical information in the literary sources; and the investigator is obliged to rely largely on archaeological evidence.[1] In agriculture, however, the case is different; for we possess a valuable collection of literary sources from which we can obtain much detailed information on the tools employed in, and the techniques applied to, many different farming operations; in the case of viticulture in particular, there

[1] See, for example, F. M. de Robertis, 'Sulla considerazione sociale del lavoro nel mondo Romano', in *Problemi economici dall'antichità ad oggi* (Milan, 1959), pp. 54–70.

is an abundance of information on all the complex and varied techniques employed. This should occasion no surprise: for agriculture enjoyed a position of unchallenged eminence. Thus on the basis of the surviving texts, supported and illustrated by the monumental evidence, together with that of surviving implements, it is possible to present a full account of agricultural activity in all its variety. Nor is our information seriously limited either in time or place; our major literary sources cover a span of more than five centuries, and although there are large gaps in the record, phases of progress and of decline can be assessed; and while Italy occupies a pre-eminent place, the agricultural history of some at least of the provinces can be pieced together.

In working through the Roman authorities for details of agricultural operations I have frequently run into difficulties of interpretation. Many of these difficulties are due to lack of precision in the translation of Latin terms for implements and operations in lexica, dictionaries of antiquities and the commentaries on the ancient texts. Since a knowledge of the precise function of an implement is often critical for a full understanding of the technique in question, I have compiled the following monograph, in which I have attempted to clear up a number of these problems.

The volume of material to be dealt with is considerable: M. G. Bruno[1] has provided a list of sixty verbs employed in the texts to describe various agricultural operations, and of sixty implements or parts of implements. Correlation of the literary evidence with surviving examples of implements is by no means easy, for the following reasons:

(*a*) Very few of the implements referred to by the writers are described in sufficient detail to enable one to reconstruct the essentials of shape and design (a notable exception is the clear description of the complex form and varied functions of the *falx vinitoria* given by Columella (4. 25).[2]

(*b*) The surviving implements in the museum collections have rarely been accurately classified; iron implements, which require careful protection against rust, are rarely found in a good state of preservation, and are frequently discovered, especially in some of the larger museums, lying unprotected and unidentified, save for the find-spot, in the basements. Notable exceptions are the collection of agricultural implements

---

[1] 'Il lessico agricolo latino e le sue continuazioni romanze', *Rend. Ist. Lomb.* XCI (1957), 381–406, and 921–1035 (on the agricultural vocabulary) (= Bruno, *Lessico*); idem, 'Apporti delle Glosse alla conoscenza del lessico agricolo latino', *Rend. Ist. Lomb.* XCIII (1959), 115–54 (on the value of the Glossaria) (= Bruno, *Apporti*).

[2] See the excellent article by E. de St-Denis, 'Falx vinitoria', *Revue Archéologique*, XLI (1953), 163–76; also the detailed discussion of pruning implements and operations by L. Savastano, *L'Arboricoltura* (Naples, 1914) (= Savastano, *Arboricoltura*). This comprehensive work covers in detail all the technical processes of silviculture, with special reference to the cultivation of vines, olives and orchard trees.

from Boscoreale near Pompeii, now housed in the Natural History Museum at Chicago,[1] and the collections of tools and weapons assembled in the reconstructed German frontier station at Saalburg, near Frankfurt.[2]

(c) The representations of implements on surviving monuments are not always sufficiently precise to make identification certain; nor are the solutions of these technical problems made any easier by the inaccurate pronouncements often made by the compilers of the standard dictionaries of antiquities.[3]

Since form and function are closely related, it seems that the first task in this enquiry should be to consider in detail what is known about the functions of the various implements, grouping them into broad general classes, such as spades, mattocks, knives, forks and so on, and then, within this framework, to discuss each implement in turn, giving first the lexicographical information, then the principal literary references (technical sources first, followed by non-technical), and then the monumental evidence. It is of course obvious that a classification by functions cannot be precise; there is much overlapping, since the same tool was frequently employed for more than one operation, and the same operation was carried out with many different tools. But it is hoped that this method will help to clear up some of the difficulties, and make some contribution, however tentative, to the study of Roman agricultural techniques.

[1] See H. F. Cou, *Antiquities from Boscoreale in the Museum of Natural History, Chicago* (Chicago, 1912), pp. 210 ff., and pls. 143–6.

[2] Saalburgmuseum, Frankfurt am Main. Numerous photographs and drawings of objects from the rich Saalburg collections are to be found, with full documentation, in L. Jacobi, *Das Römerkastell Saalburg* (Homburg von der Höhe, 1897), and in the *Saalburgjahrbuch*, Frankfurt am Main, 1910–). By contrast, many of the items from the rich collection of agricultural implements in the Museo Nazionale at Naples have never been catalogued, though many of them are known through reproductions in comprehensive works such as Petrie's *Tools and Weapons* (see p. 20, n. 1).

[3] E.g. Ch. Daremberg and Edm. Saglio, *Dictionnaire des antiquités grecques et romaines* (Paris, 1877–1919) (= Daremberg–Saglio); in this work the literary references are usually exhaustive, but many of the references to monumental sources refer to obsolete or inaccessible publications; the treatment of implements is very uneven. A. Rich, *A Dictionary of Roman and Greek Antiquities* (4th ed. London, 1874) (= Rich, *Dict. Ant.*) is particularly sound on technical matters; the figures in the text are usually clear, and the comment informative; the monumental references are unfortunately vague. The treatment of implements in Pauly–Wissowa–Kroll, *Real-Encyclopädie der Classischen Altertumswissenschaft* (= R-E) is also uneven. Some important implements (e.g. 'marra', 'mergae', 'rutrum'), are not mentioned; in other cases (e.g. 'ascia') the technical aspects are either ignored or given very cursory treatment.

2. EVOLUTION OF IMPLEMENTS AND SPECIALIZATION OF FUNCTION

The study of the historical evolution of tools is no mere academic exercise for supporters of the 'diffusionist' or 'separate invention' schools. It is a matter of considerable interest for the student of social and economic history. Some implements, invented at a very early stage in the history of cultivation, or even antedating the beginnings of agriculture, have retained their basic shape and function almost unchanged for many centuries until the advent of the machine; such is the case with the sickle.[1] In other cases, the replacement of a particular tool by an improved type, or the introduction of a more efficient one, may be correlated with changes in the pattern of land use in a given area, or with the results of conquest. Unfortunately, it is only in recent years that accurate listing of artefacts found on specific sites has become standard practice, so that many surviving implements cannot with certainty be ascribed to their source. As we have already noticed this is particularly evident in the case of iron tools; large numbers of such artefacts may be seen lying unclassified in the basements of museums, most of them now so badly corroded as to make identification impossible. In spite of these difficulties of identification and ascription, some attempt is made in the following pages to suggest historical connections where there seems to be sufficient evidence to justify them.

3. DIVERSITY IN THE DESIGN OF IMPLEMENTS

The list of agricultural implements discussed in the following pages comprises fifty separate items, including twelve distinct types of *falx*. There are two main reasons for this remarkable variety of types and designs of implement: (1) the adaptation, over many centuries of experience, of a single, basic implement, e.g. the digging-hoe, to the varying requirements of the different soils and climatic conditions which are to be found in the various regions of Italy; (2) the complicated régimes of cultivation demanded by individual plants, such as the vine, and by the systems of intercultivation of sown and planted crops which came to prevail in different areas. The study of the implements themselves cannot be divorced from that of the operations involved in each particular system of cultivation. In the following pages the documentation of the

---

[1] See A. Steensberg, *Ancient Harvesting Implements*, translated by W. E. Calvert (Copenhagen, 1943) (= Steensberg). This comprehensive work, based primarily on the Copenhagen collection, and on actual experiments with surviving implements, includes an historical classification, and a full bibliography.

sources of information has been made as complete as possible, and each particular context is set out, so that the design and functions of each implement may be studied in its operational context.

4. CONTINUITY AND SURVIVAL OF TYPES OF IMPLEMENT

Regional differences both in designs and names of implements go far back into Roman history, and continue to survive in areas where manual cultivation is still the rule, for example in South Italy and Sicily, as well as in parts of North Africa, Spain and France. The survival of the name of a Roman implement is of course no guarantee that the implement employed by the Italians, French or Spanish farmer is identical with its Roman prototype; but from the evidence furnished by historians of husbandry it is clear that traditional types have persisted for centuries, and that implements, like yoke and harness systems, are strongly regionalized so far as their design is concerned.[1] Like Greek tragedy, they have attained the shape and pattern most convenient for their purpose, and have persisted unchanged over long periods of time. Valuable evidence on the survival of the names of implements and processes is to be found in Walde-Hofmann's *Lateinisches etymologisches Wörterbuch,* and in the recent work of M. G. Bruno already referred to above (p. 2). Such survivals are mentioned in the notes on individual implements in the following pages.

5. NOTES ON THE SOURCES

1. *Lexicographical*

The ancient lexica and glossaries seldom provide information which cannot be obtained in more precise detail from other sources. Usually they are too generalized to be of any help: for example, Hesychius, s.v. μάρρον, the Roman *marra,* merely reports that it is a tool made of iron, while the Glossaries equate the term *ligo* with an astonishing variety of implements both Greek and Latin, giving little help towards solving the problem of identification. It is essential, however, that this class of evidence should be thoroughly sifted, for it may throw valuable light on the meaning of a term or an operation. M. G. Bruno's lexicon is most valuable as a comprehensive word-list of agricultural terms, and is

[1] See G. E. Fussell, *The Farmer's Tools, 1500–1900* (Melrose, 1952) (on the history of English farm implements); C. Jaberg and J. Jud, *Sprach- und Sachatlas Italiens und der Südschweiz* (Zürich, 1928–40) (= Jaberg–Jud). This invaluable work of reference contains a full classification of farm implements within the selected area, with drawings to scale of numerous surviving types, together with maps showing the regional distribution of the various implements and their local names.

particularly helpful in furnishing lists of surviving terms of Latin origin in the Romance languages, both obsolete and contemporary. But it does not pretend to be more than a word-list. The etymological dictionaries of Meyer–Lübke, Walde–Hofmann and Ernout–Meillet may often be consulted with profit, but ill-founded conjectures are all too frequent where silence would be appropriate, while at the same time there are rare items where no help whatsoever is to be found in any of them; thus the word *scudicia*, which appears in Isidore's list of *instrumenta rustica* (*Etym.* 20. 14), and is there described by him as a trenching tool equivalent to *fossorium*, is not mentioned by Meyer–Lübke. The word appears in Walde–Hofmann as neuter plural instead of feminine singular, is defined as a spade (*Grabscheit*) or a hoe (*Hacke*), and given a most unlikely derivation from *excudere*, to beat out, which is not at all the action required from the implement as described by Isidore.

2. *Ancient lists of agricultural equipment*

Five such lists have survived from Roman times. Varro's list of *instrumenta rustica* (*LL* 5. 134 ff.), which includes milling equipment, baskets and other containers as well as field implements, mentions only ten items out of more than sixty discussed in the present work. The notes are very brief, rarely lucid, and are usually accompanied by ridiculous etymological explanations. Isidore's list (*Etym.* 20. 14) contains twice as many items as that of Varro; the definitions are in many cases precise, and may well be derived from reliable earlier sources. He includes some terms (e.g. *falcastrum*, a later term synonymous with *runco*), several of which, though not found elsewhere, survive in the Romance languages. Two of the agricultural writers, the earliest and the latest of the surviving Roman authorities, include lists of implements and equipment. Cato (*De Agri Cultura* 10 and 11) provides complete inventories of equipment required for stocking an oliveyard of 240 *iugera* and a vineyard of 100 *iugera* respectively; but these are merely lists of items for the farmer's stock-books, and contain no explanatory information. Palladius concludes the first book of his *De Re Rustica* (1. 43) with a comprehensive list of farm requirements, including a few items of clothing and surgical equipment as well as a list of tools. Thirteen manual implements are included, and some of the less common items (e.g. the *lupus*, a special type of pruning saw designed for working in a confined space), are fully defined. In the other writers, uncommon or complicated tools are often described in some detail; the classic example is the careful description of the six parts of the *falx vinitoria* (the vine-dresser's knife) given by Columella (*RR* 4. 25).

6

3. *The Roman writers*

Apart from the lists cited in the previous section, the Roman agricultural writers provide a considerable amount of information on the various operations carried out with the aid of the implements that they mention. Some of these, e.g. harvesting, hoeing and weeding, are very fully documented, while for others information is often scanty. It should be remembered that our surviving authorities are handbooks for farmers, not scholarly treatises. Other non-technical sources often furnish valuable information (e.g. on *marra* and *falx*), so that by piecing together a number of scattered references it is often possible to obtain a fairly clear picture of both the form and the functions of a particular implement. Nevertheless, great care must be exercised in using this class of evidence. For example, it would be dangerous to conclude, on the basis of Ovid's *longi ligones* (*Pont.* 1. 8. 59), and in the absence of collateral evidence, that the *ligo* was a long-handled implement.

Vergil's *Georgics* contain very little information on manual implements. The list of *arma* (*G.* 1. 160) consists almost entirely of animal-drawn implements; and the endless editorial discussions of the meaning of *currus, traheae* and *iniquo pondere rastri* might have been more profitably devoted to some of the difficult problems presented by our major sources. In particular, the lack of modern commentaries on Columella and Palladius is a major handicap to those engaged in the study of the technical aspects of Roman agriculture.

4. *References to implements in non-technical sources*

Since agriculture occupied so large a place in Roman life at all periods, it is not surprising to find that, apart from the technical treatises, references to tools and operations abound in literature, in both prose and poetry. As one might well expect, many of the references in this category are quite unspecific: thus *rastrum*, specifically the multi-tined heavy clod-breaking implement, occurs very frequently in non-technical sources, and commonly symbolizes, in a general way, the hard manual labour of the field or orchard. Frequently, however, the references in non-technical writers help to complete our knowledge of the form or functions of a particular implement. A good example of the value of this class of evidence is to be found in the references to the *ligo*, one of a large category of mattock-type implements, which was so common that none of the agronomists gives details of its design. Two passages, one from Statius and the other from Ovid, provide useful information concerning its design and the method of using it, while a third, from Martial, gives information on

the regional distribution of the implement.[1] In general, however, great care should be exercised in dealing with casual references to familiar implements in non-technical writers. Editors and translators frequently make serious errors of interpretation, especially of terms (e.g. *falx*) which cover a range of different meanings. The appropriate meaning can usually be inferred from the context, provided that the editor of the text in question has some knowledge of the particular operation. In view of the special difficulties concerning *falx*, a comprehensive collection of literary references, based almost entirely on the references provided in the *Thesaurus*, s.v. 'falx', has been compiled, with cross-references under each heading to the discussion in the text (Appendix E, p. 205).

The ancient commentaries on the agricultural writers, notably that of Servius on Vergil's *Georgics*, are another important source. Although his interpretations are frequently wrong, Servius, who wrote in the fourth century A.D., occasionally reflects aspects of the changing pattern of agricultural practice, and gives information which is useful, if carefully sifted and placed in its historical context. A good example of the strength and weakness of Servius is his interpretation of the word *currus* as part of a wheeled plough at *Georgics* 1. 174, where his account seems clearly anachronistic, and presumably reflects the conditions of his own day.

5. *Tools found on Roman sites*

Iron tools are the bane of archaeologists and museum authorities, owing to the notorious effects of corrosion upon the shape and size. In addition, many of the collections in the larger and older museums have never been classified, since excavators in earlier times did not think it worth while to annotate such humble items at the time of their discovery, so that they are often of little or no use to the investigator. Amongst the notable exceptions already mentioned (above, p. 3) is the small but fine collection of agricultural implements found at the *villa* of Herennius Florus at Boscoreale on the slopes of Mount Vesuvius, and now in Chicago; but not all of these implements have been correctly identified (see Appendix B, p. 198). A new standard of classification and documentation in this department was set by those concerned with the arrangement of the Saalburg collections (above, p. 3), and their example has been followed with regard to more recent finds in other Roman centres, e.g. at the Roman frontier post of Newstead, near Melrose, Scotland (see J. Curle, *A Roman Frontier Post and its People*, Glasgow, 1911). A vast amount of research has been done on the problems associated with the designs of

[1] Ovid, *Amores* 3. 10. 31; Statius, *Thebaid* 3. 587; Martial, *Epigrams* 4. 64. 32.

Roman ploughs.[1] But no attempt has been made to study systematically the numerous surviving iron ploughshares of varying shape, size and weight, in order to amplify and clarify the often intractable literary and monumental evidence. Other agricultural implements have been very inadequately studied. Apart from the work of E. Werth,[2] there is nothing on spades or mattocks to match the magnificent monograph of A. Steensberg on ancient harvesting implements from Scandinavia, or that of G. E. Fussell on the manual implements of the English farmer (p. 4, n. 1; p. 5, n. 1).

The local and regional distribution of implements, apart from ploughs, is among the many neglected aspects of the subject. The topic is briefly referred to by Lynn White,[3] who suggests that iron implements seem to have been more prevalent in the northern provinces than to the south. Of equal importance is the question of the efficiency of the implements used by Roman farmers. Much light, for example, might be thrown on problems concerning trenching and hoeing if Steensberg's example were to be followed, and implements of Roman type constructed and used experimentally, as is now being attempted with Stone Age implements and Iron Age ploughs by investigators in Britain. To divorce the study of the implement from that of its operation is disastrous. The latest work in English on Greek and Roman farm implements, that of E. M. Jope,[4] is not only far from complete as a factual survey, but contains almost no information as to how the implements described were used. E. de St-Denis's article on the *falx vinitoria*, and some recent studies of Palladius' reaping machine,[5] remain isolated examples of what ought to be done.

---

[1] See P. Leser, *Die Entstehung und Verbreitung des Pfluges* (Münster-i.-Westph. 1931) (contains classification of ploughs by families, and many illustrations of ploughs from all parts of the world); A. G. Haudricourt and M. J.-B. Delamarre, *L'Homme et la charrue à travers le monde* (3rd ed. Paris, 1955) (with full bibliography). This latter work, as its title implies, attempts to relate differences in design to regional and local conditions.

[2] E. Werth, *Grabstock, Hacke und Pflug* (Ludwigsburg, 1954).

[3] Lynn White, jr., *Mediaeval Technology and Social Change* (Oxford, 1962). The vast collection of agricultural implements from the neighbourhood of Pompeii, now in the Naples Museum, hardly bears out the author's impression of first century A.D. Pompeii as 'still living more in a Bronze than an Iron Age' (*op. cit.* p. 40).

[4] *Art.* 'Agricultural implements' in *A History of Technology*, ed. C. Singer and others (Oxford, 1956), II, 81–102 (= Jope, *HT*).

[5] De St-Denis, *art. cit.* (p. 2, n. 2, above); M. Renard, 'Technique et agriculture en pays trévire et rémois', *Latomus*, XVIII (1959), 77–109, 307–33 (with full bibliography to date, and numerous illustrations of reconstructions of the reaping machine (the *vallus*) (=Renard)); add now J. Kolendo, 'La moissonneuse antique en Gaule romaine', *Annales* (*ESC*), XV (1960), 1099–1114 (with observations on many of the technical questions concerning the design and operation of the *vallus*) (=Kolendo).

6. *Representations of implements on monuments*

Valuable evidence is available in the various museum collections, including representations on gems, reliefs and so forth. The vivid pictures of farming operations in Imperial Roman mosaics, especially on those from North African sites, are particularly important. Most of these latter are available for study under excellent conditions in the Musée du Bardo at Tunis. Scenes showing actual operations in progress such as those on the Zliten mosaic, where threshing with horses and oxen is depicted with consummate skill, are far more valuable than the cult figures of gods or heroes carrying implements which provide the bulk of the illustrations supplied by the standard dictionaries of antiquities. The Zliten mosaic has been accurately described and discussed by S. Aurigemma,[1] and more briefly by M. Rostovtzeff,[2] while the agricultural life of Roman Tripolitania has been fully documented with reference to the surviving monuments by P. Romanelli.[3] The monumental evidence from Gaul and Germany is covered by the comprehensive inventories of E. Espérandieu.[4] The indexes to these two latter works provide easy reference to tools and operations, but the standard of reproduction leaves much to be desired. Fortunately good replicas of many of the items listed are available for study in the museum of national antiquities of France at St Germain-en-Laye, within easy reach of Paris. Other valuable collections of sources are those of P. Gauckler and others[5] on the mosaics of Gaul and Africa. Finally, there is the first volume of a new series on Italian Africa, edited by S. Aurigemma.[6] This volume sets a very high standard of reproduction, which is so necessary for detailed study of the evidence, and also makes the evidence available without recourse to works which have been long since out of print. A recent publication of the University of Tunis[7] provides a brief account of the information on the rural life of Roman North Africa which may be

---

[1] 'I mosaici di Zliten', *Africa Italiana*, II (1929), 85 ff.

[2] *Social and Economic History of the Roman Empire* (2nd ed. Oxford, 1958), I, 313, pl. 59 (= Rostovtzeff, *SEHRE*²).

[3] P. Romanelli, 'La vita agricola tripolitana attraverso le rappresentazioni figurate', *Africa Italiana*, III (1930), 53–75.

[4] E. Espérandieu, *Recueil général des bas-reliefs, statues et bustes de la Gaule romaine* (Paris, 1907–29) (= Espérandieu, *Gaule*); idem, *Recueil général des bas-reliefs, statues et bustes de la Germanie romaine* (Paris, 1930).

[5] P. Gauckler, *Inventaire des mosaïques de la Gaule et d'Afrique* (Paris, Acad. des Inscr. et des Belles Lettres, 1909–15).

[6] S. Aurigemma, *L'Italia in Africa*. Le scoperte archeologiche, Tripolitania I, I monumenti di arte decorativa, i, I mosaici (Rome, 1960).

[7] Th. Prêcheur-Canonge, *La vie rurale en Afrique d'après les mosaïques*, Paris (Publ. de l'Univ. de Tunis), n.d. (1961).

extracted from the mosaics, together with a useful inventory, grouped under various subject-headings, of the surviving mosaics; the photographic coverage is incomplete and of rather poor quality. In general this class of evidence should be treated with caution. How far may a work of art be taken as giving an accurate representation of an implement or of a process? This question is particularly relevant to the consideration of such complex technical problems as those concerned with plough-design or harnessing systems.

7. *Evidence from manuscripts*

The contribution to our knowledge of rural life in medieval Europe, and especially that of the major tasks of ploughing and harvesting, provided by contemporary illuminated manuscripts is well known.[1] By comparison the material surviving from early manuscripts of the Roman period is very small indeed. Apart from isolated marginal illustrations such as the representations of a *bidens* or two-pronged mattock in the margin of the Vatican Terence,[2] the most valuable collection consists of the nine surviving painted illustrations of the Georgics which adorn the text of the famous Vatican Vergil.[3] These pictures, some of which are remarkably well preserved, are of far higher artistic merit than the remaining forty-five which illustrate the text of the Aeneid, and are clearly by a different hand; one can only regret the loss of the paintings which originally decorated the missing portions of the text, namely that of the first and second *Georgics*. Few as they are, the surviving paintings afford glimpses of the Italian rural scene in the late imperial period, to be set alongside the far richer evidence for African farming provided by the mosaics (for details of the scenes depicted see Appendix C, pp. 201 f.).

[1] *Les travaux et les jours dans l'ancienne France*, IVᵉ centenaire d'Olivier de Serres, 1539–1939, Exposition juin-sept. 1939 (Paris, 1939) (Catalogue of the commemorative exhibition). See also G. del Pelo Pardi, *Gli attrezzi da taglio per uso agricolo in Italia*, Nuovi Annali dell'Agricoltura (Roma, 1933) (= del Pelo Pardi). This work contains numerous reproductions of harvesting scenes from illuminated manuscripts.

[2] Vat. lat. 3226.

[3] Vat. lat. 3225; for a full documentation of the illustrations, see F. Ehrle, *Fragmenta et picturae Vergilianae codicis Vaticani 3225 phototypice expressa* (Romae, Danesi, 1899). The photogravure reproductions of the first edition are far superior in quality to those of the second and third editions (1931 and 1945).

6. ARRANGEMENT OF THE WORK

The distribution of the material is as follows:

Manual Implements	*Machines*
1. Spades and shovels.	7. Ploughs.
2. (*a*) Mattocks and hoes.	8. Harrows.
(*b*) Axes.	9. Drags and threshing machines.
3. Knives and sickles.	10. Reaping machines.
4. Forks.	
5. Saws.	
6. Shears.	

A classification along the above lines is bound to involve the investigator in numerous difficulties. It is easy to begin with hard and fast distinctions, but examination of the evidence soon discloses the fact that rigid distinction either of names or types cannot be upheld: tools of a given type appear in many shapes, and one type merges into another. Thus the distinction between spades and shovels must not be pressed too hard (see the discussion s.v. 'pala lignea', p. 31). Similar caution must be exercised in dealing with mattocks and rakes (see the notes s.v. 'rastrum', pp. 52–5, and 'bidens', pp. 47–50). Another difficulty arises from the existence of general and local names for the same implement; and in the light of this some lexicographical distinctions turn out to be quite artificial. Columella's preservation of common names with phrases such as *quod vulgo nominatur*, *quod rustici vocant*, and the like, are particularly valuable.

7. THE DISTINCTION BETWEEN IMPLEMENTS AND MACHINES

The harnessing in recent times of powerful sources of energy as the prime movers of an astonishing variety of complicated machines has tended to produce some confusion of thought about the essential differences between implements and machines. Thus the standard definition of a machine as 'an apparatus for applying mechanical power, consisting of a number of inter-related parts, each having a definite function' (*OED* s.v. 'machine' 4) is far from satisfactory; the emphasis on multiplicity of parts functioning jointly is correct, but the use of the term 'mechanical power' is unfortunate, since 'mechanical' and 'machine' are related terms, and the author has not yet precisely defined his adjective while employing it to define the noun. Furthermore, the source and nature of the power applied to the machine is irrelevant: a crane is a machine, whether it be a modern derrick operated by electricity or an ancient Roman type operated by slaves working a treadmill. The basic dis-

tinction between implements and machines is twofold: it lies in the multiple organization of parts combining to effect the operation, and in the resultant redirection of effort. Manual implements are classified as depending on the muscular energy of the operator, transmitted through the hand or the foot or through a combination of both. Such implements may be described as no more than extensions of the limbs. Machines, however, whether operated by muscular power, as in the treadmill, or by the action of natural forces, such as animals, steam or electrical energy, belong to a different class: whatever the source of motive power, they are all 'contrivances for the redirection of effort to better advantage.[1]

The distinction was partially recognized in ancient times: 'There seems to be this difference between machines and instruments, that machines are driven by several workmen, as by a greater force producing its effects, for example, projectile engines or wine presses, but instruments carry out their function by the careful handling of an individual work-man.[2] In Roman farming practice, as in other sectors of the economy, the intrusion of animal traction only occurs where the extreme difficulty of manual methods (e.g. in breaking the soil), the risk of damage to the crop by bad weather during extended manual operations (e.g. threshing), or shortage of man-power lead to the adoption of time- or labour-saving devices. It is true that even in the small-holding economy of early Rome the ox-drawn plough is already an essential part of the farmer's equip-ment: yet in many parts of Italy the breaking-up of the fallow was carried out by means of the hoe; and in many parts of Central Italy, where intensive exploitation of the soil became the rule and cereals were grown, not in separate fields, but in combination with vines or olives, the ploughman 'needed to use the axe as much as the plough' (Colum. 2. 2. 28). Roman agriculture never underwent the kind of revolution which was inaugurated in eighteenth-century England by Jethro Tull's horse-hoeing husbandry; and in all but a few operations such as harrowing and threshing, the cultivator, armed with a variety of manual implements, reigned supreme. It is significant that the two most important machines, apart from the plough, which came into use, the *vallus*, or animal-driven reaping machine, and the *plostellum poenicum* or *punicum*, an improved type of threshing-sledge, are reported from the large estates of Gaul and from Spain respectively and are not found in Italy. Apart from these inventions, neither of which was of Roman origin,[3] there are few signs of

---

[1] A. R. Ubbelohde, *Man and Energy* (2nd ed. revised, Harmondsworth, 1963), p. 23.

[2] Vitruvius, *De Architectura*, 10. 1. 3.

[3] The mechanical inventiveness of the Gauls is well attested. The great majority of horse- and mule-drawn carriage-types used in Roman times were of Gallic origin (e.g. 'carpentum', 'cisium', 'essedum', 'petorritum', 'rhaeda'); see J. Carcopino, 'Ce

mechanical improvements in the routine processes of agriculture. On the other hand, the list of additions and improvements to existing equipment is important. Referring to the ploughs in use in Roman Britain F. G. Payne ('The plough in ancient Britain', *Arch. Journ.* CIV, 1947, 109), after reviewing the variety of types represented, writes: 'Thus, beyond the normal development of existing material, the future had only to contribute the true mouldboard and the asymmetrical winged share that is its complement. Even here, the first stage in the development of one (i.e. the ground-wrest), and therefore the need for the other, was already present.'[1]

8. NOTE ON SPADE-TYPE AND MATTOCK-TYPE IMPLEMENTS

Implements for working the soil may be broadly classified in terms of their basic functions. In order to prepare the soil for the reception of the seed or the plant, the surface must first be broken, and the clods turned over; this operation may be carried out with a plough, or by the use of one or other type of manual implement. The same operation may be done manually, by cutting and lifting the clods with a spade or a fork with multiple tines. The surface may also be broken by striking the earth with blows from above, using an implement of the pick or mattock type. There are two important differences between the action of spades and forks on the one hand, and picks and mattocks on the other; first, the spade and the fork press into and lift up the earth, while the pick and the mattock dislodge it by striking; secondly, the digger with spade or fork works backwards from the starting-point, while the striker with pick or mattock works forwards. These distinctions are important for understanding the directions given by the Roman writers on the various ways of preparing seed-beds or plantations under different conditions;[2] deep penetration of the soil, as in trenching for vines and olives, involves the use of several types of implement in combination.[3]

que Rome doit à la Gaule', *Points de vue sur l'impérialisme romaine*, Paris, 1936; M. Renard, 'Technique et agriculture en pays trévire et rémois', *Latomus*, XVIII, 1959, 107, nn. 8 and 9). On the advanced agriculture of Gaul during the Roman empire, A. Grenier, *La Gaule romaine*, in T. Frank, *ESAR*, III, 496 ff.

[1] In a recent discussion on Roman ploughs Mr W. H. Manning pointed out to the writer that winged shares have already been found on sites in Roman Britain, showing a further improvement on the simple Mediterranean ard. This and other technical problems concerning Roman ploughs in Britain are fully discussed in his article 'The plough in Roman Britain', *JRS*, LIV (1964), 54–65. Further reference to these problems will be found in Appendix G, pp. 213 ff.

[2] See, for example, Colum. 3. 13. 8–10; Pliny 17. 159; cf. Colum. 5. 4. 2.

[3] See further E. Werth, *op. cit.* (p. 9, n. 2, above); H. J. Hopfen, *Farm Implements for Arid and Tropical Regions* (FAO Publications, Rome, 1960) (= Hopfen, *FIATR*).

DESCRIPTION OF MANUAL
IMPLEMENTS

1

SPADES AND SHOVELS

The basic difference between spade-type and mattock-type implements has already been explained (Introduction, p. 14). Shovels, again, though similar in basic design to spades, are used for removing, lifting or throwing material lying on the surface of the ground, whereas spades are used for digging and trenching. The latter were chiefly employed by the Roman farmer in drainage operations, and in garden and orchard work, where deep digging is required. Two important differences should be noticed between Mediterranean practice and that of northern Europe: first, the heavy, four- or five-pronged fork of the northern farmer or gardener does not appear in the Mediterranean farmer's equipment in either ancient or modern times; secondly, Roman spades were both lighter in weight and different in design from those of northern Europe. Five tools of this type are mentioned in our sources: the PALA, the BIPALIVM, the VANGA, the FERREA and the FOSSORIVM (FERRVM) = SCVDICIA. Close examination of the evidence makes it almost certain that only three distinct types of spade were in use in Roman times, namely *pala*, *bipalium* and *scudicia*; the terms *bipalium* and *vanga* are undoubtedly earlier and later names for the same implement, that is, the long-handled foot-rest spade; and *ferrea*, commonly regarded as an iron spade, is much more likely to have been a fork: since the matter is controversial, the implement is discussed both in this section and s.v. 'forks'. Separate entries have also been made for *bipalium* and *vanga*.

SPADES

1. PALA   2. BIPALIVM   3. VANGA (= *Bipalium*)   4. FERREA (*pala?*)
5. FOSSORIVM (*ferrum*) = SCVDICIA

1. Pala (-ae, f.), *spade*

R-E XVIII. 2, cols. 2441–3 [Schuppe].

(*a*) Varro, *LL* 5. 134. 'The *spade* (pala) takes its name from "driving in" (*pangere*)':
pala a pangendo.
    Varro is perhaps right here; according to E-M pala derives from *pag*-sla; cf. Gk. πήγνυμι = drive; W-H regard the origin as uncertain, and prefer *past*-la; cf. *pastinum*, *pastinare*, to trench.

Fig. 1. Pala

(b) Not in Palladius' list, where it is replaced by the later word *vanga* (q.v.).

(c) Not in Isidore, except with the same meaning as *ventilabrum* = winnowing-shovel (q.v.). This is the standard meaning in ecclesiastical Latin.

(d) *Corp. Gloss.* s.v. 'pala'. Pala πτύον II 141. 24; III 195. 62; 263. 3; 368. 66; 502. 33. scoful saxonice *gloss. Werth.* (Gallée 340, cf. Suppl.) θρῖναξ III 263. 7 (*unde?*). V. paleta, palmula.

(e) Cato 10 (olives). '4 *spades*': *palas* IV.

(f) *Ibid.* 11 (vines). '6 *spades*': *palas* VI.

(g) Colum. 10. 45–6. 'Then, to be sure, let the sweet soil with the strength of iron-shod *spades* be turned . . .':

> tum mihi ferrato versetur robore *palae*
> dulcis humus . . .

(h) Pliny 18. 46. 'A sedgy field should be turned over with the *spade*; or if the ground is stony, with the two-pronged mattock': iuncosus ager verti *pala* debet; aut in saxoso bidentibus.

(j) Livy 3. 26. 9. 'Digging a ditch, pressing down on his *spade*': fossam fodiens *palae* innisus.

(k) *Edict. Diocl.* 15. 45. πᾶλα (M; μάκ[ελλαν] G.) X δ′
    shovel (pick)   den. 4.
    πᾶλα must be a small wooden shovel, at the price; perhaps a cooking utensil (Schuppe, *R-E* s.v.); see below, p. 31.

DISCUSSION

1. *Design*

The *pala* is the long-handled spade still commonly used in many parts of southern Europe and the Middle East, and not unknown in some of the remoter parts of the British Isles under the name of the Devon or Cornish spade. It differs from the northern garden spade in four ways: (a) it is normally of lighter weight; (b) the blade is commonly triangular or shield-shaped, though square blades do occur; (c) the blade is usually set at a very distinct angle to the haft, as contrasted with the northern spade, which normally has very little deflection of blade from haft; (d) the handle has no cross-bar or other form of hand-grip. These differences of form are closely related to fundamental differences in operational technique. The shape is familiar from the monuments. The implement is still used all over Italy and is commonly known as the *vanga* (q.v.). The term *pala*, on the other hand, now normally denotes a shovel, though the term is sometimes used, e.g. in parts of Sicily, to refer to the long-handled spade. The few references in the Glossaries, equating it with the Greek πτύον and θρῖναξ, the winnowing-shovel or winnowing fork, are concerned with a very

different implement, the *pala lignea* or *ventilabrum*; they are of some value, however, as indicating an important change in nomenclature (see the discussion s.v. 'ventilabrum', below, nos. 8 and 9).

2. *Functions*

The *pala* was normally used for turning over light or well-worked soils, especially in gardens and orchards (Cato, Columella, Pliny, *locc. citt.*). In hard, stony ground this task was performed, then as now, with various types of mattock, e.g. the *bidens* (Pliny, *loc. cit.*). For deep digging and trenching its place was taken by the common *bipalium* (later designated *vanga*); this change accounts for its non-appearance in Palladius and Isidore. That its use was limited is evident from Cato's inventories; he requires only four *palae* for working his olive grove, as against six ploughs. The two additional *palae* required for the vineyard are easily accounted for: the closer spacing of vines would require far more plants to the acre.

3. *Operational technique*

In light or well-worked soils a mere stirring of the top spit of earth is all that is necessary; the triangular or shield-shaped *pala*, which is still used for this task in central Italy, is very well suited to the work. When used for trenching or making ditches, as shown in the passage from Livy cited above, its shape was equally convenient, since a V-shaped ditch was commonly required for drainage purposes or for leading irrigation water into the kitchen garden or the orchard. Drainage works involving deeper digging would require the heavier *bipalium*. Soils with a high proportion of stone or gravel are common in the Mediterranean area, and for digging in these soils the pointed *pala* has a great advantage over the square-bladed type of spade. The point can be used like a pick to break the surface (some contemporary Italian specimens have the point specially reinforced for the purpose). In operation the hands grip fairly close together, so that considerable force can be exerted at the point of impact.

4. *Monuments*

(a) *Extant representations.* The *pala* appears frequently both in sculpture and painting. Rich (*Dict. Ant.* p. 464 s.v. 'pala') reproduces the figure of a workman from a burial monument of the early Christian era, who carries one on his shoulder. Representations of the *pala* in action seem to be rare: Espérandieu (*Gaule*, 5. 4044), in a series of important reliefs from Arlon in southern Belgium, containing scenes from the life of a wealthy fruit-grower, shows a panel depicting two labourers, one plying the hoe, while the other digs with a *pala*, with the hands set close together.

Fig. 2. Pala (Italian)

(*b*) *Extant specimens.* Flinders Petrie,[1] *Tools and Weapons*, pl. 67, fig. G 21, features a large *pala* with a shield-shaped blade and an internal socket-block, which may be that of a *bipalium* (see pp. 21 f.). The Saint-Germain collection contains several good specimens, including a broad, shield-shaped *pala* with a sharp point for stony ground (Reinach, *Cat. Ill.* fig. 277, no. 17806—provenance unknown). The Naples collection includes a *pala* of unusual shape (no. 71749). The blade is square and slightly wider than it is long, and there is an iron sleeve for the haft. Daremberg–Saglio (t. IV, 1, s.v. 'pala') show cuts of three extant specimens, all from Pompeii, and now in the Naples museum; only the first of these is a *pala*, the other two are *sarcula*.

5. *Survival*

(*a*) *Of the implement.* The *pala* is still widely used in orchards and vineyards in South Italy and Sicily. The accompanying illustration of a triangular *pala* from Mandanice, near Messina, north-east Sicily, shows the survival both of the type and the name; the blade is slightly dished.

(*b*) *Of the name.* The word 'pala' in Italian denotes a shovel, 'vanga' being the ordinary term for a spade. But the term survives here and there, as indicated above, to denote the simple long-handled spade.

2. Bipalium (-i, n.) = Vanga, *foot-rest spade*

(*a*) *R-E* III. 1, cols. 487–8 [Olck].

(*b*) Not in Varro or Isidore; mentioned by Palladius in the later form *vanga* (q.v.).

(*c*) *Corp. Gloss.* s.v. 'bipalium'. *Bipalium* [-llum *codd.*] ferramentum rusticum IV 25. 60.

(*d*) Cato 6. 3 (for planting a reed-bed): repeated by Varro (*RR* 1. 24. 4, by Columella (4. 30. 3), and by Pliny (16. 173). 'The method of planting (a reed-bed) is as follows: turn the soil over with the *foot-rest spade*': id (harundinetum) hoc modo serito: *bipalio* vertito.
    Cf. *ibid.* 46. 1 (olive-nursery); 48. 1 and 151. 2 (making a cypress nursery).

(*e*) Cato 45. 1 (trenching and manuring the olive-nursery). 'The bed should be thoroughly worked over with the *foot-rest spade*, and the earth made really soft and friable': locus *bipalio* subactus siet beneque terra tenera siet beneque glittus siet.

Fig. 3. Bipalium

(*f*) Varro, *RR* 1. 37. 5 (for tree-planting). 'For certain types of cultivation the ground must be turned over with the *foot-rest spade* to a greater or less depth': ad quaedam *bipalio* vertenda terra plus aut minus.

[1] (Sir) W. M. Flinders Petrie, *Tools and Weapons* (London, 1917) (= Petrie, *TW*). This work, though based on the author's personal collection of ancient Egyptian material, now in University College, London, contains line-drawings of a great variety of implements from many parts of the ancient world, together with a valuable commentary on the implements and their distribution.

(*g*) Colum. 3. 5. 23 (for a vine-nursery). 'The ground should first be turned over with the *foot-rest spade*, which equals the depth of the trenching when the ground is turned over to a depth of two and one-half feet': isque (ager) *bipalio* prius subigi debet, quae est altitúdo pastinationis, cum in duos pedes et semissem convertitur humus.

(*h*) Colum. 5. 6. 6 (for an elm-nursery); cf. Pliny 17–69 (ditto); cf. *ibid*. 18. 230 (vine-nurseries); 18. 236 (vines or roses). 'We shall therefore dig over the ground with the *foot-rest spade* where the soil is rich and moderately moist': igitur pingui solo et modice humido *bipalio* terram pastinabimus.

(*j*) Colum. 11. 2. 17 (trenching for vines). 'A *iugerum* of land is trenched in such a way as to be dug to the depth of . . . a *foot-rest spade*, which is two feet, by forty labourers (in one day)': pastinatur autem terreni iugerum ita, ut solum . . . ad *bipalium,*★ quae est altitudo duorum pedum, operis XL. (★ vipedalium AS)

(*k*) Colum. 11. 3. 11 (preparing a kitchen garden). 'But where you can irrigate, it will suffice to have the fallow turned over with a not very deep *foot-rest spade,*★ that is, to a depth of less than two feet': at ubi copia est rigandi, satis erit non alto *bipalio,*★ id est minus quam duo pedes ferramento novale converti. (★ bipalo SA)

(*l*) Colum. *De Arb*. 1. 5 (for a vine-nursery). 'It will suffice to turn it over with the *foot-rest spade* which the country folk call a "two-and-a-half-footer"': sat erit *bipalio* vertere quod rustici vocant sestertium.

(*m*) Pliny 17. 159 (preparation of nursery-bed or vineyard). 'The soil whether in a nursery or a vineyard should be exposed to the sun and should be as soft as possible, and it should be turned over with a two-pronged mattock to a depth of three feet, and thrown back with a *foot-rest spade* or mattock to swell naturally in ridges four feet high, so that the trench moves forward two feet at a time . . .': solum apricum et quam mollissimum[1] in seminario sive in vinea bidente pastinari debet ternos pedes, bipalio aut[2] marra reici quaternum pedum fermento, ita ut in pedes binos fossa procedat . . .

Note: The word *bipalium* is purely technical, and does not occur in any non-technical author. This would explain the fact that, unlike *bidens*, *marra* and other terms, it has not survived in any of the regional dialects of Italy.

DISCUSSION

1. *Design*

As in the case of other common implements, no description of the *bipalium* has survived: the prefix suggests that it is a double *pala*, that is, a tool made up of two triangular or shield-shaped blades joined together (cf. 'bipennis', an axe with two blades). There is a heavy English digging-spade of this type, consisting of two rectangular blades, welded together at the base and along the sides, the upper section having a wedge-shaped

[1] mollissimum? *Mayhoff*: amplissimum *codd.*   [2] Warmington: alto *codd.*

socket-block driven in to receive the shaft; the narrow upper ledge makes a good foot-rest for digging in hard ground. Among the implements found near Pompeii was a *pala*-blade with a socket-block rather similar to the above.[1] Two-faced *bipalia* of this type are known both among surviving specimens (e.g. in the Saint-Germain collection—Reinach, *Cat. Ill.* fig. 277, no. 29021, from Compiègne), and in existing Italian types (e.g. Jaberg–Jud, Karte 1429, no. 26). Many of the surviving specimens are single-bladed, with a projection on the face of the blade to enclose the lower portion of the shaft (e.g. the very large blade from the Naples collection (inv. no. 120661), for trenching heavy soil. As the passages cited above indicate, the *bipalium* was chiefly used for deep trenching, especially for vines, where depths of up to 3 ft were required. The ancient Roman digging-spade, like the Italian *vanga*, had neither a cross-bar nor an inset hand-hole, and deep trenching was done by driving down with both hands on the long handle, the action being assisted in the *bipalium* by the foot-rest attachment. The addition of the foot-rest gave a greater depth of cut, depths of $2\frac{1}{2}$ ft being common (passages (*g*) and (*l*) above). That there were short-cut and long-cut foot-rest spades seems a reasonable deduction from passages (*k*), (*l*) and (*j*), which imply short, medium and long varieties. The Italian *vanga* has a single foot-rest (see Figs. 4 and 5, p. 23), but the only surviving representation of the ancient implement (Fig. 1, p. 17) has its cross-bar projecting on both sides, which would be natural if the foot-rest was fixed.

2. *Functions and operational technique*

These are clearly indicated in the passages cited above. The *bipalium* was essentially a *trenching* implement: it was employed for deep digging over of heavy ground without much inversion of the sod ('defodere' is the technical term), and for digging with inversion, where the terms are 'vertere', 'convertere' and 'pastinare'. As Cato informs us (151. 2) the implement was regularly used for the dual task of digging over the soil for planting, and incorporating into the top spit a layer of manure previously spread over the surface. In deep trenching operations it was, as the frequency of references indicates, the standard implement, though here the *bidens* (see passage (*m*)), was also employed. The foot-rest enabled the digger to penetrate deeply after the digging and removal of the first spit, as in English double-trenching. In spite of the textual difficulties in passage (*m*) it is a process very like double-trenching which Pliny appears to be describing; the triangular blade and the foot-rest make the *bipalium* a most efficient implement for this task. In ordinary digging-over of the

---

[1] Petrie, *TW*, pl. 67, fig. G 21.

ground for planting, the foot-rest spade as used in Italy today can turn about half as much soil again as a plain *pala* of the same shape. Some commentators (e.g. H. B. Ash in the Loeb edition of Columella at 3. 5. 3)[1] seem to imply that it could reach a depth of 2½ ft; hence the common local term 'sestertium' (= '2½-footer'), applied to a deep trenching spade ('altum bipalium'), as reported by Columella (*l*). The common Italian *vanga* varies between 7 and 12 in. in depth of blade (contrast Fig. 4, with a 7 in. blade, and Fig. 5, with a shield-shaped blade 12 in. deep).[2] Fig. 4, with its broad, shallow blade is very suitable for ordinary digging, or for making wide, shallow drainage ditches, while Fig. 5, from the same area, is a deep trenching spade. With its 12 in. blade and a foot-rest set 6 in. above it, trenching to a depth of 2½ ft presents no problems; this is the sort of implement required by Columella (*k*) for preparing a kitchen-garden.

Fig. 4. Bipalium (Italian)

3. *Monuments*

(*a*) *Extant representations.* Representations of the *bipalium* are not very common. This is not surprising, since trench-digging was the most despised of all operations on the land (cf. Catullus 22. 10: 'Like some wretched goatherd or navvy'—'tamquam unus caprimulgus aut fossor'), and was commonly assigned to slaves in the chain-gang (Juv. *Sat.* 11. 80, etc.). It was obviously inappropriate to monumental representation. Rich (*Dict. Ant.* s.v. 'bipalium') shows a reproduction from a funerary bas-relief from the Catacombs of Callistus in Rome (Fabretti, *Inscr. antiq. Romae*, 1699, c. VIII, no. LX, p. 514; R. Thielscher, *Des Marcus Cato Belehrung über die Landwirtschaft*, Berlin, 1963, Abb. 3). The monument is commonly dated to the fourth century A.D., and is thus probably contemporary with Palladius. The foot-rest is shown as a cross-bar, whereas the modern Italian *vanga* has only a single adjustable projection on one side. In the absence of other monumental evidence we must assume that the Roman implement had a cross-bar, and that 'altum' and 'non altum bipalium' (Colum. 11. 3. 11) refer to spades with the cross-bar fixed at varying distances from the blade. The identical drawing appears in the article in Daremberg–Saglio (t. 1. 1, 711, fig. 859), but no provenance is given. The provision of a cross-bar where only a single foot-rest was required may have been due to the method of securing the bar to the haft so as to withstand the heavy downward pressure.

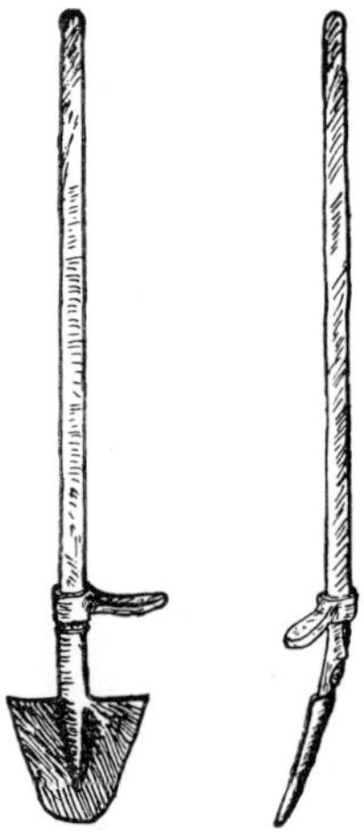

(*b*) *Extant specimens.* Since only the metal blades have survived, it is

Fig. 5. Bipalium (Italian)

[1] 'The *bipalium* had a cross-bar fitted to the handle at some distance above the blade, which allowed the spade to be pushed by the foot two spits deep, twice the depth of the ordinary spade (*pala*)', Columella, *De Re Rustica*, ed. by H. B. Ash (Loeb Classical Library, London, 1948), I, 266, n. 2.
[2] Jaberg–Jud, Bd. VII, Karte 1429, figs. 27 and 28.

impossible to distinguish *palae* from *bipalia*. For extant *palae* see above, s.v. 'pala', p. 20. There is a very large shield-shaped blade in the Naples collection (inv. no. 120661), which is 30 cm wide and 45 cm deep. It consists of a single blade with the massive handle-socket forged on. Its great size suggests a *bipalium*; equipped with a foot-rest it could presumably penetrate the soil to a depth of $2\frac{1}{2}$ ft (*c.* 65 cm) in two successive 'bites' (see the discussion of the problem of deep trenching, above, p. 22). The large square blade from Naples (inv. no. 71769, Plate 2 (*a*)), is wider than it is deep (38 cm against 30 cm). It would be an excellent implement for deep trenching in vineyards or orchards. The type is, however, rare.

4. *Survival*

(*a*) *Of the implement.* Implements of similar design, but with adjustable foot-rests, are still in use in several areas of Italy (see Figs. 4 and 5 above, p. 23), both from the Po Valley, north Italy. For the fixed cross-bar type see Hopfen, *FIATR*, 37, fig. 21 *c* (from Afghanistan).

(*b*) *Of the name.* The term *bipalium*, being superseded in imperial times by *vanga*, has not survived.

3. **Vanga** (-ae, f.) = Bipalium, *foot-rest spade*

(*a*) Not in Varro, *LL*; not in Isidore; among agricultural writers not before Palladius, and used only once by him, in the inventory of equipment.

(*b*) Pallad. 1. 43. 3. 'Small saws, *foot-rest spades*, and grubber-spades, with which we attack the brambles': serrulas minores, *vangas*, runcones, quibus vepreta persequimur.

(*c*) *Corp. Gloss.* s.v. 'vanga'. *Vanga* est pala cum ferro v 625. 1. *vangas* spaedun (*AS*) v 423. 25 (Gregor. *dial.* 3. 14) = v 399. 43 (spadan). Cf. Ducange.

(*d*) *Ducange*, s.v. 'vanga'. sarcula. Ugutio et Jo. de Janna: *vanga, genus fossorii, quia vagando fodit*. Glossae MSS: *vanga, pala cum ferro*. Lexic. Lat. Gall.: *vanga*, Besche. Italis vanga idem sonat quod bipalium.

Vanga appears to be a loan-word of Germanic origin (Meyer–Lübke, Walde–Hofmann, s.v.); it is the standard medieval term for a metal spade (*Corp. Gloss.* v 625. 1) the equivalent of the Anglo-Saxon 'spaedun', Eng. 'spade'. The Glossary phrase 'pala cum ferro' ('spade with iron'), presumably refers to the iron-shod wooden spade which appears to have been very common (see p. 27). The term is still in ordinary use in many parts of Italy to denote the foot-rest spade (see above, s.v. 'bipalium', p. 22), as distinct from the simple, long-handled spade (see above, s.v. 'pala', pp. 17 ff.).

4. Ferrea (? = Pala ferrea), *iron spade ?*

Cato 10. 3 (oliveyard inventory). '8 *iron spades*' (?): *ferreas* VIII.

Cato 11. 4 (vineyard inventory). '10 *iron spades*' (?): *ferreas* X.

Varro, *RR* 1. 22. 3 (quoting Cato).

DISCUSSION

The word occurs nowhere else in an agricultural context. It is obviously a common term, used to describe a familiar implement, like the English word 'iron', which can mean a great variety of things, including a flat iron and a golf club. Since it is a feminine adjective, it must represent an implement made wholly or substantially of iron, and one common enough to have lost its substantive. The choice is thus narrowed down to *furca ferrea*, an iron fork, or *pala ferrea*, an iron spade. Wooden spades (*palae ligneae*) were an essential item in the equipment for the vineyard (see below, s.v. 'pala lignea' no. 8, p. 31), and wooden forks (*furcae, furcillae*) were used for a variety of purposes, as in haymaking, stacking and loading (see below, section 4, nos. 1 and 2, pp. 104 ff.). Iron forks have survived from Roman times; they include pitchforks of iron from northern France, and small garden forks from central Italy (section 4, pp. 107 ff.). The majority of commentators identify the *ferrea* as a fork; E. Brehaut[1] thinks that the evidence does not admit of certainty, adding 'it may have been a type of spade with heavier iron in the blade than the *pala*' (*loc. cit.*). In favour of this view it may be urged that the heavy *bipalium* or foot-rest spade occurs five times in the text of the *De Agri Cultura* (6. 3; 45. 1; 46. 1; 48. 1; 151. 2), but is missing from Cato's inventories; the simple conclusion is that *ferrea* is a synonym for *bipalium*. Unfortunately there are other omissions from the inventories. The chief argument against identification with any form of spade is the fact that there appear to be enough spades in the inventories already, without a large additional quota of digging implements. On balance, then, it would seem more plausible to regard *ferrea* as = *furca ferrea*; in that case the most likely implement would be the two-pronged dibble used for planting vines and trees in the nursery (Columella's *pastinum*; see the discussion in full s.v. 'ferrea', section 4(3), pp. 107 ff.).

5. Fossorium (ferrum) = Scudicia (-ae, f.) '*grubber*'-*spade* (?)

(*a*) Isid. 20. 14. 7. 'The *scudicia* is so called because it opens the earth around the base (of the plant); and although it is used for other operations, it still retains its name from the base (*codex*). Others commonly call it a *trenching tool*, as if

---

[1] E. Brehaut, *Cato the Censor on Farming* (a translation of the *De Agri Cultura* with commentary) (New York, 1933), p. 22, n. 14.

Fig. 6. Scudicia
(Italian)

the word were derived from *fovea* (a hole)': *scudicia* dicta eo, quod circa codicem terram aperiat; et quamvis eius usus in reliquis operibus habeatur, nomen tamen ex codice retinet. hanc alii generaliter *fossorium* vocant, quasi *fovessorium*.

(b) *Corp. Gloss.* s.v. 'fossorium'. *Fossorium* ὄρυξ III 204. 52. *fonsarium* (!) ὀρυγεύς III 326. 25. *cavatorium*,[1] *sarculum* V 501. 45. *rastrum* II 591. 9. *rutrum* II 591. 45; *sarculum fosorium* II 591. 63; *sarcula fosorium* II 591. 64.

(c) *Gloss. Ansilenbi* 252. Is. 20. 14. 7 fossoria. V. fossorium = *raster, rutrum, sarculum*.

(d) Meyer–Lübke, p. 3462. *fossorium*, 'Grabscheit' (a spade).

(e) Ernout–Meillet, p. 243, s.v. 'fodio': *fossorium* (n.), 'bêche'.

Note

It seemed desirable to present a somewhat fuller range of lexicographical references for this implement, since Isidore is the only author who uses the term 'scudicia' and that only once. The *fossorium* references must be discussed, since Isidore employs it as the common equivalent of the specialized term *scudicia*. The authorities, both ancient and modern, are evidently at sea about the meaning of *fossorium*; some of the Glossary entries make it an adjective, and the majority of them equate it with the *sarculum*. There is clearly much confusion, culminating in *Gloss. Ansilenbi* 252, which identifies it with three unrelated implements. By contrast, Isidore, or his source, is in no doubt as to what a *scudicia* is; he describes it as so called because it opens up the earth round the base of the plant (*circa codicem*). This important operation in the cultivation of the vine is well known to us from technical sources; Palladius, in describing the process known as 'ablaqueation' (*ablaqueatio*) of the vine, cites the verb *excodicare*, which he says is an Italian dialect word, meaning 'to dig round the base of the vine'. This operation, which was designed to remove the deleterious surface roots, and at the same time provide a reservoir of moisture for the growing plant, was carried out early in January (Colum. 2. 14. 3; Pallad. 2. 1); The earth was carefully removed so as to form a circular hole or depression (*lacus*—hence *ablaqueatio*), and the surface roots thus exposed were carefully scraped off; the earth that had been removed was heaped up between the rows to be replaced (*adcumulare*) later in the season, after the vinestock had been exposed to the action of the sun and rain (Pallad. *loc. cit.*). The derivation of *scudicia* from the same root which appears in the verb *excodicare* seems to be reasonable, but the etymologists are almost

---

[1] *Cavatorium*: 'strumento per scavare e zappare' (Bruno, *Apporti*, 128, 78).

Fossor, a digger, navvy, is common in classical Latin, but both *cavare*, to excavate, dig up, and *cavator* are late; *cavatorium* (scil. *ferrum*) only here. *Cavator* survives in Italian as 'cavatore' (m.), a digger. Cf. Fig. 6 (above) 'vanga da cavatore'.

unanimous in deriving it from the verb *excudere*, to 'beat out', which is the most inappropriate verb one could choose to describe the operation referred to by Isidore, as well as by the agronomists. In modern Italian viticulture a small specialized type of spade has been developed for this purpose; it has a semi-cylindrical blade, which is drawn to a point (see Figure 6, p. 26 from L. Savastano, *Arboricoltura* 743, fig. 259, no. v). I have not been able to examine all the spades in the great Naples collection; but it would not be unreasonable to regard Isidore's *scudicia* as the ancestor of the Italian 'vanga accartocciata' which is still used in the Campanian vineyards.

6. Pala cum ferro, *spade shod with iron*

Not in any of the agricultural writers.

Corp. Gloss. s.v. 'vanga'. Vanga est *pala cum ferro* v 625. 1.

Note

No. 5 completes the list of iron spades mentioned by the classical authorities. There is, however, some evidence of the widespread use in Roman Gaul and Britain of a type of spade not noticed by the literary sources, which consisted of a wooden blade shod with iron. P. Corder ('Some spade-irons from Verulamium', *Arch. Journ.* c, 1945, 224–31), reporting on a collection of these iron 'sheaths' found at St Albans (Verulamium), an important British colony and a considerable centre of commerce and industry, notes that three types of spade were in use in the Roman period: the first was a common *pala* with an iron blade and long wooden handle; the second was made entirely of wood (see under 'pala lignea', no. 7, p. 31); the third consisted of a wooden blade shod with iron; of these types the third is by far the most common in the Verulamium collection. The choice of the term 'pala cum ferro' for this group is based solely on the evidence of the Glossaries; one may suppose that by the time *Corp. Gloss.* v 625. 1 was compiled, iron-shod wooden spades had become very common.

Extant specimens. Apart from the Verulamium group mentioned above, there is a representative collection, including variations in size and weight, in the Saint-Germain collection (Reinach, *Cat. Ill.* fig. 279, nos. 15914, 15914A and B, 29021, 29021A (all from Compiègne); *ibid.* fig. 50840 (from Alise Ste-Reine, a large specimen with a rounded blade). Our illustration is of a spade-iron from Pompeii, now in the Naples museum (cat. no. 71764). In the first two specimens mentioned the nails which attached the iron to the top of the blade are still to be seen. Both groups come from areas close to military occupation zones, and the prevalence of

Fig. 7. Pala cum ferro

the type may perhaps reflect a local shortage of iron for agricultural implements, the greater part of the available supply being required for army purposes.

On the other hand, wooden spades are still used in England for digging out heavy clay. They are preferred to iron spades since the clay does not clog the blades.[1] For the same reason farmers working in heavy clay soils in England used to prefer a wooden mouldboard. The fact that most of the spade-irons reported come from sites in north-west Europe may lend support to this interpretation. Local preferences often account for the prevalence and persistence of a particular type of implement or of a particular method.

SHOVELS

7. RVTRVM   8. PALA LIGNEA   9. VENTILABRVM

The basic distinction between spades and shovels is that the blade of the former is either almost flat or slightly dished, while that of the latter is scoop-shaped, i.e. upturned at the sides to enable it to retain a quantity of soft material such as soil, sand, gravel or concrete-mix. In both categories there are wide varieties of shape and weight, the result of regional and local preferences or of the special nature of the material to be dug or shovelled.

Fig. 8. Rutrum

7. Rutrum (-i, n.), *shovel*

(*a*) Varro, *LL* 5. 134. '*Rutrum*, "shovel", previously *ruitrum*, from *ruere*, "to pile in a heap"': *rutrum ruitrum a ruendo.*
    Not in Isidore.

(*b*) Festus, s.v. 'It is called *rutrum*, "shovel" because it is used for digging out sand': *rutrum dictum, quod eo harena eruitur.*

(*c*) *Corp. Gloss.* s.v. 'rutrum'. *Rutrum* ἄμμη II 531. 57 (*sutrum*); 546. 50 (v. *aratrum*); III 23. 39; 325. 70. ἄμη III 204. 33. ἄπη II 505. 19 (ἄμη). σκυτάλη III 197. 34; 263. 14. *fos⟨s⟩orium* II 591. 45. *a radendo* v 651. 33 (Non. 18. 17). Cf. *ruculum* σκυτάλη II 531. 58 (= rutlum, ruclum).

(*d*) Cato 37. 2 (making manure from olive-vat screenings). 'Mix it up well with the *shovel*': *permisceto rutro bene.*

(*e*) *Ibid.* 10. 3 (equipment for the olive plantation). '5 *shovels*': *Rutra* v.

(*f*) *Ibid.* 11. 4 (for the vineyard). '4 *shovels*': *rutra* IV.

[1] Private communication from Mr J. W. Anstee of the Museum of English Rural Life, Reading; on spades and digging techniques see now the excellent article by A. Fenton, 'Early and traditional cultivating implements in Scotland', *Proc. Soc. Ant. Scot.* XCVI (1962–3), 264 ff.

(g) Pallad. 1. 15 (for mixing plaster). 'This mixture must be worked for so long that when we lift up the *shovel* with which we mix the lime, it is clean': quae inductio tam diu subigenda est, ut *rutrum*, quo calx subigitur, mundum levemus (cf. Cato 128).

(h) Livy 28. 45 (in a long list of equipment provided for the fitting-out of a fleet). 'The people of Arezzo promised ... axes, *shovels*, sickles, buckets, grinding mills ...': Arretini secures, *rutra*, falces, alveolos, molas ... (polliciti sunt).

(j) Vitruv. 7. 3. 'Until the lime is so tempered that it does not stick to the *shovel* while being worked': dum ita materies temperetur, uti cum subigitur non haereat ad *rutrum*.

(k) Vegetius, *De Re Militari* 2. 25 (in a list of tools required for a legion of the later Roman Empire). 'Two-pronged hoes, hoes, mattocks, spades, *shovels*': bidentes, ligones, palas, *rutra*.

(l) Ovid, *Fasti* 4. 843 (Remus killed by a blow from a *rutrum*). 'Instantly Celer struck the rash fellow with a *shovel*': *rutro* Celer occupat ausum.

This is the only account which mentions the *rutrum* as the implement which dealt the fatal blow; Dionysius of Halicarnassus uses the general word σκαφεῖον (= spade, hoe or mattock, LSJ s.v.); in Aurelius Victor (*De Vir. Illust.* 1. 4) it is a *rastrum*.

DISCUSSION

1. *Form*

The problem of identification is difficult. Espérandieu contains no representation. The implement illustrated by Rich (s.v. 'rutrum') is not a shovel, but a hoe; it is in fact a rather inaccurate representation of a hoe-blade from the Boscoreale collection in Chicago; this blade could not be inserted into its shaft except at a right-angle or thereabouts. The type suggested by the literary evidence is, however, well represented in a group of tools on display in the Saalburg Museum.[1] The longer of the two implements resembles closely the modern coal shovel; the other is much shorter in the blade (see Figs. 8 and 9). In both examples the blade is set at an obtuse angle to the handle. The Saalburg collection to which these items belong probably represents a standard set of soldier's entrenching tools; the items shown, except for the turf-cutter (a very important item in Roman military life on the frontier), do not differ much from a modern soldier's kit.

Fig. 9. Rutrum

2. *Functions*

The *rutrum* was evidently a multi-purpose shovel, used for scraping and throwing up sand (Festus, s.v.), and for blending and chopping up concrete and plaster mixes (Vitruvius, Palladius). The surviving literary references do not make the agricultural uses of the implement clear; Varro is extremely

[1] C. Blümlein, *Bilder aus dem römisch-germanischen Kulturleben* (München/Berlin, 1926), 86, Abb. 267, nos. 5 and 6 (= Blümlein, *Bilder*).

unreliable as an etymologist, but his derivation from *ruere* seems obvious (passage (*a*)). The phrase *eruere terram* clearly means ripping up the ground, but the meaning of *eradere* is not very clear. The ordinary meaning of this verb is to scrape off; perhaps *eradere* means to turn over lightly, by contrast with *eruere*, which suggests a deeper and more thorough process. Here then we have a shovel-type implement which in agriculture does the job of a spade. There are no precise references in the authorities to the *rutrum* as an agricultural implement, but Forcellini s.v. 'rutrum' appropriately cites what is evidently a rustic proverb, recorded by Pomponius (*ap.* Non. I. 66); 'sarculum hinc illo profectus, illinc redisti rutrum'; i.e. 'you have suffered a total reverse of fortune', the first task in arable farming being the digging over with the *rutrum*, and the last a light hoeing with the *sarculum*. Daremberg–Saglio (t. IV, 2, s.v. 'rutrum') seem to have been persuaded by the passages from Vitruvius and Palladius that the implement *they* refer to is the ordinary mason's trowel (*trulla*), and then to have decided that the design of the agricultural *rutrum* can be inferred from a similarity of function; but Vitruvius and Palladius (*locc. citt.*) are both referring to the mixing of plaster in quantity before application to a wall, and this requires a shovel, not a trowel. That there were both short-handled and long-handled versions of the implement is a necessary inference from the literary references, the former being required for the mixing of concrete and plaster, while the latter would be needed for digging. The evidence as a whole strongly supports identification of the *rutrum* with the implement now known as a 'grubber', and with the Saalburg examples mentioned above.

3. *Monuments*

(*a*) *Extant representations*. No clearly identifiable example seems to be known from the monumental sources. The illustration provided by P. Gauckler (Daremberg–Saglio, t. IV, 2, fig. 5982) to support his view that the mason's trowel (*trulla*) and the *rutrum* are similar in design is too mutilated to be of any use. The ordinary builder's trowel is common enough on funerary monuments; but E. Pottier's illustration (Daremberg–Saglio, t. V, s.v. 'trulla', fig. 7135) is very different in design from the Saalburg *rutra* illustrated above (Figs. 8 and 9, pp. 28 and 29) and closely resembles the modern implement.

(*b*) *Extant specimens*. See Figs. 8 and 9 (both from the Saalburgmuseum).

4. *Survival*

(*a*) *Of the implement*. The examples shown above are both from Roman Germany: an implement of the same design is still in common use among

German farmers for light turning over of the soil.[1] This form of shovel is very common in many Mediterranean countries, and is the standard type of excavator's shovel used in archaeological excavations in Greece, Palestine and North Africa.

(b) *Of the name.* Sp. 'ru(d)ro', a tool used for cleaning the threshing-floor (Meyer-Lübke, s.v. 'rutrum'). This implement is evidently a scraping tool.

8 Pala lignea, *wooden spade, shovel, trowel*

Not in Varro, *LL*; not in Isidore.

Cato 11. 5. 'forty *wooden shovels*': *Palas ligneas* XL.

Wooden shovels are well attested. Cato's equipment for a vineyard of 100 *iugera* (= 66 acres) includes forty wooden shovels (or scoops?). Their purpose is not disclosed, but the large number indicates a very common operation, probably performed simultaneously by members of a large gang. Wooden shovels were used from early times for winnowing grain, but corn production is only ancillary to a vineyard, and forty implements of this sort would clearly be excessive; in Cato's account the item is immediately preceded by the item forty 'planting baskets' or 'troughs' (*quala sataria vel alvei*); and it seems fairly likely that these *palae ligneae* were short-handled trowels used in planting the vines in an *arbustum*, which is the only form of viticulture mentioned by Cato. In this system the vines were 'married' (*maritare*) to trees and carefully trellised; they were planted in holes, not in trenches; this explains the use of trowels. The common use of the term *pala* for this trowel-type implement demonstrates clearly that distinctions between categories must not be pressed too closely; *pala* was a general term, and could as well be applied to scoop-shaped as to spade-shaped implements (see the discussion s.v. 'rutrum', above, pp. 29 f.). The contention that the term 'pala' covers several distinct implements is borne out by Isidore's note on *pala = ventilabrum* (see below, s.v. 'ventilabrum' (9)). Wooden shovels are invariably used for shifting grain in non-mechanized systems. The πᾶλα priced at 4 den. in Diocletian's *Edict* (above, p. 18) need not be merely a small kitchen utensil. Wooden spades can be produced very cheaply: A. Fenton (*Proc. Soc. Ant. Scot.* XCVI, 1962–3, 264 f.) notes that wooden digging spades were being imported into Scotland from Norway in the eighteenth century, and sold for 5*d.* each.

---

[1] Private communication from Dr C. Hofmann, University of Ibadan, Nigeria (on German spades). Spades of this type were still in demand in parts of Wales and South-west England as late as the end of the last century, and the 'Devon spade' is still in use. On the resemblance of current German spades and Roman types see Schuppe, *R-E* XVIII. 2, s.v. 'pala'.

Fig. 10. Ventilabrum
(Cretan)

9. Ventilabrum (-i, n.), *winnowing fork* (= Isidore's *pala*)

Walde–Hofmann, s.v. 'ventus', p. 752, connect the ending -*lābrum* with *flābrum*, a blast of wind, from *flāre*, to blow, making *ventilabrum* equivalent to a 'wind-blower'.

(*a*) Varro, *LL* 5. 138. 4. 'It is called a *wind-blower*, because with it the corn is blown in the breeze': *ventilabrum quod ventilatur in aere frumentum.*

(*b*) Isid. *Etym.* 20. 14. 10 (pala = ventilabrum). 'The *shovel*, commonly called "wind-blower", which takes its name from the fanning of the chaff' (i.e. tossing the chaff in the air): pala, quae *ventilabrum* vulgo dicitur, a ventilandis paleis nominata.

(*c*) *Corp. Gloss.* s.v. 'ventilabrum'. *Ventilabrum* λικμητήριον II 360. 69. λικμητήρ II 528. 22. λικμητρίς II 506. 10. πτύον II 425. 47; 523. 57; III 263. 3. *pala ventilandi* II 596. 36. *ventilatorium* IV 578. 38. *velabrum, velatorium, vel ventilatorium* V 631. 66. *instrumentum quo palea ventilatur* V 252. 20; cf. Isid. 20. 14. 10.

(*d*) Varro, *RR* 1. 52. 2 (on winnowing). 'After the threshing the grain should be tossed from the ground when the wind is blowing gently, with winnowing scoops or *shovels*. The result is that the lightest part of it, called *acus* and *palea*, is fanned outside the threshing-floor, whilst the grain, being heavy, comes clean to the basket': iis tritis oportet e terra subiectari vallis aut *ventilabris*, cum ventus spirat lenis. ita fit ut quod levissimum est in eo atque appellatur acus ac palea evannatur foras extra aream, ac frumentum, quod est ponderosum, purum veniat ad corbem.

(*e*) Colum. 2. 10. 14 (on threshing with the flail, and winnowing). 'For the seeds that have been beaten out will lie on the floor, and the other bundles will be threshed out on top of them, little by little, in the same manner. The hardest chaff will be knocked off and separated by the beaters, but the fine chaff which has fallen from the pods along with the beans will be separated in another way: that is, when the mixture of chaff and seeds has been heaped together in one pile, let it be tossed some distance away, a little at a time, by *winnowing shovels*; and by this means the chaff, being lighter, will fall short, and the beans, which are thrown farther, will arrive clean at the spot where the winnower throws them': nam semina excussa in area iacebunt, superque ea paulatim eodem modo reliqui fasciculi excutientur, ac durissimae quidem acus reiectae separataeque erunt a cudentibus, minutae vero, quae de siliquis cum faba resederint, aliter secernentur. nam cum acervus paleis granisque mixtus in unum fuerit congestus, paulatim ex eo *ventilabris* per longum spatium iactetur, quo pacto palea, quae levior est, citra decidet, faba, quae longius emittitur, pura eo perveniet, quo ventilator eam iaculabitur.

(*f*) Colum. 2. 20. 4–5 (various methods of threshing and winnowing corn).' It is better, however, if the ears themselves are beaten with flails and cleaned in winnowing baskets. But when the corn is mixed in with the chaff, they are separated *by the wind* . . . If however there is no wind for several days, let them be cleaned with winnowing baskets . . .': ipsae autem spicae melius fustibus cuduntur[1] vannisque expurgantur. at ubi paleis inmixta erunt frumenta, *vento* separantur . . . at si compluribus diebus silebit aura, vannis expurgentur . . .

[1] *cuduntur* SA ä: *tunduntur* Lundstr.

DISCUSSION

1. *Design*

'*Ventilabrum* was a winnowing shovel (Gr. πτύον), by which the corn was thrown up in the air across the wind. Winnowing seems to have been done in the same way in Homer's as in Varro's time. Cf. *Iliad* 5. 499.'[1] That this is the correct identification of the implement is clear from the authorities cited above. The identification of *ventilabrum* as a shovel is also supported by the Glossaries (see the references above and also *Corp. Gloss.* s.v. 'pala'). In spite of the unanimous evidence of our sources, the word is commonly mistranslated as 'winnowing fork', or simply as 'fork'.[2] The common view involves two difficulties: (i) It contradicts the express evidence of the Glossaries with their known Greek equivalents (*c*), and that of Isidore (*b*);[3] this difficulty could be explained away by supposing that the form of the implement had changed in the centuries after Columella's time; (ii) it is difficult to see how the task described in such detail by two Roman authorities could have been effected with a fork. The longer account, that of Columella (*e*), refers to the use of the *ventilabrum* in separating a mixture of fine chaff (*minutae acus*) and beans, the latter having been previously beaten out of their pods by means of flails. To catch and toss up such a mixture would clearly be impossible with a fork. Daremberg–Saglio (t. v, s.v. 'ventilabrum') appear to confuse the issue further by stating that the implement was both a wooden spade and a fork; in fact this statement seems to be an unconscious stumbling on the truth. The problem of the *ventilabrum* was neatly solved long ago by J. Harrison,[4] who showed that the *ventilabrum* was a similar implement to the *vannus* or winnowing basket, that is, a cross between a fork and a shovel, the prongs sliding more easily under the mixture, and the scoop-shaped portion enabling the operator to throw the contents into the air.

[1] L. Storr-Best, *Varro on Farming*, a translation of the *De Re Rustica* (Bohn Library, London, 1912), note on *RR* 1. 52. 2.

[2] Rich (*Dict. Ant.*) s.v. 'ventilabrum': 'the instrument was a fork with three or four prongs'. Rich claims that the practice was still (1874) in use in Spain, where a similar name, 'aventador', was employed for the implement; he gives no illustration of its design. The Loeb editor of Varro, at *RR* 1. 52. 2 translates *ventilabra* as 'forks', adding no comment.

[3] See the Glossary references (*a*), p. 18, where *pala* is identified with πτύον, the ordinary Greek word for a shovel, and with θρῖναξ, a forked shovel (*c*), p. 32, where *ventilabrum*, is equated with λικμητήριον, 'a winnowing-fan', 'shovel' (LSJ) and with πτύον, and further defined as 'pala ventilandi', 'a winnowing-shovel'; cf. Isid. 20. 14. 10.

[4] 'Mystica vannus Iacchi', *JHS*, XXIII (1902), 292–304; XXIV (1904), 241–54.

2. *Ventilabrum, vannus and vallus*

In spite of the similarity of their shapes *vannus* and *ventilabrum* employ quite different methods of separating the grain from the chaff. With the *vannus* the mixture is separated by a shuttling motion inside the scoop, the separated grain remaining in the closed end; the *ventilabrum*, on the other hand, is used to fling the mixture into the air where the lighter chaff is carried away by the breeze. It is also evident from Varro (passage (*d*), above) that his *vallus* is merely another type of shovel for throwing the grain. At *RR* 1. 23. 5 Varro states that the *vallus* is made of wicker-work. It may thus have differed from the *ventilabrum* only in the material of which it was made. Comparative lightness would be an essential quality to both varieties of the implement.

3. *Operational technique*

The method of operation is carefully described by Columella: the *ventilator* or winnower tossed up a shovelful of the mixed chaff and grain into the wind, which must not be too violent or gusty—'Favonius . . . levis aequalisque perflat' (2. 20. 5). The lighter chaff will thus be blown away, and the heavier grain will fall back on the threshing-floor. He also clearly distinguishes between the two methods; with the winnowing basket (*vannus*) the grain is separated from the fine chaff by a delicate sifting action inside the 'cradle'. This process is slower, and therefore can only be used when there is no wind ('si . . . silebit aura' (f.)); bad weather is always possible, and speed is of the essence of the operation.

Note. Of course a fork may be used for winnowing if the crop has been trodden out by cattle or horses; in that case the chaff mixture will be dense enough to be picked up by a fork; indeed wooden forks with broad tines are still used in several areas for this purpose (see the 'forca da ventolare' from North Italy, illustrated s.v. 'furca' (below, p. 35, Fig. 12)). But Columella's description does not refer to that method. Much of the confusion in modern accounts of winnowing arises from a failure to distinguish between these two different methods of separating the grain from the straw. Where manual methods prevail it is the familiar Biblical method of treading out the grain that has usually survived.

4. *Monuments*

(*a*) *Extant representations*. Simple winnowing shovels (i.e. without the toothed blade), are often found on ancient Egyptian harvesting scenes (e.g. the XVIIIth Dynasty sculptured relief now in the Bologna Museum, Italy (*Cat. Antich. Egiz.* no. 1912, p. 187, reproduced by J. Harrison (*JHS*,

Fig. 11.
Ventilabrum
(Greek)

xxiv, 1904, 242)). The winnowing fan (*vannus*) is commonly displayed on Roman monuments, but I have not been able to identify the *ventilabrum*: neither Rich nor Daremberg–Saglio carries an illustration of it. The shape of both types of the implement may well have resembled the surviving specimens discussed by Harrison (*art. cit.* above, p. 33; Figs. 10 and 11, pp. 32, 34).

(*b*) *Extant specimens.* I cannot trace any surviving specimens of Roman origin. For Greek examples see Figs. 10 (from Crete, now in the Museum of Archaeology and Ethnology, Cambridge, England), and 11 (from Tripolis, Arcadia, Greece, also in Cambridge (Museum of Archaeology and Ethnology)—cat. no. 1904·161).

5. *Survival*

(*a*) *Of the implement.* Rich (*Dict. Ant.* s.v. 'ventilabrum') claims that this implement, which he erroneously describes as a fork with three or four prongs, was still in use in Spain in his time (late nineteenth century), under the name 'aventador'. It is well known that winnowing with fork and shovel, and with winnowing baskets (*vanni*), still survives in parts of southern Europe and the Middle East. The Cretan θυρνάκι now in Cambridge corresponds very closely with the requirements of shape (see Fig. 10). For good illustrations of surviving forks ('forche da ventolare') and shovels ('pale da ventolare') from northern Italy see Figs. 12 and 13 (= Jaberg–Jud, Karte 1485, nos. 1 and 10).

(*b*) *Of the name.* It. 'ventolaio' (m.), winnowing fan.

Note. On the regional distribution in Italy of the deep *ventilabrum* (Fig. 13) see Parain, *Verbreitung*, 361.

Fig. 12.
Ventilabrum
(Italian)

Fig. 13.
Ventilabrum
(Italian)

2

MATTOCKS, HOES AND AXES

Fig. 14. Sarculum

Fig. 15. Dolabra

This class comprises a great variety of implements used for different purposes. Mattocks differ from axes in the relation of the blade of the implement to the haft. In mattock-type implements the haft is set at right-angles to the width of the blade, while in axes the edge of the blade lies parallel to the haft. A glance at the accompanying illustrations will make the difference clear. Both types employ a striking or dragging action, and are thus clearly distinguished from spades and shovels, which employ a downward pressing or a forward scooping action. Picks and mattocks are primarily used as strikers, biting into and loosening rock, masonry, hard ground, etc., while axes are mainly used for chopping, cutting and splitting, especially timber. The common English mattock combines both types in a single dual-purpose implement; several such double-headed tools are known from Roman practice (see below, pp. 67 f., s.v. 'ascia'). In agricultural parlance the term 'hoe' is commonly used to cover all the implements of the mattock type, as when we speak of hoe cultivation in contrast to cultivation with the plough. The term 'sarculum', which has a specific meaning in the agronomists, is often used quite generally by non-technical writers, like the English word 'hoe'. The range of these implements in Roman agricultural practice, and the numerous variations in weight, shape and length of blade, and angle with the haft, reflect the variety of soil conditions encountered, and the need to suit the implement to the local conditions.[1] Some of these implements (e.g. the *rastrum*) have no counterpart in English, and their functions have often been misunderstood. The common rendering of *rastrum* as 'rake' is entirely misleading. In these cases, confusion will be avoided if a specific English term is employed throughout in translating the texts. The following renderings have been adopted in this section: *bidens*, two-pronged drag-hoe; *capreolus*, weeding-hoe; *ligo*, mattock; *rastrum*, drag-hoe; *sarculum*, hoe. In the case of the *marra*, there is so much uncertainty about its design that it has been thought best to retain the Latin name. Few of the dictionaries give any help in sorting out the implements of this class: 'a sort of hoe' is the common resort of ignorance.

[1] Regional differences in the design of common implements are exhaustively analysed by Jaberg–Jud; cf. esp. Bd. III, 1 (scythes and hatchets), Bd. VII, 1 (sickles and forks).

MATTOCKS AND HOES

1. LIGO   2. MARRA   3. SARCVLVM   4. BIDENS   5. RASTRVM
6. RASTELLI (= *Rastri lignei*)   7. CAPREOLVS   8. OCCA (dub.)

1. Ligo (-onis, m.), *mattock*

R-E XIII. I, col. 525 [Hug].

(a) Varro, *LL* 5. 134. 'The *ligo*, so called because its width enables it to lift up (*legere*) what lies beneath the earth': *ligo, quod eo propter latitudinem quod sub terra (est) facilius legitur.*

(b) Isid. 20. 14. 6. '*Ligones*, because they lift up the earth like "lifters"': *ligones, quod terram levent, quasi levones.*

(c) *Corp. Gloss.* s.v. 'ligo'. μακέλη II 123. 17; III 325. 68; μάκελλα III 368. 76; 454. 58. ὄρυξ II 387. 31; III 262. 63. ἀξίνορυξ III 325. 69. δίκελλα, μακέλη, τὸ τζάπιον III 262. 62 (unde?). σκαπάνη καὶ σκάφη III 262. 61 (unde?). ἡ ἀμ[μ]οδικέλη (*del. Buech. coll.* schol. Theocr. 4. 10). ἤτοι λίσχον II 550. 51; macellum II 586. 38 (= macella). tinctura (*ad* lix?) vel fossorium V 572. I. *ligones* genus ferri V 308. 23. rastri, bidentes IV 255. 16. rastros IV 361. 5. fossoria V 218. 4. V. ligonas.

(d) Cato 135. '... spades, *mattocks*, axes ... (should be bought) at Cales and Minturnae': *Calibus et Minturnis ... palas, ligones, secures.*

(e) Colum. 10. 88–9 (preparing beds in the kitchen-garden). 'Then with the tooth of the marra or of the split *mattock* let him thoroughly smash the clods with their living turf': *mox bene cum glebis vivacem caespitis herbam / contundat marrae vel fracti dente ligonis.*

(f) Pliny 18. 41 (in the inventory of a farmer's tools). '... his iron tools of excellent make, heavy *mattocks* ... ponderous ploughshares ...': *ferramenta egregie facta, graves ligones, vomeres ponderosos ...*

(g) Hor. *Epod.* 5. 30 (digging a grave). 'He with hard *mattocks* was digging out the earth, groaning over his painful task':

ligonibus duris humum
exhauriebat ingemens laboribus.

(h) Hor. *Od.* 3. 6. 38–9 (on the decline of the yeoman farmer). '... virile sons of peasant warriors who had learnt to turn the sod with Sabellian *mattocks*':

... rusticorum mascula militum
proles, Sabellis docta *ligonibus*
versare glebas ...

(j) Ovid, *Am.* 3. 10. 31. '... when the well-swung *mattocks* hammered the ground': *... cum bene iactati pulsarent arva ligones.*

(k) Ovid, *Pont.* 1. 8. 59 (the poet longs for a plot of land to cultivate). 'I should straightway clean the ground with long *mattocks*':

nec dubitem longis purgare *ligonibus* herbam.

Fig. 16. Ligo

37

(*l*) Martial 4. 64. 32–5. 'You who now count everything paltry subdue cool Tivoli or Praeneste with a hundred *mattocks*, and hand over the steep slopes of Setia to a single settler':

> vos nunc omnia parva qui putatis
> centeno gelidum *ligone* Tibur
> vel Praeneste domate, pendulamque
> uni dedite Setiam colono.

(*m*) Statius, *Theb.* 3. 587. 'now in the greedy furnace ploughs, drag-hoes and incurved *mattocks* glowed terribly':

> iam falces at aratra caminis
> rastraque et incurvi saevum rubuere *ligones*.

(*n*) Vegetius, *De Re Mil.* 2. 25 (in a list of tools stocked by a Roman legion of the late imperial period). '... two-pronged hoes, *mattocks*, spades, shovels': ... bidentes, *ligones*, palas, rutra.

DISCUSSION

1. *The ordinary ligo: design and functions*

From the numerous literary and lexicographical references cited above the shapes, sizes and functions of the various types of *ligo* may be determined with some degree of accuracy. The common type consisted of a broad, inward-curving blade of iron (*m*) attached to a handle (*k*). The implement was swung above the head so as to strike the ground with some force on the downswing (*j*). The curved blade made it useful for trenching in garden and orchard (*e*), and for uprooting and destroying weeds and scrub (*a*), (*b*), (*k*). In hilly areas it took the place of, or rather was not displaced by the plough; heavy mattocks of this type are still in common use in many of the mountainous districts of Italy and Sicily, and it is still a familiar sight in the vegetable-growing areas of the Mediterranean (see Figs. 17–20, pp. 39–40). The Glossaries are very confused on the identification of the *ligo*, but it seems to be identified with the Greek μάκελλα, a mattock (*Corp. Gloss.* III 368. 76), and with the later word τʒάπιον, which survives in the Italian 'zappa' and 'zappone' a mattock (see below on Survival, p. 40). That it was a very common implement is evident from several texts, especially those cited from Statius (*m*) and Vegetius (*n*).

2. *The fractus ligo*

In addition to the single-bladed type, there was a *ligo* with a notched blade. Literary references to technical matters, especially in poetry, are often ambiguous, and should be treated with caution; the notched type (*fractus ligo*) is mentioned only once, in a well-known passage from Columella's poem on gardening (*e*), where he describes the use of the *ligo*

or the *marra* (below, no. 2), for breaking up garden ground in the spring. It has been suggested (e.g. by Thédenot (Daremberg–Saglio, s.v. 'ligo')) that *fractus* in this passage means 'curved'. But this would be a very abnormal use of the adjective, which simply means 'broken'. Still less convincing is the suggestion advanced by the Loeb translators (Forster–Hefner *ad loc.*) that the gardener is to use a broken mattock for this heavy task. A much more likely explanation is that given by Rich (*Dict. Ant.* s.v.), who assumes that the implement in this instance had a divided blade. Other implements of this type, e.g. the *sarculum* (below, no. 3), are found either in a straight-bladed form (*s. simplex*) or armed with a double blade (*s. bicorne*), the latter term (= 'two-horned') giving a precise indication of the shape produced by notching the blade (see Fig. 16, p. 37). For 'bidens' = 'two-pronged' and its shape see the discussion on the *bidens* (no. 4 below). Yet another suggestion takes 'fractus' as referring to the acute angle between the blade and the haft in this type of implement, and identifies 'fractus ligo' with the Italian 'zappone', which has a sharp angle; the *fractus ligo* will then have been a special type adapted for use in the kitchen garden, the ordinary type being aptly described as 'bent inwards' ('incurvus'). That some *ligones* had long handles is proved by the second passage from Ovid (*k*), but Ernout–Meillet (s.v. 'ligo') are surely wrong in deducing that all *ligones* had long handles.

Fig. 17. Ligo
(Italian)

3. *Monuments*

(*a*) *Extant representations.* Trajan's Column, with its numerous scenes of camp-building and fortification involving excavation (see p. 67, n. 7), might have been expected to yield representations of excavating tools, including the *ligo*, in operation. Unfortunately, the actual trenching taking place below ground level is not visible on the reliefs. Rich (*Dict. Ant.* s.v.) shows a representation from an engraved gem (provenance not given), depicting Saturn in the guise of an agricultural labourer. The implement has an inward-curving, notched blade which fits our definition of the *fractus ligo*.

(*b*) *Extant specimens.* I have been unable to identify the implement in any of the collections that I have studied.

Fig. 18. Ligo
(Italian)

4. *Survival*

(*a*) *Of the implement.* Manual cultivation with various types of mattock is common enough in Greece, Italy and Spain. Of eight examples of surviving single-bladed hoes with long handles from contemporary Italy illustrated in Jaberg–Jud, two, nos. P 375 and P 559, have the incurved blade and long handle characteristic of the *ligo*; two, nos. P 520 and P 740 have the notched blade (see Figs. 17–20).

Fig. 19. Ligo
(Italian)

Fig. 20. Ligo
(Italian)

(b) *Of the name.* Meyer-Lübke, *op. cit.* s.v. 'ligo': 'Spanish "legón" (m.) —"Karst"' (i.e. a two-pronged hoe). They also report two provincial variations of the Spanish word, each bearing the meaning single- or two-pronged hoe. The Greek word λισγάριον, 'mattock', Schol. Theocr. 4. 10, Suid. s.v. 'σκαφείδιον', survives in Mod. Gr. λισγάρι, a kind of rake or harrow. In Italian *marra* (2) and *sarculum* (3) survive in numerous dialect forms, but *ligo* has disappeared. Yet the distinction between single- and double-bladed types is preserved in the separate forms 'zappa' and 'zappone'.

Fig. 21. Marra
(Italian)

2 Marra (-ae, f.), *mattock*

(a) Not in Varro, *LL*; not in Isidore; not in Palladius' list.

(b) *Corp. Gloss.* s.v. marra. *Marra* ἄμ[μ]η (r)utrum III 23.39. σκαφίον (= σκαφεῖον) III 325. 71 (*praecedit* ἄμμη rutrum). V. mappa.

(c) Hesych. μάρρον· ἐργαλεῖον σιδηροῦν (an iron implement). According to Walde–Hofmann, s.v., the word is of Semitic origin; they compare Assyr. *marru*, 'hoe', perh. fr. Sumer. *mar*.

(d) Colum. 10. 72–3 (on preparing the kitchen-garden). 'Do not spare to scrape out her inmost parts with *marrae*, and mix them still warm with the top layer of turf...':

tu penitus latis eradere viscera *marris*
ne dubita, et summo ferventia caespite mixta
ponere ...

(e) Colum. 10. 88–9 (on preparing the kitchen-garden: second stage). 'Then with the tooth of the *marra* or of the split mattock let him thoroughly smash the clods with their living turf':

mox bene cum glebis vivacem caespitis herbam
contundat *marrae* vel fracti dente ligonis.

(f) Pliny 9. 45 (on fishing). 'It is particularly on the Main, a river of Germany, that the silurus is hauled out with a team of oxen, and on the Danube by means of *marrae*': (silurus) praecipue in Moeno Germaniae amne protelis boum et in Danuvio mar⟨r⟩i⟨s⟩* extrahitur. (* marris *Hard.*: mario *Gel.* mari *ll.*)

(g) Pliny 17. 159 (on trenching for vines). 'The soil whether in a nursery or a vineyard should be exposed to the sun and should be as soft as possible. It should be trenched with the two-pronged hoe to a depth of three feet, and should be thrown back again with the double spade or *marra* so as to swell naturally to a height of four feet...': solum apricum et quam mollissimum[1] in seminario sive in vinea bidente pastinari debet ternos pedes, bipalio aut[2] *marra* reici quaternum pedum fermento ...

(h) Pliny 18. 147. 'Lucerne should be scraped down to ground level with *marrae* when it is three years old': medica ad trimatum *marris* ad solum radi (debet).

[1] mollissimum? *Mayhoff*: amplissimum.　　[2] alto *MS*: out *Warmington*.

40

(*j*) Juv. 3. 310–11. 'An enormous quantity of iron is used up for chains, so much indeed that one is afraid of a shortage of ploughshares, *marrae* and hoes':

> maximus in vinclis ferri modus, ut timeas ne
> vomer deficiat, ne *marrae* et sarcula desint.

(*k*) Juv. 15. 166–8. 'The first smiths, since they were only in the habit of firing drag-hoes and hoes, and being worn out after forging *marrae* and plough-shares, did not understand how to beat out swords':

> . . . cum rastra et sarcula tantum
> adsueti coquere, et *marris* ac vomere lassi
> nescierint primi gladios extendere fabri.

DISCUSSION

1. *General observations*

The above references appear to be exhaustive, yet neither the shape nor the functions of this implement can be precisely determined from the evidence. The Glossary references are few and singularly unhelpful; the equation with ἄμμη and *rutrum* implies a shovel-shaped implement, while σκαφεῖον (= a 'digger') (*b*) is imprecise, and may refer to a spade or a mattock (cf. LSJ s.v.). The scholiast to Juv. 3. 311 (*instrumenta sunt, quibus terra colitur*) is a model of imprecision. It must have been a common enough implement, or it would surely not have appeared in Juvenal's list (*j*), along with ploughshares and hoes. If it had been uncommon, it would have been absurd for the satirist to suggest that the cutting-off of supplies of *marrae* would cause alarm.

2. *Design and operational technique*

Blümner (*Privataltertümer*, p. 566) follows the Glossaries in assuming the *marra* to have been a kind of spade, but states that nothing certain can be said about its form. The etymological evidence, however, suggests a mattock-type implement, and this is supported by the second passage from Columella (*e*); there the *marra*, like the *ligo*, is described as a toothed implement, and must be a kind of mattock. It would be very difficult to use a Roman spade for the operation of breaking up clods with the living turf attached to them; and it is clear that Columella is recommending his gardener to use one or other type of hoe. This view is also supported by Saglio (DS s.v. 'marra'), who notes that it must have been an implement with strong tines like the French 'houe à main', and not a rake-like imple-ment with shallow teeth, such as that envisaged by Rich (*Dict. Ant.* s.v.). The latter describes the *marra* as 'a kind of hoe . . . used for tearing up and clearing away weeds and other fibrous encumbrances from the ground'. He illustrates his text with a drawing of an implement found in a Christian

martyr's tomb near Rome, which is declared to be the instrument with which he was tortured.[1] A saw-toothed hoe is otherwise unknown, and in any case Rich's implement would be useless for the purposes he mentions. The narrowly spaced, shallow teeth would easily clog, and would not help in weeding lucerne. In fact they would do no more than scratch the topmost layer of soil, dislodging only the very shallow surface weeds. A tined implement such as the *rastrum* would be the correct tool for weeding; such an implement would be required for the removal of the matted surface growth on a stand of lucerne, which is what Pliny is presumably referring to at 18. 147 (*h*). The phrase 'shave to the ground' (*ad terram radi*) seems inappropriate, unless it refers to the matted growth, and not to the lucerne plants themselves, which would certainly not stand being scraped down. It is most unfortunate that there are serious textual difficulties in both the other passages from Pliny. At 9. 45 (*f*) the conjecture *marris* clearly points to a narrow-bladed implement used here as a gaff for a very large fish. But it remains no more than a brilliant conjecture. At 17. 159 (*g*), a mattock does not seem to be an appropriate implement for returning soil to a trench; but the text appears suspect. On the balance of the evidence, the *marra* will perhaps have been a single-bladed hoe, lighter in weight than the ordinary *ligo*, but heavier than the sarculum. Closer identification seems to be impossible.

3. *Monuments*

No attempt, other than that reported by Rich, and rejected as unsound (above, p. 41), appears to have been made to identify the implement from any monumental source.

4. *Survival*

(*a*) *Of the implement.* Of the many surviving single-bladed hoes studied by Jaberg–Jud (*op. cit.*), no. P 522 from Carmignano near Acerra, south Italy, and known locally as 'la marrucola', has the narrow, incurved blade, and corresponds closely to the design tentatively suggested in the foregoing discussion (see Fig. 21, p. 40). Hoes with a similar narrow tongue-like blade occur in later English practice. There are several specimens in the Museum of English Rural Life at Reading.

(*b*) *Of the name.* The name survives in Italian, Spanish, Portuguese and French; the relevant meanings are as follows:

(1) It. 'marone' (m.): (i) a broad, short-handled hoe, (ii) a hoe-like

---

[1] The implement is certainly not a *marra*, but the blade is similar to that of the French 'sarcloir' (see, for example, *Larousse du XXᵉ siècle*, t. VI, s.v. 'sarcloir'), and may have been a variety of weeding-hoe used for destroying small surface weeds.

instrument used in mixing mortar, (iii) the fluke of an anchor. Jaberg–Jud (*op. cit.*), Karte 1429, no. P 520, provide an illustration of a notched hoe still in use in Camaiore in northern Tuscany, where it is known as 'il marone'.

(2) Sp. 'marrazo' (m.), a mattock.

(3) Pg. 'marra' (f.), a weeding hoe.

(4) Fr. 'marre' (f.), reported from various parts of France, especially the central and western areas, a hoe. Two additional items, noted by Larousse (s.v. 'marre'), are of some interest in connection with the identification of *marra*: (*a*) 'marre du fer', used of the flukes of an anchor (*obs.* fifteenth to eighteenth centuries); (*b*) 'prise du marre', the seizure of a farmer's implements for non-payment of tax.

The effect of these references is to rule out any suggestion that the implement is not of the mattock type. Furthermore, the two references to the survival of the word, with the meaning 'fluke of an anchor', point to the shape and suggest a narrow-bladed hoe.

3. Sarculum (-i, n.), Cato, Varro (-us, -i, m.), Pallad., Isid., *hoe*

(*a*) *R-E* I A. 2, col. 2436 [Orth].

(*b*) Varro, *LL* 5. 134. 'The *hoe* takes its name from sowing or hoeing': *sarculum ab serendo ac sariendo.*

(*c*) Isid. 20. 14. 'The *hoe*. They are either simple or two-pronged': *sarculus. sunt autem vel simplices vel bicornes.*

(*d*) Pallad. 1. 43. 3. 'The *hoe*. They are either simple or two-pronged': *sarculos vel simplices vel bicornes.*

Fig. 22. Sarculum

(*e*) *Corp. Gloss.* s.v. 'sarculum'. *Sarculum* σκαλίς, σκαφίον II 178. 50. *sarculum et sarcula* σκαλίς II 432. 29. *sarculum* σκαλίς II 505. 26; III 94. 10–11; 204. 29; 325. 67. *sarcula* σκαλίς III 262. 64 (unde?). sarculum ὄρυξ II 387. 31; III 262. 63. *sarculum* id est ferrum uueadhoc (AS).[1] v 388. 41. *sarculus* fos⟨s⟩orium II 591. 63. *sarcula* fos⟨s⟩orium II 591. 54. V. sacculus.

(*f*) Cato 10. 3. 'eight *hoes*': *sarcula* VIII. (Not in vineyard inventory.)

(*g*) Cato 155. 1. 'When the rains start, the entire household must turn out with shovels and *hoes*, open the drainage channels, turn the water into the roads and see that it flows off': cum pluere incipiet, familiam cum ferreis *sarculisque* exire oportet, incilia aperire, aquam diducere in vias et curare oportet uti fluat.

(*h*) Varro, *RR* 1. 22. 3 (quoting Cato 10. 3).

(*j*) Colum. 2. 10. 33 (on the régime for fenugreek). '(the seed must be thinly covered) and for this reason some people break the ground with the smallest size of plough, then scatter the seed without preparation, covering it with *light hoes*': propter quod non nulli prius quam serant, minimis aratris proscindunt atque ita iaciunt semina et *sarculis* adobruunt (adruunt *S. Lundström*).

[1] I.e. 'weedhack'.

43

(*k*) Colum. 2. 15. 2 (on manuring for grain). '(if you have been unable to apply manure at the proper time), a second method is . . . to broadcast goat manure by hand and then thoroughly stir up the earth with *hoes*': caprinum manu iacere atque ita terram *sarculis* permiscere.

(*l*) Colum. 2. 17. 4. 'We shall break the clods with *hoes*': glaebas *sarculis* resolvemus.

(*m*) Colum. 5. 9. 4. 'When you start tilling your nursery with two-pronged mattocks or *hoes*': cum bidentibus aut *sarculis* seminarium colere institueris.

(*n*) Colum. 10. 91–3 (making garden-plots). 'Then let him take the shining *hoe*, worn by the soil, and trace straight, narrow ridges from the opposing bounds and these across with narrow paths divide':

> tunc quoque trita solo splendentia *sarcula* sumat,
> angustosque foros adverso limite ducens,
> rursus in obliquum distinguat tramite parvo.

(*o*) Pliny 18. 178 (on hilly ground). 'Hilly ground is ploughed only across the slope of the hill . . . and man has such capacity for labour that he can actually perform the function of oxen—at all events mountain folk dispense with this animal and do their ploughing with *hoes*': in collibus traverso tantum monte aratur . . . tantumque est laboris homini ut etiam boum vice fungatur: certe sine hoc animali montanae gentes *sarculis* arant.

(*p*) Pliny 18. 186 (to revive crops that have been eaten down by cattle). 'The crops that have been eaten down as pasture have to be revived with the *hoe*': quae depasta sunt *sarculo* iterum excitari necessarium.

(*q*) Pliny 18. 241 (on hoeing beans). 'They should be cleaned with a *light hoe* rather than dug over': *levi sarculo* purgare verius quam fodere.

(*r*) Pliny 18. 295 (operations of late summer). 'Cleaning seed-beds with the *hoe*': seminaria purgare *sarculo*. Cf. 18. 146; 157.

(*s*) Pliny 19. 109 (on cultivating leeks). 'The modern practice is to separate the roots gently with the *hoe* . . .': nunc sarculo leviter convelluntur radices . . .

(*t*) Horace, *Odes* 1. 1. 11 ff. 'The man who joyfully cleaves his ancestral fields with the *hoe* . . . will never be persuaded . . . to cleave the sea':

> gaudentem patrios findere *sarculo*
> agros . . . numquam dimoveas ut . . .
> . . . secat mare.

(*u*) Jerome, *in Is.* 28. 23, p. 385 (on the order of operations in preparing the soil for cereals). 'Will he not first break the ground, then turn over the furrow-slice with the ploughshare, and break up the clods that are lying with the clod-breaker and the *hoe*?': nonne prius proscindet humum, et vomere sulcos revolvet, iacentesque glebas rastro franget et *sarculo*?

This implement is more frequently mentioned both by technical writers and elsewhere than any other member of the hoe family. In the above list only passages which throw light on the design or function of the implement are cited. That it was among the commonest of all agricultural implements is evident from, for example, Ovid, *Fasti* 4. 977–8, where it is featured with the *bidens* and the *vomer* as constituting the wealth of the countryside.

1. *Design*

Precise information on the shape is lacking in the literary sources. Like many other articles in common use, it was too familiar to be described. Nor is there anything of value in the lexicographers or the glossaries. Among the monuments Rich, *Dict. Ant.*, and Daremberg–Saglio, s.v. 'sarculum', mention a bas-relief containing a representation of a light hoe used for drawing shallow furrows across the arena: the design of the blade is similar to that of the French *sarcloir*, having a rounded cutting edge. That there were *sarcula* of various weights is evident from a comparison of passages (*o*) and (*q*) above.

2. *Function*

The *sarculum* was employed in a wide variety of tasks both in the cultivation of field crops and in the orchard. The heavier form had two main uses. In hilly country it was used, like the *ligo* (q.v.) in place of the plough, for breaking and turning over the ground (*o*) and (*t*). It was also used, like the *rastrum* (q.v.), to break up the clods left after ploughing (*l*) and (*u*). The lighter type also had a wide range of uses. In cereal and legume cultivation, frequent hoeings were essential during the growing period, to keep down the weeds and prevent the surface soil from 'caking'. This process was known as *sartio* (*q*) and (*r*). Our best source of information on this is Columella 2. 11 (an entire chapter devoted to the hoeing of cereals and legumes). The process is repeated in condensed form by Palladius (2. 9). The *sarculum* was used not merely for stirring and aerating the soil, but for earthing up the plants so as to make them bush out (*fruticare*) at the base, a procedure which is the only one that will make thinly sown Mediterranean wheat 'head'.

Palladius (*d*) distinguishes two different forms, a single-bladed (*simplex*) and a two-pronged (*bicorne*) type.

Four of the remaining passages cited involve rather delicate tilling or mixing operations requiring a light implement; Columella advises the use of the *sarculum* for covering small seeds (*j*), and for working manure carefully into the surface layer (*k*), while Pliny recommends it for reviving crops that have been grazed down (*p*) (a light implement would be essential to avoid disturbing the roots of the growing corn while loosening the earth impacted by the hoofs of the grazing animals) and for separating the roots of the leek during growth. The implement was also used in irrigated lands for opening and closing drainage channels (*g*). Some authorities (e.g. Daremberg–Saglio, t. IV, 2, s.v. 'sarculum') assert that it was used for

45

removing the surface roots of vines and olives. But it does not figure in Cato's inventories, nor does any surviving description of this process (e.g. Columella 5. 9. 12 ff.) refer to the *sarculum*, the *fossorium* or *dolabra* (qq.v.) being normally employed for this.

3. *Monuments*

(*a*) *Extant representations*. According to Daremberg–Saglio (t. IV, 2, 1075), the *sarculum* is often found on monuments. Their sole illustration from this source, however, is that of a square-bladed implement from the Antinous statue in the Richelieu collection in the Louvre, which is untypical in design (*loc. cit.* fig. 6116). Rich (*Dict. Ant.* s.v.) is also inadequate: his only illustration is of a light *sarculum*, with a convex cutting edge, taken from a Roman bas-relief (no provenance given), and said to have been commonly used for making a defining ring at the broad end of the arena for boxing and *other* contests (see Fig. 14, p. 36). This is the weight of *sarculum* required for marking out garden-plots (passage *n*).

Fig. 23. Sarculum

(*b*) *Extant specimens*. Two specimens of the *sarculum* are reported by H. Sandars[1] from the well-known site of Linares in Spain. Both are illustrated in Daremberg-Saglio, *loc. cit.*, figs. 6117 and 6118. The swan neck design of no. 6117 is still common in many parts of Europe, including France and Great Britain. Good ancient specimens of this variety are to be seen in the St-Germain collection (Reinach, *Cat. Ill.* fig. 279, nos. 15880, 15880A, 15881). The Chicago collection from Boscoreale contains seven iron hoe-blades, one of which is pear-shaped (cat. no. 26154), the other being of the common flat-edged type (cat. nos. 26150–3, 26155). The two types are illustrated on Plate 2. The pointed blade of no. 26154 identifies it as a *sarculum*, while the others are square-bladed versions of the same implement.[2]

4. *Survival*

Fig. 24. Sarculum (French)

(*a*) *Of the implement*. The swan-neck weeding hoe reported from the Linares relief (below, n. 1: Daremberg–Saglio, t. IV, 2, 1075, fig. 6117) is of the type still commonly used by gardeners in many parts of the world. The shallow-bladed French weeding hoe, the 'sarcloir', has the same swan neck curved in a third- or quarter-circle to suit the angle required (see, for example, Larousse du XXᵉ siècle, t. VI, s.v. 'sarcloir'). The term σκαπάνη (see the *Corp. Gloss.* references s.v. 'ligo', above, p. 37) is still applied to a hoe used in many of the Greek islands, which is identical in shape to

---

[1] *Archaeologia*, LIX (March 1905), pl. 70, figs. 2 and 4.
[2] All these implements are illustrated in *Field Mus. Nat. Hist. Anthr.* VII, no. 4 (Publication 152). Both types are illustrated in Petrie, pl. 67 G, nos. 2 and 9.

Sandars's second specimen (above, p. 46, no. 6118). The σκαλίς used by Greek vinedressers is identified with the two-bladed *sarculum* by H. de Villefosse[1] (see the *Corp. Gloss.* references, above. p. 43).

(*b*) *Of the name*. The name survives in the Italian forms 'sarchio' (m.) a light hoe, 'sarchiella' (f.) and 'sarchiello' (m.) a garden hoe. The *sarchio* is used chiefly in orchards and gardens, and for weeding in grainfields. An Italian agronomist has pointed out that the *sarculum* was the present-day 'zappetta', which still retains its ancient name in the less common terms 'sarchio' and 'sarchiello' (see Bruno, *Lessico*, s.v.). Both ancient *sarculum* and modern 'zappetta' perform the same operations: (*a*) replacing the plough on stony soils (Pliny 18. 178); (*b*) covering the young plants to make them bush out (Colum. 2. 11. 2); (*c*) cultivating in between the growing plants (Colum. 2. 11. 7 ff.); (*d*) cleaning the ground (Lat. *politio*).

Fig. 25. Sarculum (Italian)

4. Bidens (-ntis) (scil. rastrum), *two-pronged drag-hoe*

(*a*) *R-E* s.v. 'bidens': III. 1, col. 428 (2) [Olck].

> *Note:* In order to avoid confusion and duplication, only the plain *bidens* is discussed here. The double-headed implement known as 'ascia/rastrum' is discussed s.v. 'ascia', pp. 67 f.

(*b*) Not in Varro, *LL*; not in Isidore; not in Cato's lists.

Fig. 26. Sarculum (Italian)

(*c*) Pallad. 1. 43. 1 (the inventory). '*Two-pronged drag-hoes*, hatchets and pruning-hooks which we are to use for trees and vines': *bidentes*, dolabras, falces putatorias, quibus in arbore utamur et vite.

(*d*) *Corp. Gloss.* s.v. 'bidens'. *Bidens* δίκελλα II 277. 33; 490. 30; III 204. 54; 440. 31; 466. 38; 477. 35. δίκελλον III 23. 40; 326. 1. δίκελλα, μακέλη, τὸ τзάπιον III 262. 62 (unde?). bidens et bidentis δίκελλα II 29. 52. bidento fodio IV 25. 47; 211. 41. fodeo IV 488. 52; 592. 17; V 172. 39. bidentat fodit V 172. 34.

(*e*) Colum. 3. 13. 3 (on the furrow system of vine-planting). 'Then leaving a space, varying with each man's custom of cultivating either with the plough or the *two-pronged mattock*, they set out the next row': tum deinde relicto spatio, prout cuique mos est vineas *colendi vel aratro vel *bidente*, sequentem ordinem instituunt. (* colenti SAcM, *et plerique*: colendi *a*, Ursinus, Schn.)

Fig. 27. Bidens

(*f*) Colum. *De Arb*. 12. 2 (on preparing the soil for a vineyard). 'It is more effective to turn over the soil with *two-pronged mattocks* than with the plough. The mattock turns over the whole piece of ground evenly; as for the plough, apart from the fact that it makes ridges, there is also the fact that the oxen which do the ploughing break off a considerable number of the shoots, and from time to time whole vines': *bidentibus* terram vertere utilius est quam aratro. bidens aequaliter totam terram vertit: aratrum praeterquam quod scamnum facit, tum etiam boves, qui arant, aliquantum virgarum et interdum totas vites frangunt.

---

[1] H. de Villefosse, 'La mosaïque des quatre saisons', *Gaz. Arch.* (1879), pl. XXII (illustrating a *sarculum bicorne* [= Gk. σμινύη]).

(*g*) Colum. 4. 5. 1 (on frequency of hoeing the vineyard). 'No limit should be set to the number of times that the ground is to be turned with the *two-pronged mattock* ... But ... most people have thought it sufficient to dig over newly planted vineyards every thirty days from 1 March to 1 October ...': numerus autem vertendi soli *bidentibus* ... definiendus non est, sed ... satis plerisque visum est, ex Kalendis Martiis usque in Octobres tricesimo quoque die novella vineta confodere.

(*h*) Colum. 4. 14. 1 (on the cultivation of young vines trained on the frame system). (After fastening the cuttings to the frame) 'then follows the digger, to break up the surface soil evenly and finely with many strokes of the *two-pronged mattock*': insequitur deinde fossor, qui crebris *bidentibus* aequaliter et minute soli terga comminuat.

(*j*) Colum. 5. 9. 12 (on cultivating olives). 'But it (i.e. the olive plantation) ought to be ploughed at least twice a year and dug deeply all round the trees with the *two-pronged mattock*': sed id minime bis anno arari debet: et *bidentibus* alte circumfodiri.

(*k*) Pliny 17. 54 (on the use of lupins as green manure). 'No manure is more beneficial than a crop of lupins turned in with the plough or *two-pronged mattock* before the plants form pods': nihil esse utilius lupini segete priusquam siliquetur aratro vel *bidentibus* versa.

(*l*) Pliny 18. 46 (on keeping land clear of weeds). 'Land overgrown with rushes should be turned over with the spade after being first broken up with *two-pronged mattocks*': iuncosus ager verti pala debet, ante infractus *bidentibus*.

(*m*) Pallad. 2. 10. 2 (on the furrow system of planting vines). 'Furrows are therefore made ... 2½ or 3 feet wide, in such a way that two diggers linked together can cover with their *two-pronged mattocks* an area marked out by a cord to a depth of 3 or 2½ feet': fiunt ergo sulci ... latitudine pedum duorum et semis, vel trium, ita ut iuncti duo fossores designatum linea spatium *bidentibus* persequantur altitudine trium vel duorum et semis pedum.

(*n*) Pallad. 4. 7. 1 (on pulverizing and digging round the soil of young vines). 'In this month (March) we must begin covering the young vines with dust; this must be kept up every first day of the month until October, not only to keep down the weeds, but in order to prevent the young shoots, which are still tender, from being pinched by the impacted soil': hoc mense novella vinea incipit pulverari, quod nunc et deinceps per omnes Kalendas, usque ad Octobres, faciendum est, non solum propter herbas, sed ne tenera adhuc semina solidata terra constringat.

(*o*) Pallad. 8. 5 (on eradicating grass). 'Also, if *two-pronged mattocks* are made of cypress-wood, and dipped in goat's blood ... these implements will, according to the Greek authorities, eradicate grass, after uprooting': item (Graeci asserunt) si *bidentes* cyprei fiant, et sanguine tingantur hircino, ... per eos erutum gramen extingui.

(*p*) Verg. G. 2. 355–6 (after planting vines). 'After the shoots have been planted, there remains the task of cleaving the earth often and (drawing it up) to the crowns, and plying the tough *two-pronged mattocks*':

> seminibus positis superest diducere terram
> saepius ad capita et duros iactare *bidentis*.

(q) Verg. G. 2. 399–400 (on repeated turning over of the soil in the vineyard). '... and the clods must be everlastingly broken up with the *two-pronged mattock* reversed':

glaebaque versis
aeternum frangenda *bidentibus*.

DISCUSSION

1. *General design and functions*

The *bidens*, as the name indicates, was a hoe fitted with a pair of teeth, like the Greek δίκελλα, with which the Glossaries equate it (d). It was amongst the commonest manual implements, mentioned frequently both by the agronomists and elsewhere (e.g. by Lucretius, Ovid, Tibullus and Juvenal), and by the latter writers as the obvious symbol of hard manual labour. Most of the commentators, however, are unsatisfactory in their accounts of its design. Rich (*Dict. Ant.* s.v. 'bidens') assumes it to be a variety of *ligo*, and uses an identical illustration for both implements. R. Billiard, however,[1] shows a drawing of what he describes as a Gallo-Roman *bidens* found at Autun in central France. If this identification could be proved, it would show the *bidens* as differing considerably in design from the split variety of *ligo*, the *bidens* consisting of two separate parallel blades united to the handle, while the *fractus ligo*, as we have seen (above, pp. 38 f.), had a single blade with a notch in the middle. An implement so designed would be very suitable for reducing the surface soil in a young vine-plantation to a fine powder (g) and (o), but it would not be suitable for deep digging operations (m), for breaking up a matted surface (j), or for clod-breaking (p). The explanation of these disparities lies in the term itself: *bidens* was in origin an adjective. In the passages in which the context clearly calls for a heavy implement, *bidens* is just a common and natural abbreviation for *bidens rastrum*, to distinguish it from *rastra* fitted with more than two tines. The fundamental distinction in design between light and heavy *bidentes* was recognized by Olck, *R-E* III. I, s.v. 'bidens' col. 428. 2), who cites the important monumental evidence (see below, s.v. 'Monuments', and Figs. 29 and 30).

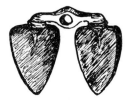

Fig. 28. Bidens

2. *Classification of types*

Surviving specimens may be classified in the following ways: (i) according to weight (see section 1 above); (ii) more specifically, according to the design of the blades or tines, and the method by which they were attached to the bar.

Examination of the numerous surviving specimens indicates a functional

[1] R. Billiard, *La Vigne dans l'antiquité* (Lyon, 1931), p. 323 (=Billiard, *La Vigne*).

difference between two types: (1) those with two or more wide blades for biting into and moving soil horizontally; (2) those with two or more round or square tines for biting into and stirring soil without appreciable horizontal displacement.

Implements of this type were of either single or double construction, either forged from a single piece of iron to form a U-shaped bar as in Fig. 29, or having the tines forged on to a horizontal bar as in Fig. 28. The latter method was normal in multi-tined *rastra*, which thus resemble the modern garden rake. Implements of the bladed type would be needed for chopping up rush-grown land (passage (*k*)), the tined varieties for the clearing and tilling operations required in the vineyard.

3. *Function and operational technique*

Fig. 29. Bidens

(*a*) The heavy *bidens*, as both literary and monumental references prove, was commonly used for breaking the soil in stony ground, especially where vines and olives were to be planted, and where the land was infested with bracken or rushes (*l*). In both cases the double-tined implement had the advantage over a single-bladed *ligo* or *marra*, since it attacked the surface like a pair of pickaxes, being equally effective in breaking through a stony or a matted surface (see the Istanbul mosaic, Plate 3).

It was also regularly used as a clod-breaker, as was the *rastrum* (*k*). For clearing an old plantation, which involved the removal of stumps as well as the clearing away of bracken and other surface growth, a double mattock, consisting of a narrow blade on one side and a *bidens* on the other, was employed in later times (see Palladius 1. 43. 3—*ascias in aversa parte referentes rastros*, and the discussion s.v. 'rastrum' (no. 5 below)).

Fig. 30. Bidens

(*b*) A *bidens* of lighter weight was in constant use in the vine nursery and the vineyard. Equipped with round or square tines it would be an ideal implement for dislodging and stirring soil around the roots of vines without cutting them (passages (*e*), (*f*), (*l*), (*n*)). Here the *bidens* was preferred to the plough, as Columella explains (*f*). Trenching was dangerous in an established vineyard, since it tended to expose and dry out the surface roots, while ploughing was not recommended, since it involved the risk of breaking off the roots of the vine (Columella, *De Arb.* 10. 5), as well as making ridges, instead of the unbroken surface required for this type of cultivation. Good drainage is absolutely essential for success in viticulture, and the process known as *pulveratio* ('powdering'), described by Palladius (*n*) is still the rule in the great vine-growing areas of France, and is still performed with the aid of an implement very similar to the light-weight *bidens* (see below, under 'Survival').

4. *Monuments*

(*a*) *Extant representations.* Rich (*Dict. Ant.* s.v. 'bidens') describes the implement as a strong, heavy two-pronged hoe, and illustrates the text with a cut of an engraved gem in which the god Saturn is depicted as an agricultural slave. Since he uses the identical cut to illustrate the *ligo*, his identification of one or the other must be wrong. The implement is most likely to be a *fractus ligo* (see above, s.v. 'ligo', pp. 38 f.). The implement is rarely depicted on this class of monument. A heavy type of *bidens*, shaped somewhat like a horseshoe, but with long, backward-curving tines, is known from a finely preserved mosaic pavement of superb workmanship in the Great Palace of the Byzantine Emperors at Istanbul.[1] The mosaic, which is still *in situ*, presents a vigorous picture of two men hoeing in échelon formation in an orchard or olive grove; the workman in the foreground has just completed the stroke, while his companion, working just ahead of him, has reached the top of his swing (see Plate 3). Orchard and market garden cultivation with two men working in échelon is still common practice in southern Europe. A rather similar implement of horseshoe shape, with its curved blades set at an acute angle to the shaft, appears as a marginal illustration in an ancient MS of Terence in the Vatican (Vat. lat. 3226), where the text refers to *rastri*.[2] Similar in design is the 'vineyard bidens' used chiefly for the winter operation known as 'ablaqueatio' (above, p. 50), which is represented on a number of monuments, including the celebrated mosaic from Cherchel, Algeria (see Plate 4), published by J. Bérard (*MEFR*, LII, 1935, pl. XI, p. 120). The two lower registers depict this operation being carried out with great vigour by two pairs of labourers each directed by an overseer. The long, widely spaced tines are set at an acute angle to the handle, enabling the implement to claw away the earth from around the base of the vine (see also Gauckler, *Inv. des mos. d'Afrique*, III (Algérie), no. 350, for an identical *bidens*). The bas-relief from the Catacombs of Callistus (see p. 23) shows a light *bidens* with a short handle.

(*b*) *Extant specimens.* The simple *bidens* is not common; the annexed illustrations (Figs. 27 and 29) are taken from a heavy specimen from Greece, probably of the Roman period, now in the Polytechnic Museum, Athens. The tines are long and thick, with a wide gap. Examples of the dual-purpose *ascia/rastrum* are very common (see Figs. 42–7, pp. 67 f.). The heart-shaped blades of the small vineyard *bidens* from Autun (Fig. 28,

---

[1] *The Great Palace of the Emperors*, 2nd report, ed. by D. Talbot Rice (Edinburgh, 1958), pl. 47 (mosaic from the north-east portico).

[2] R. Billiard, *L'Agriculture dans l'antiquité d'après les Géorgiques de Virgile* (Paris, 1928), p. 58 (=Billiard, *L'Agriculture*).

p. 49) are unique. Implements of such delicate construction have a poor chance of survival.

5. *Survival*

(*a*) *Of the implements.* Jaberg–Jud have collected several specimens from the Po Valley and the Piedmont of northern Italy (e.g. Bd. VII, Karte 1429, no. 18, from S. Elpidio a Mare, in the foothills of the Marche, south of Ancona), and many others not illustrated (nos. 453, 584, 590, 612, 616, 625, 654). They appear to belong to the heavier category used for ground-opening and clod-breaking. Savastano's comprehensive catalogue of manual implements still used in Italian vineyards[1] includes three single-bladed hoes, but no *bidens*, but I found the lighter type still in use, under the name 'arpiots' (cf. 'erpice'?) in Ibiza in 1964.

(*b*) *Of the name.* The name survives in a wide variety of dialect forms in northern and central Italy; Jaberg-Jud (Bd. VII, Karte 1429) cite 'ubbidente', 'abbidente', 'ubbiende' and many other forms of the name.

Fig. 31. Bidens (Italian)

5. **Rastrum** (-i, n.) (pl. *rastri* more freq. than *rastra*), *drag-hoe*

Note: (1) The form *raster seems to have been inferred erroneously from the pl. *rastri,* and commonly appears as the standard form in the dictionaries of antiquities (e.g. Blümner, Daremberg–Saglio, Rich, the last-named also offering *rastrus).

Note: (2) Although *bidens* (i.e. *bidens rastrum*) is a sub-species of *rastrum,* references to it are so numerous that it seemed convenient to allocate a separate section (no. 4 above) to the two-pronged implement, leaving the four- and six-pronged varieties to be discussed here.

Fig. 32. Rastrum quadridens

(*a*) *R–E* I A. 1, cols. 257–8 [Orth].

(*b*) Varro, *LL* 5. 136. '*Drag-hoes*, that is, toothed implements with which they thoroughly scrape away and dig up the ground. From this digging-up they get the name *rastri*': rastri, quibus dentatis penitus eradunt terram atque eruunt, a quo rutu *rastri* dicti.

(*c*) Isid. 20. 14. 6. '*Drag-hoes* also, so called because they scrape the ground, or because the teeth are *rari* (i.e. widely spaced)': rastra quoque aut a radendo terram aut a raritate dentium dicta.

(*d*) Pallad. 1. 43. 3. 'Or narrow mattocks fitted with *drag-hoes* on the opposite side': vel ascias in aversa parte referentes *rastros.*

(*e*) *Corp. Gloss.* s.v. 'bidens'. *Rastrum* bidens II 277. 33.

(*f*) *Ibid.* s.v. 'ligo'. *Rastri,* bidentes IV 255. 16.

(*g*) *Ibid.* s.v. 'raster'. δίκελλα II 169. 4; 490. 53; 513. 17; 539. 13; 551. 36. δίκελλα rastrum hic raster hic bidens II 277. 33. *rastrum* δίκελλα II 277. 33. σκαπάνη II 432. 36. σκαπάνη καὶ σκάφη III 262. 61 (unde?). δίκελλα, μακέλη,

[1] A. Savastano, *Arboricoltura* (Napoli, 1914), p. 743, fig. 249, nos. I, II, III.

τὸ τζάπιον III 262. 62. *rast⟨r⟩us* (raster?) σκαφεῖον II 169. 3 (ratis *c*). *rastrum* fossorium vel ferramentum duplex II 591. 9. genus strumenti (= instr.) rusticorum V 327. 41. ferramentum culturae; aut a ra⟨d⟩endo terram aut a raritate dentium rastros dicimus; et est generis masculini pluraliter hi rastri et hos rastros his rastris (et aratra dicuntur rastri (= Abstr.)) V 141. 16; 239. 20 (cf. Serv. *Georg.* 1. 94; Isid. 20. 14. 6). *rastro* ligone IV 160. 26; 278. 6; 560. 25; V 239. 19. *rastros* ligones IV 384. 39; V 388. 17. ligones, id est mettocas (*vel* metticas AS) V 387. 28.

(*h*) Cato 10. 3; 11. 4. 'two four-pronged *drag-hoes*': *rastros* quadridentes II.

(*j*) Colum. 2. 10. 23 (preparing ground for turnips). 'Turnips demand a soil that has been thoroughly worked by repeated operations with the plough or the *drag-hoe*': rapi subactum solum pluribus iterationibus aratri vel *rastri* postulant.

(*k*) Colum. 3. 11. 3 (after clearing bush on virgin land by cutting and stumping). 'The little that remains in the lower layer of soil may be dug out with *drag-hoes* . . .': quod superest inferioris soli *rastris* licet effodere . . .

(*l*) Pliny 18. 180 (further preparation of the soil after ploughing). 'After the cross-ploughing has been done there follows the harrowing of the clods with a wicker frame or a *drag-hoe* where circumstances require it': aratione per transversum iterata occatio sequitur, ubi res poscit, crate vel *rastro*.

(*m*) Verg. *G.* 1. 94–5 (on preparation of the soil for cereals). 'He also much improves the fields who breaks the sluggish clods with *drag-hoes*, and draws wicker-work harrows over them . . .':

> multum adeo, *rastris* glaebas qui frangit inertis
> vimineasque trahit cratis, iuvat arva . . .

(*n*) *Ibid.* 1. 166–7 (short list of implements). '. . . the wicked weight of *drag-hoes*': . . . iniquo pondere *rastri*.

(*o*) Catull. 64. 40 (fields deserted at the marriage of Peleus and Thetis). 'No more is the sprawling vine kept clean with curved *drag-hoes*': non humilis curvis purgatur vinea *rastris*.

(*p*) Ovid, *Metam.* 11. 36. 'Hoes, and heavy *drag-hoes*, and long-handled mattocks': sarculaque *rastrique* graves longique ligones.

(*q*) Ovid, *Fast.* 1. 699–700. 'Hoes were idle, mattocks were turned into javelins, and a helmet was fashioned out of a weighty *drag-hoe*':

> sarcula cessabant, versique in pila ligones,
> factaque de *rastri* pondere cassis erat.

(*r*) Seneca, *De Ira* 2. 25. '. . . digging, and lifting his drag-hoe rather high': . . . fodientem et altius *rastrum* allevantem.

DISCUSSION

1. *Design*

The principal Glossary references, which are unusually extensive for this implement, equate it with the δίκελλα, which is the generic name for a mattock or pick (*Corp. Gloss.* III 262. 62—(*e*)), and with two other Greek implements whose names derive from the root σκαπ, to dig. This last identification with a spade-type implement is clearly unsound; the word 'rastrum' is formed from the root *rad*, 'scrape' (cf. 'rostrum', beak, from 'rodere', to gnaw), and both Varro (*b*) and Isidore, at his first attempt (*c*), are on the right track. The further Glossary reference (*Corp. Gloss.* II 277. 33), defining *bidens* as *rastrum bidens*, i.e. a two-pronged *rastrum*, coupled with Cato's references to *rastri quadridentes* (*k*), makes it clear beyond doubt that *rastrum* was a generic term for a striking mattock with multiple tines. The two-pronged variety was evidently so common that it was known simply as 'bidens', i.e. a 'two-pronger'.[1] A *rastrum* with four or more tines bears a close resemblance to our garden-rake, an implement used for removing surface rubbish and levelling off the soil after digging, and is commonly mistranslated 'rake'. But the literary references which describe the action of the *rastrum* (e.g. (*b*), (*j*), (*k*), (*m*)) make it quite clear that it was not a rake, but a mattock. Rakes are either *rastri lignei* or *rastelli* (see below, no. 7).

2. *Types*

Four-pronged and six-pronged varieties are attested by surviving examples in the Naples Museum.[2] That its teeth were set farther apart than those of the ordinary rake is evident from the false etymology in Isidore ('from the widely spaced teeth'—'a raritate dentium' (*c*)).

Descriptive epithets are rare: Vergil (*n*) and Ovid (*p*) refer to the weight of the implement, and the *rastri* that Menedemus is invited to lay down, in the first scene of Terence's *Self-Tormentor* (Ter. *Heauton.* I, i, 36–7 (see below, p. 55)), are obviously heavy. All the surviving specimens I have seen have a backward curve on the tines (see passage (*o*)), and this is also evident on the monumental examples. The curvature both strengthens the implement against the effect of the pulling action and also assists the clearing

---

[1] E.g. Colum. 4. 14. 1; 17. 8, etc. (cultivating in the vineyard); idem, 5. 9. 12 (olive cultivation); Pliny 17. 159 (preparing the soil for vines); idem, 18. 46 (clearing the land of rushes); Pallad. 4. 7. 1 (loosening the soil around young vines).

[2] Reproduced by Petrie, pl. 67, nos. 51 (two-pronged), 55, 56 (four-pronged). The Chicago collection from Boscoreale includes a well-preserved six-pronged *rastrum* (cat. 26159), which is wrongly described as a rake; the same error is repeated by Rostovtzeff, *SEHRE*[2], pl. XI, 2. Other examples from the Naples Museum are mentioned at pp. 55 f., under 'Extant specimens'.

process when the implement is used for breaking up heavy ground (see section 3 below). While most of the literary references imply a heavy implement, the Catullus passage (*o*) requires a lighter type, as does Vergil's reference to removing weeds with *rastri* at G. 1. 155.

3. *Functions*

The *rastrum* was a multi-purpose implement, being employed, like the single-bladed mattock, for digging and clearing the surface of the soil (*b*) (cf. Verg. G. 3. 534), for breaking the ground as substitute for the plough, especially in hilly terrain (*j*), and particularly for reducing the large clods left after ploughing (*l*), (*m*). This clod-breaking activity, which is frequently mentioned in our sources, was rendered necessary by the conditions imposed by the climate. In northern Europe the clods left after the autumn ploughing are soon broken down by the winter frosts, but in the Mediterranean lands, where the principal grain crops must be sown before the onset of winter, the clods must be broken down by clod-breaking equipment, either manual or mechanical. A second use for the *rastrum* was for the removal of roots from the lower layers of soil (*k*). From the evidence of Palladius (*d*) it appears that some *rastri* resembled the English mattock in having an adze-shaped blade (*ascia*) projecting from the opposite side to the prongs, which was used for chopping out the roots encountered when a worn-out vineyard was being converted to pasture or cereal growing. This dual-purpose implement is fully discussed (s.v. 'ascia', pp. 66 ff., Figs. 42–5). A lighter type was used for weeding in the vineyard and elsewhere (*o*).

4. *Monuments*

(*a*) *Extant representations*. The heavy, multi-tined *rastrum* is not, so far as I know, depicted on any of the well-known series of sculptured monuments; for representations of the *bidens* see p. 51. The implement in the margin of the MS of Terence in the Vatican library, Rome (Vat. lat. 3226), which purports to illustrate the words 'these mattocks', 'istos rastros', at *Heauton Timorumenos*, I, i, 36, is in fact a *bidens* with a horse-shoe blade (see the discussion, s.v. 'bidens', p. 51).

(*b*) *Extant specimens*. Only the two-tined (*bidens*) and the four-tined (*quadridens*) varieties are mentioned in the literary sources. The museum collections also include five- and six-tined specimens. There is a heavy five-tined specimen in Florence (Museo Archeologico, inv. 10779 (Plate 5 (*a*)) with close-set tines, for clod-breaking. The Naples collection includes six *rastri quadridentes* (inv. nos. 71733–8), and two well-preserved specimens of the six-tined variety, one of which is remarkable for its very thin prongs

(for light work in the vineyard?); the other resembles closely the specimen from Boscoreale, now in Chicago (Plate 5 (b)). This latter specimen is also reproduced by Rostovtzeff (*SEHRE*², pl. xi, 2, facing p. 65), but wrongly identified as a rake.

5. *Survival*

(a) *Of the implement.* While the heavy *bidens* and the dual-purpose *bidens/ascia* still survive in many districts of Italy (above, p. 52 and Figs. 31, 47, 48), *rastri* with four or more tines are rare (none in Jaberg–Jud). But they are still to be found in more remote parts. I have seen a light four-tined specimen on sale, together with several other manual implements of traditional design, in an ironmonger's shop in Ibiza (Balearic Islands).

(b) *Of the name.* Fr. 'râteau' (m.), a rake; 'ratissoire' (f.), a hoe or light rake (Fr. 'ratisser', to hoe or rake).

It. 'rastrello' (m.), a rake; 'rastrelliera' (f.), a hay-rack, dish-rack (from the shape).

6. Rastelli (-orum, m.) (= Rastri lignei—Colum.), *rakes*

(a) Varro, *LL* 5. 136. '*Rakes* are light saws resembling harrows; with this implement men scrape together the stalks in the meadows during haymaking. The name *rastelli* is derived from this scraping process': *rastelli ut irpices serrae leves; itaque homo in pratis per fenisicia eo festucas corradit, quo ab rasu rastelli dicti.*

(b) Not in Isidore; not in Palladius' list.

(c) *Corp. Gloss.* s.v. 'rastellum'. ligo ligneus v 512. 20. ligonem v 478. 38.
    Note: Daremberg–Saglio also have this late form.

(d) Varro, *RR* 1. 22. 1 (list of items to be raised or made on the farm). '... in general articles which are made of withies and of wood, such as hampers, baskets, threshing-sledges, fans and *rakes*': ... ut fere sunt quae ex viminibus et materia rustica fiunt, ut corbes, fiscinae, tribula, valli, *rastelli*.

(e) Varro, *RR* 1. 49. 1 (after haymaking). 'Then the straw should be scraped off with *rakes* and added to the pile of hay': tum de pratis stipulam *rastellis* eradi atque addere faenisiciae cumulum.

(f) Colum. 2. 10. 27 (on cultivating lucerne). 'When you have made the sowing, the seeds must be covered up as soon as they are put in with *wooden rakes*; they are very easily scorched by the sun ... After sowing, the area ... must be "scoffled" (i.e. lightly hoed) with *wooden rakes*, and weeded from time to time ...': quod (i.e. sementem) ubi feceris, *ligneis rastris* ... statim iacta semina obruantur; nam celerrime sole aduruntur ... Post sationem ... *ligneis rastris* sariendus et identidem runcandus est ...

(g) Colum. 2. 12. 6 (on cultivating lucerne). 'Lucerne, however, is covered, not with the plough, but, as I have said, with *wooden rakes*': at medica obruitur non aratro, sed, ut dixi, *ligneis rastellis*.

DISCUSSION

1. *Design*

The *rastellus* was a wooden implement, similar in design to the modern garden rake, except that it was made entirely of wood; that it simply meant a wooden *rastrum* is evident from the two passages from Columella cited above. Daremberg–Saglio (s.v. 'rastellum') distinguish two implements under this name: (1) a small *rastrum*, used by Nero to inaugurate the cutting of the canal through the Isthmus of Corinth (Suet. *Nero* 19); since Dio, describing the same event, calls the implement a δίκελλα, they assume that it was a *bidens*, but the Suetonius reference is unique, and this implement is not separately listed here, inasmuch as it was evidently a ceremonial implement, like the ceremonial spades used today for cutting the first sod; (2) 'a rake with wooden or iron teeth used for various purposes': this is incorrect: none of the passages cited refers to iron teeth; and there is no authority, other than the Glossaries, for the neuter form.

2. *Functions*

Three main uses are mentioned: (1) for covering the fine seeds of plants such as lucerne, which would be buried too deep for successful germination if ploughed in with the *aratrum* (*f*), (*g*); (2) for 'scoffling' (i.e. gently loosening the top layer of soil in the lucerne beds or in the kitchen-garden around plants too delicate even for the light hoe or *sarculum* (*f*); (3) for raking up hay, straw, etc., at harvest time (*e*). It is curious that the implement does not appear in either of Cato's inventories. Although hay and fodder crops were subsidiary in his system to vines and olives, a supply of rakes of this type will have been essential.

3. *Monuments*

No representations or specimens of the implement appear to have been recorded.

4. *Survival*

(*a*) *Of the implement.* The wooden rake survives in many areas where the task has not been completely mechanized, or where the hand-rake has not yet been superseded by the horse-drawn rake.

(*b*) *Of the name.* It. 'rastrello', a rake, or grass-cutter, also 'rastrellare' to rake; cf. Ir. 'rastal', a rake.

7. Capreolus (-i, m.), *weeding-hoe*

Fig. 33. Capreolus
(Portuguese)

(*a*) *R-E* III. 2, cols. 1548–50 [Olck].

(*b*) Not in Varro, *LL*; not in Isidore.

(*c*) Colum. 11. 3. 46 (on cultivating asparagus). 'The soil should be stirred with *weeding-hoes*. This is a two-pronged iron implement': *capreolis, quod genus bicornis ferramenti est, terra commoveatur.*

DISCUSSION

1. *Design*

The *capreolus* was a two-pronged light weeding-hoe, shaped, as the name implies, like the close-set horns of the chamois, or wild mountain goat.

2. *Function*

Columella (*c*), in the only surviving reference to the implement, recommends its use in the delicate operation of loosening the surface of the asparagus bed before the shoots begin to sprout. A small, delicate implement with close-set prongs would be necessary for this operation, since hoeing with a larger tool would easily damage the tender shoots lying just below the surface.[1]

3. *Monuments*

(*a*) *Extant representations.* Rich (*Dict. Ant.* s.v.) shows a drawing taken from an ancient ivory carving now in Florence, Italy, where the implement 'appears in the hands of a figure standing, with a goat by its side, in the midst of a vineyard, thus identifying its object and name'. The implement as it appears in Rich's drawing, does not resemble the horns of a goat; it appears to be a pole with two crossed sticks at the end, and it does not seem to be made of iron. The identification is certainly wrong.

(*b*) *Extant specimens.* None recorded.

4. *Survival*

(*a*) *Of the implement.* Light hoes with a pair of close-set tines are familiar items in the gardener's tool-shed. The illustration above (Fig. 33) is of a heavier implement of the same basic type, from Portugal (Hopfen, *FIATR*, XLII, fig. 27B (right)).

(*b*) *Of the name.* M. G. Bruno (*Apporti* 150, no. 230, s.v. 'sappa') cites etymological evidence in support of the derivation of the familiar Italian terms 'zappa', 'zappetta', etc., from *capreolus*; cf. also Meyer-Lübke, 9599.

[1] The Portuguese implement has straight tines, but the name 'capreolus' suggests that it was fitted with curved prongs resembling the horns of a goat.

8. Occa (-ae, f.), (dubious)

Not attested before the Glossaries (the reading 'occa' at Columella 2. 17. 4 is suspect). The word is included here as a possible colloquialism for 'rastrum' (*Corp. Gloss.* s.v.). The verb 'occare' is common in all the technical writers for weeding.

(*a*) *Gloss. Isid.* occa, rastrum. *Gloss. Philox.* occa βωλοκόπτημα.

(*b*) †Colum. 2. 17. 4 (on laying down a meadow). '. . . we shall then break down the clods with hoes, and bring on an "occa" to level off the surface . . .': . . . tum glaebas sarculis resolvemus et inducta *occa*[1] coaequabimus . . .

(*c*) Veget. *De Mulomedicina* 1. 56. 5 (on hay-racks for horses). 'The hay-rack, for which the common name is "occa",[2] must not be too high up for the height of the horses . . .': cratis, quae *occa*[2] vocatur a vulgo, pro equorum statura nec minus alta sit . . .

DISCUSSION

On the strength of the two Glossary references, coupled with the possible use of the term 'occa' in later Latin to designate a hay-rack for feeding horses in the stall, it is just possible that *occa* was a vulgar term for *rastrum*, and that it has crept into the text of Columella as a gloss for *crate*. But this is no more than a conjecture.

AXES

9. SECVRIS   10. DOLABRA   11. DOLABELLA   12. ASCIA

Certain implements corresponding to our axe, hatchet and adze may be considered here. Some (e.g. the *ascia*) closely resemble the *ligo* (pp. 37 ff.); in others (e.g. the *dolabra*) the blade is set differently on the haft; but in all of them the action of splitting or chopping (as with an axe), or of chipping or whittling (as with an adze), is effected by swinging and striking, as in the case of most of the implements so far discussed under the general heading of mattocks. Some were exclusively employed in forestry, others in mining as well as in forestry and agriculture proper. One preliminary distinction should be noticed: axes and hatchets are clearly distinguished in form from adzes and mattocks; the former have their blades set parallel to the line of the haft, while in the latter the edge of the blade is set at an angle to the haft (see the illustrations of *securis*, e.g. Fig. 34, and 'ascia', e.g. Fig. 41, p. 66).

[1] *Sed exemplaria castigatiora praebent* crate (Forc.).
[2] iacca, cocca, zaca: *codd.*; *sed* occa *leg. esse vid. Schneidero* (Forc. *ad loc.*).

Fig. 34. Securis

9. Securis (-is, f.), *axe, hatchet*

Securis is the general term for the implement which corresponds to our axe and hatchet.

(*a*) Not in Varro, *LL*; not in Isidore.

(*b*) Pallad. 1. 43. 3. '*Axes* are either simple or fitted with a hatchet': *secures simplices vel dolabratas.*

(*c*) *Corp. Gloss.* s.v. 'securis'. securis πέλεκυς II 181. 8; 496. 10; 520. 47; 541. 40. III 325. 57 = 503. 23 (secoreis securis), etc. . . . securis ἀξίνη III 23. 34. secure axnari (ἀξινάρι) Buecheler II 563. 36.

(*d*) Cato 10. 3. '3 axes': *securis* III.

(*e*) Cato 11. 4. '5 axes': *securis* V.

(*f*) Colum. 4. 25. 1. 'The section placed above it (the "beak"), and shaped like a half-moon, is the "*hatchet*"': cui (i.e. rostro) superposita semiformis lunae species *securis* dicitur.

The use of *securis* is frequent in the other agronomists in the general sense of the woodman's axe; common in the same sense in other literature, both prose and verse; also used generally of the miner's axe and the headsman's axe.

DISCUSSION

Fig. 35. Ascia/securis (Italian)

1. *Design*

The basic shape is familiar enough: the sides of the blade are more or less concave in profile, while the cutting edge is more or less convex. The blade is wedge-shaped in section, its thickness decreasing from the narrow haft end to the broader cutting edge; and the blade is socketed to receive the haft. In its Roman form it might be either single- (*s. simplex*) or double-bladed (*s. dolabrata*), having a vertical cutting edge on the one arm, and a horizontal one on the other. The term *bipennis* (i.e. double-axe) is normally used only to denote the double-bladed battle-axe, though it may occasionally be used in poetry as equivalent to the *securis*, as in Horace, *Odes* 4. 4. 57.

The term was also used, as in Columella (*f*) and elsewhere in the agronomists, for the axe-shaped part of the vine-dresser's knife (the *falx vinitoria*). From surviving examples, which are very numerous, it is clear that *secures* varied considerably in size, weight and shape. Those used for felling trees may be easily distinguished from the short-handled types used for chopping small timber by differences in the width and convexity of the cutting-edge. The woodman's axe was both wider and more convex than that used by the carpenter or the butcher.

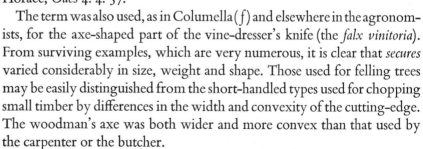

2. *Functions*

Heavier long-handled types were used for felling standing timber; lighter types for splitting logs, chopping out roots, making stakes, and for many other tasks. The double-bladed type, which closely resembled the English mattock, was an excellent implement for clearing overgrown land, when both stumping and chopping out of roots were required.

3. *Monuments*

(*a*) *Extant representations*. Axes appear very frequently on extant monuments. Trajan's Column in Rome, with its numerous tree-felling scenes, provides six examples of soldiers felling trees with the wide-bladed *securis* and two with the shorter hatchet[1] (there is a replica of the Column in the Victoria and Albert Museum, London). From the study of these examples it is evident that the official headsman's axe, which was carried with the bundle of scourging-rods by the lictor, was only a slightly modified form of the standard type used in tree-felling.

(*b*) *Extant specimens*. Fine collections of these implements may be seen in the Naples Museum, where there are more than seventy, discovered in Pompeii and the neighbourhood. Petrie (ch. II) features a large range of socketed axes from many parts of the ancient world, including several fine Roman specimens. Our illustration (Fig. 34, p. 60) is taken from the excellent collection at Saint-Germain-en-Laye, which is fully represented in Reinach.[2]

4. *Survival*

(*a*) *Of the implement*. The shape and the method of hafting have remained largely unaltered down to the present day.

(*b*) *Of the name*. The name survives with little modification in the Italian word 'scure' (f.), the general term for an axe.

10. **Dolabra** (-ae, f.), *hatchet*

(*a*) *R-E* v. I, cols. 1274–5 [Mau].

(*b*) Not in Varro, *LL*; not in Isidore, except as mining implement (18. 9. 11).

[1] C. Cichorius, *Die Reliefs der Traianssäule* (Berlin, 1896–1900) (= Cichorius, *Traianssäule*), Tafel XXXVII, p. 129, Bild 51 (a *dolabra*); Taf. LIII, 189, Bild 73 (2 *dolabrae*); Taf. LXVII, 242, 243, Bild 92 (2 *dolabrae*); Taf. LXXXVI, 315, Bild 116 (1 *dolabra*); Taf. LXXXVIII, 316, Bild 117 (1 *dolabra*); Taf. XXXVIII, 132, 133, Bild 61 (2 *secures*); Taf. XCV, 343, Bild 126 (1 *securis*).
[2] Reinach, *Cat. Ill.* p. 261, fig. 272. Small axes are well represented in finds from the Romano-British city of Silchester (Calleva Atrebatum), now on loan to the Reading City Museum. All are fully documented.

Fig. 36. Dolabra

(c) Pallad. 1. 43. 1. 'Two-pronged drag-hoes, *hatchets* . . . which we are to use on trees and vines': bidentes, *dolabras* . . . quibus in arbore utamur et vite.

(d) *Corp. Gloss.* s.v. 'dolabra'. *Dolabra* ἀξίνη τεκτονική (dolabra *codd., non* dolob.) II 54. 32. ἀξίνη III 325. 56. *dolobra* ἀξίνη III 204. 31. *dolabrum* ἀξίνη II 55. 42; 503. 37. ἀξίνη πελεκητρίς II 547. 15. *dolobra, dolobrum* ἀξίνη II 231. 43. *dolabra* πέλεκυς III 368. 62; 502. 34. ὄρυξ II 387. 31, etc. *delebra* instrumenta rusticana quos dicimus rastros V 284. 38. dolabrum est dolaturia V 287. 53 (cf. *Roensch Coll.* p. 198). V. dolamen, delabrum.

(e) Colum. *RR* 2. 2. 28 (on ploughing). 'The ploughman must use his *hatchet* as much as his ploughshare; he must dig up and . . . hunt out the broken-off stumps and surface-roots': nec minus *dolabra* quam vomere bubulcus utatur, et praefractas stirpes summasque radices . . . refodiat ac persequatur.

(f) Colum. *De Arb.* 10. 2 (on pruning vines). 'Shoots which are old and dried-out, and which cannot be cut away with the pruning-knife, should be pared away with a sharp *hatchet*': arida et vetera, falce quae amputari non possunt, acuta *dolabra* abradito.

(g) Pallad. 2. 1 (on *ablaqueatio*) '. . . the vines should be "ablaqueated" . . . that is, to open up the soil around the base of the vine carefully with the *hatchet*, and . . . to make shallow depressions': . . . ablaqueandae sunt vites . . . id est, circa vitis codicem *dolabra* terram diligenter aperire et . . . velut lacus efficere.

(h) Pallad. 2. 3 (after the first ploughing). 'All clods should be broken up with hatchets': glebae omnes *dolabris* dissipandae sunt.

(j) Pallad. 3. 21. 2 (on restoring rose-beds). 'Old rose-beds . . . are dug round with light hoes or *hatchets*': antiqua rosaria . . . circumfodiuntur sarculis vel *dolabris*.

The word occurs several times in the historians (Livy, Tacitus, Curtius) in accounts of assaults on walls and ramparts. Its chief military use was in demolishing fortifications (Livy 21. 11; Tacitus, *Hist.* 3. 20, etc.), while it was also employed in the construction of palisades (Vegetius, *De Re Mil.* 2. 25, etc.).

DISCUSSION

1. *Design*

Fig. 37. Dolabra

The shape of this implement is known for certain; a sepulchral monument found at Aquileia in north-eastern Italy, which depicts the deceased carrying an axe-type implement on his shoulders, contains also the inscription DOLABRARIVS COLLEGII FABRVM (i.e. a pick-axe maker, member of the Institute of Smiths).[1] As shown here, and on numerous other monuments, the *dolabra* was a double-headed implement having on one side a rather narrow axe-blade, counterbalanced on the other side by a narrow pick, which might be either straight or crooked (see Figs. 36–9, pp. 61 ff.). The lexicographical and literary references give no information about its design,

[1] Rich (*Dict. Ant.*), s.v. 'dolabra'; the inscription (*CIL* v, 908) reads: Ti. Claudius Ti. Claudi Epaphroditian. Vet. Leg. vii P. F. Fil. Astylus Dolabrar. Col. Fab. vivos fecit sibi et Iuliae Dionysi coniugi bene de se mer.

but three of the Glossary references (II 547. 15; III 368. 32; 504. 34) equate it with the Greek πέλεκυς, which we know to have been a double-bladed axe, the single-bladed variety being denoted by the term ἀξίνη (cf. Eng. 'axe').

2. *Functions and operational technique*

The long-handled form is well known as the excavator's and miner's pick (*dolabra fossoria*; cf. e.g. Statius, *Theb.* 2. 418). In agriculture it had two main uses. First, it was used in preparing for cultivation ground previously under timber, to root out stumps and surface-roots (passage (*c*)); frequent reference is made in the agronomists to the digging-up of worn-out vineyards for cereal or legume cultivation. Again, in the vineyard, it was used for chopping out old, dried-out shoots (passage (*d*)). The smaller type required for this operation is known from a surviving specimen found at Boscoreale, in the vine-growing area around Vesuvius (Petrie, pl. 14, no. 53). In his account of the implement Petrie (*TW*, 15), points out that many of the surviving Roman specimens resemble the mattock: 'the reason for this may be that they were for working in woodland, where a main need was the cutting of roots, so that an adze-edge was required' (*loc. cit.*). The second main use was for breaking up the clods left after ploughing. The principal reference to this (passage (*h*)) comes from the late writer Palladius, the common implement used for this purpose in earlier practice being the drag-hoe or *rastrum* (q.v.). Palladius' main concern in his *De Re Rustica* is with vines and orchard trees, and the *dolabra* is frequently mentioned in this connection, as used for the process of digging round the base of the vine (*ablaqueatio*) (*g*), digging round old rose-beds (*j*), etc.

Fig. 38. Dolabra

In addition to these uses the *dolabra* was used by woodmen for splitting logs. In the well-known scene on Trajan's Column (see below, under 'Monuments') it is the crooked-pick variety that is used.

3. *The varieties of pick*

Three types are known from finds and monuments: (i) the straight pick (Figs. 36 and 38); (ii) the down-turned pick (Fig. 40); (iii) the up-turned pick (Figs. 37 and 39). There is no dispute about the functions of types (i) and (ii). Type (ii) is the commonest, and was a general-purpose cleaver. Its downward curve was designed for dislodging stones embedded in the face of the quarry or mine-working. It is the type still used on the fireman's axe for prising open door-frames and dislodging planking. But type (iii), which is featured on Trajan's Column and in the Saalburg collection, requires explanation. Two items of forester's equipment still in use seem to suggest that it was a useful dual-purpose implement, the axe-head being

used for splitting and shaping logs and the upward-curving pick for rolling them into position. The English log-roller is known as a 'cant-hook' (Huggard and Owen, *Forest Tools and Instruments*, London, 1960, p. 77, fig. 28. 5). An Australian implement with the same upward curvature is known as a 'picaroon'. If this is the correct explanation, it would fit very well the fact that most of the examples are from military centres like Saalburg or from the representation of Trajan's Dacian campaigns, where 'log-cabin' forts were strongly featured.

4. *Monuments*

Fig. 39. Dolabra

(*a*) *Extant representations*. The most important of these is the sepulchral monument from Aquileia already mentioned (see Fig. 37), which contains the inscription that fixes the identity of the implement (above, p. 62). The implement appears frequently on Trajan's Column, most commonly in the numerous scenes depicting tree-felling by the Roman forces advancing into wooded country during the invasions of Dacia, twice in the hands of soldiers demolishing enemy defence-works, and once in a vigorous representation of a legionary soldier splitting a log in front of a fort.[1] The difference between the straight- and crooked-pick types is clearly indicated by Rich (*Dict. Ant.* s.v.), but the implement is wrongly equated there with the Greek ἀξίνη, which is a single-headed axe. Good drawings are to be found in E. Saglio's article (Daremberg–Saglio, t. II, 1, 328–9, s.v. 'dolabra', figs. 2485–8, including an example on an Etruscan mirror (*ibid.* fig. 2488)).

(*b*) *Extant specimens*. These are common in the museum collections; some of the finest are illustrated by Petrie (pl. 14, nos. 53, 57, 58 (from Boscoreale), 55 (from Velleia), 54 (from Pompeii), 56 and 60 (both from Mainz, West Germany)). Plate 59, no. T 59, an excellent example of the crooked type, was found at the Roman fortress of Newstead in Scotland, (J. Curle, *A Roman Frontier Post and its People*, Glasgow, 1911, pl. LVII, no. 5). The annexed illustrations are both from the Pompeii district of Central Italy, Fig. 36 (= Petrie 54) illustrating the heavier, and Fig. 38 (= Petrie 53) the lighter version of the agricultural type.

5. *Survival*

See below, s.v. 'dolabella'.

II. **Dolabella** (-ae, f.), *small hatchet*

Not in the lexicographers. Mentioned only in the two passages from Columella cited below.

Colum. 4. 24. 4 (a detailed account of pruning operations in the vineyard). 'Now to begin from the base of the vine, the earth around the stock must

[1] Cichorius, *op. cit.* Taf. LIII, 189, Bild 73 (Fig. 39).

always be removed with the *small hatchet*': nam ut ab ima vite incipiam, semper circa crus *dolabella* dimovenda terra est.

Ibid. 4. 24. 5 (further on in the same passage). 'But if part of the trunk has completely dried out ... or if the vine has become hollow, it will be useful to clean off all dead wood with the *small hatchet*': si vero trunci pars ... peraruit, aut ... cavata vitis est, *dolabella* conveniet expurgare quicquid emortuum est.

Fig. 40. Dolabella

DISCUSSION

1. *Design*

As the diminutive form implies, the *dolabella* was a small, short-handled *dolabra*. Rich's drawing (*Dict. Ant.* s.v.), taken from a sepulchral marble, has a straight cutting blade, like that of a chisel, on one side, and a crooked pick on the other, with a very pronounced curve, like that of a pruning-hook (see Fig. 40 above). Nisard (*ad* Colum. *locc. citt.*) wrongly translates *dolabella* by 'dolone', which is the adze.

2. *Functions and operational technique*

The first passage is concerned with the operation known as *ablaqueatio* (i.e. trenching round the base of the vine or olive so as to remove surface rootlets, and to make a shallow depression (*lacus*), admitting heat and moisture to the base of the plant). The operation is clearly described by Pliny (*HN* 17. 140). For the extreme care required in order to avoid damage to the stock see Columella, *De Arb.* 5. 3–4. This autumn operation also included root-trimming, and for this the hooked portion of the implement would be effective, the hatchet being used for chopping away the dead wood, as prescribed in the second passage above.

3. *Monuments*

(a) *Extant representations*. Rich (*Dict. Ant.* s.v.) cites Mazzocchi, *De Ascia*, 179 for a short implement of this type from a sepulchral monument. The soldier who is depicted in the act of splitting a log on Trajan's Column (Cichorius, *Traianssäule*, Taf. LIII, 73, 189) is using a short-handled implement, and grasping it at both ends of the haft, while his pose is more suited to the task of chopping a small piece of wood than to that of splitting a heavy log. Possibly the sculptor has exaggerated the girth of the log, and the implement is intended to be a short hatchet or *dolabella*.

(b) *Extant specimens*. The Naples collection, which is particularly rich in *asciae* and *dolabrae* (see Appendix B), contains a few light *dolabrae*, but no specimen with a twisted pick. There is a good example of the small chopper in the Saalburg collection (*Saalburgjahrb.* 1, 1910, Taf. 1, no. 5); the back of

the implement is squared off to form a hammer, like a modern hatchet. The implement is also well represented in Romano-British collections, e.g. Reading City Museum (from the Silchester hoard of 1890.)

4. *Survival*

(a) *Of the implements.* 'The standard form of *dolabra* corresponds to our "pioche à déchausser", known locally in the Saône-et-Loire vineyards as "besseron de Fuissé"' (A. Lagrange, 'Notes sur le vocabulaire viticole', *REL*, xxv, 1947, 79). The ancient and modern implements are basically of the same design, and the pick section is still used for cleaning the base of the vine. Lagrange found the prototype *dolabella* still in use in 1947, the pick being used to clear the earth away, the unwanted growth being trimmed off with the hatchet portion.

(b) *Of the names.* The derivations all refer to forms of the adze or axe-adze, Fr. dolabre (f.), axe-adze; Fr. doloire (f.), carpenter's adze; It. delobra (dial.), axe-adze.

12. (i) Ascia (-ae, f.), *adze* **(ii) Ascia/rastrum** *Combination mattock/2-pronged drag-hoe.*

(a) *R-E* II. 2, cols. 1522–3 [Mau].

(b) Not in Varro, *LL.*

(c) Isid. 19. 19. 12. The *adze* takes its name from the splinters (*astulae*) which it removes from a piece of wood; it has a diminutive form *asciola*. There is, however, an *adze* with a short handle which has on the opposite side a hammer with either a simple or a hollowed blade or a two-pronged drag-hoe': *ascia ab astulis dicta quae a ligno eximit; cuius diminutivum est asciola. est autem manubrio brevi ex adversa parte referens vel simplicem malleum, aut cavatum, vel bicorne rastrum.*

(d) Pallad. I. 43. 3. 'Or *narrow mattocks* fitted with drag-hoes on the opposite side': vel *ascias* in aversa parte referentes rastros.

(e) *Corp. Gloss.* s.v. 'ascia'. Ascia σκέπαρνον II 23. 58; 433. 5; 496. 26; 521. 14; 545. 2; III 23. 33; 204. 23; 325. 55; 368. 59; 503. 74. ferramentum, aecsa (*vel* etsa; *ubi* aetsa *vel* aedsa *Kluge* AS) II 568. 22.

Fig. 41. Ascia

DISCUSSION

1. *Agricultural use of the term 'ascia'*

The important distinctions in design and function between the axe and the adze have already been discussed (above, p. 59). The term *ascia*, equated with the Greek σκέπαρνον and with the English axe, covered a wide variety of implements, including the common carpenter's adze (superseded

in modern times by the plane), a mason's tool of similar design, and a bricklayer's chopper. In agriculture its use is confined to the specialized tool referred to by Palladius (d), which consisted of a narrow mattock-type blade on one side, and a two-pronged *rastrum* (i.e. a *bidens*, q.v.) on the other. This peculiar dual-purpose implement is not mentioned in any other literary source, but surviving examples are known. Dual- or multi-purpose implements are particularly useful in the complex operations of viticulture and horticulture, enabling the farmer to economize on the number of separate tools to be provided, as well as time spent on the series of operations. For other multi-purpose implements see the discussions s.v. 'dolabra', pp. 62 ff., and 'falx vinitoria', pp. 94 ff.

2. *Design*

(a) *The simple ascia.* Rich (*Dict. Ant.* s.v. 'ascia') describes the implement as a short-handled hoe, used 'for breaking up the ground, excavating earth, and similar purposes'. He then cites Palladius 1. 43. 3, which refers only to the double-headed implement. His illustration, taken from Trajan's Column, is that of a single-bladed hoe, with an adze-shaped blade and a short handle. His comparison of this implement with the short-handled 'zappa' still used in Italy today is irrelevant, since we have no evidence that the term 'ascia' was ever used of such an implement. Hoes vary greatly in shape, weight and angle to the shaft, and there is no particular reason why this shape should have acquired a specific name, which has, moreover, gone unrecorded in the literature. Forcellini (s.v. 'ascia') makes the same assumption without citing any relevant evidence. Mau (*art.* 'ascia', *R-E* IV. 2, col. 1549 (6)) offers no comment on the identity of the implement. Implements of appropriate shape and size exist (e.g. Reinach, *Cat. Ill.* fig. 277, nos. 16244, 19731, 25797, described there as 'pioche en forme d'herminette (*sape*)'), but whether they were known by the name 'ascia' is uncertain.

(b) *The double-headed ascia.* As may be seen from the specimens illustrated (nos. 43–7, pp. 67–8) this popular implement was made in a great variety of shapes and weights, varying from 15 to 45 cm in length, and with narrow or spatulate adze-blades (cf., for example, Figs. 43 and 45).

3. *Functions of the ascia/rastrum*

These implements could naturally perform all the tasks for which the separate *bidens* and *ligo* or *marra* were employed. The literary references are late and uninformative, but we may assume that they were invented in areas where such combined operations were in heavy demand, especially in the preparation of ground for growing vines, and in trenching and

Fig. 42.
Ascia/rastrum

Fig. 43.
Ascia/rastrum

Fig. 44.
Ascia/rastrum

Fig. 45.
Ascia/rastrum

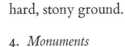

Fig. 46.
Ascia

Fig. 47.
Ascia/rastrum

Fig. 48.
Ascia/rastrum
(Italian)

soil-shifting operations generally. A spatulate blade like that of Fig. 43 would be particularly useful for ridging and earth-moving, while the spur-shaped tines of Fig. 44 indicate an implement for digging and clearing hard, stony ground.

4. *Monuments*

(*a*) *Extant representations.* The carpenter's and mason's *asciae* are very common on sepulchral monuments;[1] the double-headed implement, for reasons which are perfectly obvious, does not occur.

(*b*) *Extant specimens.* The double-headed implement is very common in the leading collections. The Naples collection includes eight specimens with the balancing hammer as described by Isidore (above, p. 66), varying from 20 to 40 cm in overall length. Petrie includes a small type from Velleia in the Po Valley, north Italy (Fig. 45), and a much larger example with a spatulate blade from Gloucestershire, England (Fig. 43). The implement is well represented in the Saalburg collection by two very large specimens and one of the smaller type, all three extremely well made (*Saalburgjahrb.* III, 1912, Taf. 8, no. 17 (= Fig. 44); VI, 1914, 1924, Taf. 10, no. 2; VII, 1930, Taf. 14, no. 13). Reinach, *Cat. Ill.* fig. 277, no. 15869, is a powerful implement of medium size, used for clearing and hoeing (from Compiègne, north-east France).

5. *Survival*

(*a*) *Of the implement.* (i) Single-bladed *ascia.* The single-bladed implement depicted on Trajan's Column in Rome (Cichorius, *Traianssäule*, Taf. XL, 56, Bild 139 (= Fig. 46)) may not have been called an *ascia*, but it bears a very striking resemblance to the short-handled 'zappa' or 'zappetta' used by Italian farm-labourers and gardeners.

(ii) The double-headed type corresponding to Palladius' description (above, p. 66) is reported by Jaberg–Jud from two distinct areas in Italy: Fig. 47 is from Palmoli in the mountainous Molise/Abruzzi region of Central Italy, Fig. 48 comes from Galliate on the river Ticino, west of Milan (Jaberg–Jud, Karte 1429, nos. 14 and 15). Their resemblance to Fig. 46 (now in the Parma Museum) is clear. See also H. Wuilleumier, *art.* 'ascia' in *Rev. de l'hist. des religions* 128 (1944), pp. 40 ff.

(*b*) *Of the name.* It. 'ascia' (f.), axe, hatchet. Fr. 'asse' (f.), 'asseau' (m., dial.), Marne, Ardennes; 'assados' (m., dial.), Languedoc: axe, hatchet.

[1] E.g. Espérandieu, *Gaule*, t. II, no. 1117, p. 158 (*ascia* on the tomb of a carpenter from Bordeaux); *ibid.* no. 1196, p. 193 (carpenter's *ascia* in a niche); *ibid.* t. VI, no. 5226, p. 408 (mason's *ascia* from Trier, West Germany).

3

KNIVES, SICKLES, HOOKS
AND SCYTHES

This section comprises all types of knives, whether straight-edged, like some forms of *culter*, or of curved form throughout, like the various types of *falx*. They differ fundamentally from the mattocks and axes in that the blade, instead of being attached to the handle at varying angles, is a continuation of it, and is usually inserted into it by means of a tapered iron prong, known as the tang. The blade with which implements of this class are equipped may be used in a variety of actions. Thus straight-bladed knives may be used with a cutting, slicing, shaving or even with a chopping action (see below s.v. 'cultellus'), while curved knives may be used with a lopping action (i.e. striking and cutting actions combined), as with the billhook (*falx arboraria, falx putatoria*, see below s.v.), or with a sawing action, as with the sickle (*falx messoria*, q.v.).

KNIVES

1. CVLTER   2. CVLTELLVS

1. Culter (-tri, m.), *knife*

(a) *R-E* IV. 2, cols. 1752–3 [Mau] (no reference to agricultural uses).

(b) Not in Varro, *LL*; not in Isidore.

(c) *Corp. Gloss.* s.v. 'culter'. *Culter* μάχαιρα II, p. xxxvii; 509. 28; III 726. 17; 530. 42 . . . colter cultella II 574. 12.

(d) Colum. 4. 25. 1. 'Now the shape of the vine-dresser's knife is so designed that the part next to the haft, which has a straight edge, is called the "*knife*", because it resembles a knife': est autem sic disposita figura vinitoriae falcis figura, ut capulo pars proxima, quae rectam gerit aciem, *culter* ob similitudinem nominetur.

(e) Pliny 18. 171. 'There are many kinds of ploughshare; *culter* (knife) is the name given to the part fixed in front of the share-beam, cutting the earth before it is broken up, and marking out the tracks for the furrows that are to be made with incisions, which the backward-sloping share is to bite out in the process of ploughing. Another kind is the ordinary share . . .': vomerum plura genera; *culter* vocatur *infixus prae dentali* priusquam proscindatur terram

secans futurisque sulcis vestigia praescribens incisuris quas resupinus in arando mordeat vomer. (* infixus prae dentali? *Mayhoff*: infelix (inflexus *Sillig*) praedensam.)

DISCUSSION

The word *culter* is of frequent occurrence in the sense of kitchen-knife and hunting-knife and is sometimes used of the barber's razor. The passages cited above appear to be the only instances of its occurrence in the agricultural vocabulary. In the first passage it is used to designate one of the six parts of the composite vine-dresser's knife (*falx vinitoria*), and is fully discussed in section 12. The vexed passage from Pliny (*e*) is concerned with the various parts of the plough and is commonly regarded as referring to what is still called the coulter of a plough, that is, a curved blade slotted into the beam, which makes a vertical cut in advance of the *vomer* or share. This suggestion must be rejected as anachronistic; the coulter belongs to a different class of plough from any known to have existed in Pliny's day; and in any case this *culter*, if it existed in Italy in Roman times, is not a manual implement, and is therefore out of place here. The reference is included in this section, since most of the dictionaries mention it in the sense of 'coulter'. For a full discussion see s.v. 'aratrum', pp. 133 ff.

2. Cultellus (-i, m.), (i) *pruning knife*, (ii) *machete*

Fig. 49. Cultellus (Nigerian)

(*a*) *R-E* IV. 2, cols. 1752–3, contains no reference to agricultural uses.

(*b*) Not in Varro, *LL*.

(*c*) Isidore 20. 14. 3. '*Pruning knives* take their name from pruning, from the fact that they were used by the ancients for pruning trees and vines before the invention of pruning hooks': cultelli a cultura dicti, eo quod ex ipsis veteres in arbore utebantur et vite, priusquam falces essent repertae.

(*d*) *Corp. Gloss.* s.v. 'cultellus'. *Cultellus* μαχαίριον II 118. 49; 119. 54; 542. 22. *cultellum* II 365. 34; III 23. 28, etc.

(*e*) Pallad. 1. 43. 2 (in the inventory of agricultural implements). 'Also small curved *pruning knives*, which make it easier to cut off dry or protruding shoots from newly-planted trees': cultellos item curvos minores, per quos novellis arboribus surculi aridi aut exstantes facilius amputentur.

DISCUSSION

The diminutive of *culter* is the common word for the barber's razor (Ulp. *Dig.* 9. 2. 11, etc.), and for various other types of knife in common use such as the carving-knife (Juv. 5. 122, etc.). As the researches of Steensberg (*op. cit.* pp. 133 ff.) have shown, the straight reaping knife preceded the

angular sickle in the evolution of harvesting implements. There is nothing inherently improbable in Isidore's theory, which would bring the evolution of pruning implements into line with that of the sickle. His etymological explanation is of course absurd. In fact the *falx vinitoria* or vine-dresser's knife, which was a highly specialized implement, appears in Cato's list of vineyard equipment. The *cultellus*, as used in arboriculture, was a knife of the simple 'machete' or 'panga' type, consisting of a long, slightly curved blade, but lacking the typical hook of the *falx arboraria* (q.v.). Knives of this type are still extensively used in tropical and sub-tropical areas for clearing paths in the forest, and for cutting sugar-cane and bamboo. Palladius' use of the adjective 'minores' (*e*) implies that there were larger and smaller versions of the implement; the diminutive, as in several other cases, has no reference to size.

1. *Monuments*

   (*a*) *Extant representations.* I have not been able to identify any implements of this type.

   (*b*) *Extant specimens.* (i) *Large type*: there are two specimens in the Museo Nazionale at Naples (nos. 3263 and 2189). 3263, which is very well preserved, is 51 cm long, and is 9 cm wide at the base, the blade widening to a terminal width of 13½ cm. The design is almost identical with that of the modern specimen from Nigeria (Fig. 49). 2189 is almost the same in size and shape. (ii) *Smaller type*: the illustration (Fig. 50) is of a specimen from Nattenheim, now in the Landesmuseum at Trier, West Germany.

Fig. 50. Cultellus

2. *Survival*

   (*a*) *Of the implement.* Large implements of this type are still in regular use in forest areas for slashing and lopping. The small curved pruning knife has been largely superseded by the secateur.

   (*b*) *Of the name.* It. 'coltellaccio' (m.), matchet, ploughshare.

SICKLES, HOOKS AND SCYTHES

3. FALX MESSORIA (= *F. stramentaria*)   4. SERRVLA FERREA
5. FALX VERVCVLATA (*denticulata, rostrata*)
6. FALX ARBORARIA (= *F. putatoria*)   7. FALX LVMARIA
8. FALCVLA RVSCARIA (= *Falx rustaria*)   9. FALX SIRPICVLA
10. FALCICVLA BREVISSIMA TRIBVLATA   11. FALCASTRVM (= *Runco*)
12. FALX VINITORIA (= *F. silvatica, F. a tergo acuta atque lunata*)
13. FALCVLA VINEATICA (= *Falcula*)   14. FALX FAENARIA

Falx (-cis, f.), *sickle, hook, scythe*

R-E, s.v. 'Sichel', II A. 2, cols. 2190–3 [Hug].

This common term covers a wide variety of iron implements, consisting of a curved blade, equipped with a single cutting edge. Numerous variations in the size and curvature of the blade, and in the length and set of the handle in relation to the blade, have been developed in course of time to meet the different conditions encountered in the various tasks of reaping and pruning for which these implements were and still are employed. Twelve apparently distinct types of *falx* are mentioned by the Roman authorities in seven lists. In order to avoid unnecessary repetition, the ancient lists of *falces* are cited once only. In the non-technical writers, the simple term *falx* is commonly used to denote several implements of this class. Appendix E contains a classified table of the main non-technical references.

I. THE LISTS OF FALCES

(*a*) Varro, *LL* 5. 137. '*Sickles* (*falces*), from "emmer wheat" (*far*), with the change of a letter; in Campania these are called *seculae*, from "*secare*", to cut; from a certain resemblance to these are named others, the "hay scythes" (*falces faenariae*), and "tree-billhooks" (*arborariae*), of obvious origin, and *falces lumariae* and *sirpiculae*, whose origin is obscure. "Thorn-cutters" (*lumariae*) are those with which they cut thorn-thickets (*lumecta*), that is, when thorns creep over the fields. They are called "thorn-thickets" (*lumecta*) because they loosen (*solvunt*), that is "free" them (*luunt*) from the ground. *Falces sirpiculae* take their name from *sirpare*, to "plait from rushes", that is to fasten (*alligare*); . . . these sickles they call *phanclae*[1] in the peninsular dialect': *falces a farre litera commutata; has in Campania seculae a secando; a quadam similitudine harum aliae, ut quod apertum unde, falces faenariae et arbor⟨ar⟩iae et quod, non apertum unde, falces lumariae et sirpiculae. lumariae sunt quibus secant lumecta, id est cum in agris serpunt spinae; quas quod ab terra agricolae solvunt, id est luunt, lumecta. falces sirpiculae vocatae ab sirpando, id est ab alligando . . . has phanclas*[1] *Cherso⟨ne⟩sice.*

(*b*) Cato 10. 3. (inventory of equipment for an oliveyard):

8 mowing scythes	*falces faenarias* VIII
5 sickles for harvesting	*falces stramentarias* V
5 billhooks for trees	*falces arborarias* V

(*c*) Cato 11. 4 (inventory of equipment for a vineyard):

5 sickles for cutting reeds	*falces sirpiculas* V
6 billhooks for cutting foliage	*falces silvaticas* VI
3 billhooks for trees	*falces arborarias* III
40 knives for cutting grapes	*falculas vineaticas* XL
10 knives for cutting broom	*falculas rustarias* X

[1] *phanclas* is presumably a by-form of the Greek word ζάγκλη, 'sickle'. Most editors prefer to read 'zanclas', making the work a direct loan-word from the Greek, or to follow Scaliger's conjecture 'zanculas', which is the better Latinized form (cf. Aesculapius from Ἀσκληπιός). See Varro, *LL* v, ed. by J. Collart (Paris, 1954), 233.

(*d*) Varro, *RR* I. 22. 5 (citing Cato's vineyard list). 'Some classes of iron tools have several subdivisions, such as the *hooks*—thus the same author (i.e. Cato) says there will be required forty knives for cutting grapes, five for reeds, three for trees and ten for broom': quorum non nulla genera species habent plures, ut *falces*—nam dicuntur ab eodem scriptore vineaticae opus esse XL, sirpiculae V, arborariae III, rustariae X.

(*e*) Ulpian, *Digest* 33. 7. 8 pr. (a list of necessary equipment on the estate which must be transferred with the property itself):

pruning hooks	*falces putatoriae*
sickles	*falces messoriae*
scythes	*falces faenariae*

This list is also found in Paulus (*Sententiae* 3. 6. 35–6).

(*f*) Pallad. 1. 43. 1–2. '. . . Pruning-*hooks*, which we are to use for trees and vines, also sickles and scythes . . . *knives* which are sharp and crescent-shaped at the back . . . also very short, toothed (?) *knives*, which we commonly use for cutting out bracken': . . . *falces* putatorias, quibus in arbore utamur et vite. item messorias vel faenarias . . . *falces* a tergo acutas atque lunatas . . . item *falciculas* brevissimas tribulatas, quibus filicem solemus abscindere.

(*g*) Isidore 20. 14. 'The billhook is the tool with which trees and vines are pruned; the implement is called a *falx* because soldiers used them in early times for cutting out bracken (*filix*)—hence the well-known expression of Martial:

The solid peace of our ruler has curved me into the uses of peace;
Once used by soldiers, I am now the farmer's tool':

falcis est, qua arbores putantur et vites; dicta autem falcis quod his primum milites herbam filicem solebant abscindere. unde est illud (Mart. 14. 34)

pax me certa ducis placidos curvavit in usus;
agricolae nunc sum, militis ante fui.

(*h*) *Corp. Gloss* s.v. 'falx'. *Falx* δρέπανον II 70. 16; 280. 58 (flax); 499. 31 (fax); 545. 34; III 23. 38; 204. 50 (falce); 299. 72 (falix); 326. 23; 448. 12; 477. 34. δρέπανος II 507. 21; 518. 44; 555. 56. *falcis* uuidubil sigdi riftr (nominat., AS) V 361. 3. *falces* quod his primum milites herbam filicem a⟨b⟩scidebant, ut illud: pax me certa. . . V 568. 49 (Martial 14. 34; cf. Isid. 20. 14. 4). V. putatoria falx, uvae falx. *falx* (falcis codd.) *faenaria* χορτοδρέπανον III 299. 73; 525. 11. *falx* (fali *h.e.* fals *cod.*) *messoria* ἅρπη III 299. 73; 525. 11.

2. DISCUSSION OF THE LISTS OF FALCES

The contents of the above lists, when combined together, give a total of twelve names of implements of the *falx* class. The first obstacle to be surmounted before we can proceed to a discussion of the design and functions of the implements of this class is to examine the list of names, and determine in each case whether we are dealing with a specific implement or with a duplicate concealed under a different name. In order to make

this task easier, the references are set out below under a series of headings, the Latin name appearing first, followed by the name of the citing authority, then, when possible, the English equivalent, or at least an English rendering of the meaning of each term.

Latin name	Authority				English term (or translation)
1. *Falx arboraria*	C	V	–	–	Tree-pruning billhook (= no. 5)
2. *Falx faenaria*	C	V	D	P	Mowing scythe
3. *Falx lumaria*	–	V	–	–	Thorn-cutter
4. *Falx messoria*	–	V	D	P	Reaping sickle (= no. 9)
5. *Falx putatoria*	–	–	D	P	Tree-pruning billhook (= no. 1)
6. *Falx ruscaria*	C	–	–	–	Billhook for cutting out
Falx rustaria	–	V	–	–	butcher's broom (*rusca*)
7. *Falx silvatica*	C	–	–	–	Vine-dresser's knife (= no. 11)
8. *Falx sirpicula*	C	V	–	–	Billhook for cutting out reeds
					(*scirpus*)
9. *Falx stramentaria*	C	–	–	–	Reaping sickle (= no. 4)
10. *Falcula vineatica*	C	–	–	–	(Col.) grape-cutting knife
11. *Falces a tergo acutae*	–	–	–	P	Vine-dresser's knife (= no. 7)
atque lunatae					
12. *Falcicula brevissima*	–	–	–	P	Bracken-cutter
tribulata					

Note: C = Cato; V = Varro, *LL*; D = Digest; P = Palladius.

To these items should be added two implements mentioned only by Columella: (i) the reference at 2. 20. 3 to a *falx veruculata* used for reaping corn, an implement which is further subdivided into *f. v. rostrata* ('beaked'), and *f. v. denticulata* ('fitted with small teeth'): there are good reasons for believing that the *falx veruculata* was a variety of sickle (*f. messoria*), not a scythe (*f. faenaria*) (a full discussion of these implements will be found below, s.v. 'flax messoria', pp. 77 ff.); (ii) the reference at 4. 25 to the *falx vinitoria* (= nos. 7, 11). Of the fourteen names mentioned only nine are beyond question the names of distinct implements, viz. nos. 1, 2, 3, 4, 6, 8, 10, 13 and 14. Four of the nine are well known from literary and monumental sources; they are (1) the tree-pruning billhook, (2) the mowing scythe, (4) the sickle, (14) the vine-dresser's knife. The remaining five are of rare (8) or unique occurrence (3, 6, 10, 13) in the authorities, and their design cannot be inferred with certainty from either category of evidence. They are fully discussed below under their several headings (pp. 82 ff.). There remain nos. 5, 7, 9, 11 and 12. Each appears to be identifiable with one or other of the eight whose identity is beyond reasonable doubt. Each of these is now discussed in turn:

No. 5: falx putatoria. This is clearly a pruning knife (from 'putare' to 'cut' or 'prune'). The name appears only in the Digest and in Palladius, while *falx arboraria*, the billhook for tree-pruning, occurs only in Cato and

Varro. J. le Gall[1] has sought to show, with good reason, that the implements are one and the same, *f. putatoria* being the term used by later writers for the earlier term *f. arboraria*.

No. 7: falx silvatica. The term occurs only in Cato. His inventory of equipment for the vineyard includes five types of *falx*; these comprise reed-cutters (*f. sirpicula*), broom-cutters (*falcula rustaria*), forty *falculae vineaticae* of uncertain identity, and six *f. silvaticae*. In the operations of the vineyard the task calling for the greatest concentration of labour at the same time is the vintage. Since no other implement in the list is required in larger quantity than ten units, it follows that *f. vineatica* is the short knife used for cutting off the bunches of grapes from the vines (hence the diminutive form *falcula*). In a valuable recent discussion of the problems of the *falces* J. le Gall argues convincingly that *f. arboraria* and *f. silvatica* as used by Cato refer to two different hooks, the former being employed for pruning the trees on which the vines were trained, while the latter, being twice as numerous, were vine-dresser's knives, used for pruning the vines themselves. *F. silvatica* is thus identified with Columella's *f. vinitoria*.

No. 9: falx stramentaria. The common term for the sickle (for reaping cereals and legumes), the *f. messoria* (from *messis* the corn harvest) occurs in all the lists except that of Cato. His list of equipment for the oliveyard contains only three *falces*, viz. *f. faenaria* (the mowing scythe), *f. arboraria* (the billhook for tree-pruning) and the *f. stramentaria*. The adjective *stramentarius* means 'of or belonging to straw', from *stramen*, 'straw'. Intercultivation of olives with corn was common,[2] and a sickle would be essential; it must be concluded that *f. stramentaria* is identical with *f. messoria*. For further discussion see below, 3, pp. 78 f.

No. 11: falces a tergo acutae atque lunatae. The term, which is found only in Palladius, suggests a composite implement having a sharp, crescent-shaped edge on the opposite side (*a tergo*) to the front of the implement. Although Palladius gives no information about the uses of the implement, the immediate context of the passage is overwhelmingly concerned with viticulture, and it is therefore reasonable to suppose that he is referring, in a rather odd way, to the *f. vinitoria* (q.v.). The crescent-shaped part opposite the pruning blade of the vine-dresser's knife, known as the 'hatchet' (*securis*, Columella 4. 25. 1), is certainly its most distinctive feature, and this may well account for Palladius' descriptive phrase.

No. 12: falciculae brevissimae tribulatae. This term also occurs only in Palladius. Beyond the fact that it was a very small *falx* with a very short

---

[1] J. le Gall, 'Les "falces" et la faux', *Annales de l'Est*, Mém. no. 22, 4 (1959), p. 58 (= Le Gall).

[2] See Colum. 5. 9. 10–12 (the olive only bears heavily in alternate years). This type of combination-cropping is common today in South Italy and South Spain.

handle (*brevissima*) identification is difficult. Le Gall,[1] who seems to ignore the clear reference in the text to its use as a bracken-cutter, classes it rather doubtfully with the *f. sirpicula*. The adjective *tribulatus* surely means simply that it was fitted with teeth, like a *tribulum* or threshing-sledge (q.v. pp. 152 ff.) to enable the blade to bite into the tough stems of the bracken.

Other evidence

(1) The evidence obtained from the Glossaries, which is not of any great value, and that derived from the monuments, which is important, are discussed under the headings of the separate implements.

(2) The evidence of the agronomists, apart from the information contained in the lists discussed above, is set out in the usual way.

(3) Survivals of the name *falx* are set out at the end of the first discussion, that on *f. messoria* (the reaping sickle).

3. ARRANGEMENT OF THE MATERIAL

The implements of this class, which is a rather numerous one, are grouped for convenience of study and reference in four subdivisions.

(i) Sickles

3. *F. messoria* = *f. stramentaria* (Cato)	Reaping sickle
4. *Serrula ferrea*★ (Varro)	Special toothed reaping implement
5. *F. veruculata*★ (Colum.) (i) *dentata*, (ii) *rostrata*	Special variety of reaping sickle

(ii) Billhooks

6. *F. arboraria* (Cato, Varro) = *f. putatoria* (Dig., Pallad.)	Tree-pruning billhook
7. *F. lumaria*★ (Varro)	Thorn-cutter
8. *F. ruscaria*★ (Cato) = *f. rustaria*★ (Varro)	Butcher's broom-cutter
9. *F. sirpicula* = *f. scirpicula*	Reed-cutter
10. *Falcicula brevissima tribulata*★ (Pallad.)	Bracken-cutter
11. *Falcastrum*★ (Isid.) = *runco*	Bramble-cutter

(iii) Vine-dresser's knives

12. *F. vinitoria*★ (Colum.) = *f. silvatica* (Cato) = *f. a tergo acuta atque lunata*★ (Pallad.)	Vine-dresser's pruning knife
13. *Falcula vineatica*★ (Cato)	Grape-cutter

(iv) Scythes

14. *F. faenaria*	Mowing scythe

★ means that the word occurs only once in this technical sense.

The range and variety of this class of implement reflect certain characteristics of the Roman agricultural scene. There is first the special importance of the

---

[1] Le Gall, p. 69, n. 2.

foliage of trees and shrubs as fodder for animals, secondly the cultivation of reeds and osiers as well as of suitable trees to provide the large quantities of fencing-poles, vine-props, hurdles and wickerwork containers of all kinds required on the farm. Hence the specialized types of billhook such as *f. ruscaria* and *f. sirpicula*; hence also the large numbers of surviving specimens to be found in the museums, especially in the great Naples collection.

Hafting and variation in length of handle

In this class of implement the length of the handle is often critical for the operative technique. Since the handles have not survived, the method of hafting can often provide a clue: short and medium-sized handles are usually tanged, while a long socket (e.g. that of Fig. 63) implies a long handle.

3. Falx messoria (Pallad.) = Falx stramentaria (Cato), *sickle*

4. Serrula ferrea★ (Varro), *sickle*

5. Falx veruculata★ (i) denticulata★, (ii) rostrata★ (Colum.), *sickle*

R-E, s.v. 'Sichel', II A. 2, cols. 2190–3 [Hug] (brief and not very informative).

R-E, s.v. 'Ernte', VI. 1, cols. 477–82 [Olck].

R-E, s.v. 'Getreide', VII. 1, cols. 1347–9 [Orth].

Fig. 51. Falx
messoria

DISCUSSION

1. Terminology

A glance at the above list shows at once some of the major problems of interpretation that are involved here. Of the four terms employed one (*f. veruculata*) is known only from a single reference in Columella (2. 20. 3), while the terms *messorius*, 'harvesting', and *stramentarius*, 'of or belonging to straw', only appear once as qualifying adjectives with the word *falx*. The dictionaries of antiquities are very misleading on this topic; Rich (*Dict. Ant.* s.v. 'falx') has attempted a fairly full classification of the *falces*, but erroneously classifies Columella's *f. veruculata* as a scythe, and then confuses the same implement with Varro's special reaper (*RR* I. 50. 2), while Daremberg–Saglio furnish the student with a fairly comprehensive set of literary references to the shape of the sickle (*f. messoria*), the majority of which do not refer to this implement, but to the billhook (*f. arboraria, putatoria*, q.v.).[1] In any case, literary references, except in the technical

---

[1] E.g. Verg. G. 2. 420–1 (pruning the olive), etc.; three well-known passages in Juvenal refer to the *f. messoria* (8. 201; 13. 39; 14. 149).

writers, are of little or no importance in connection with the sickle; its design is well known from the large number of surviving examples from many parts of the Roman world, and there is an extensive literature on the historical development of the implement.[1] So far as Roman practice is concerned, the evidence of the agronomists is particularly informative. Varro's discussion (1. 50. 1) is of great value, and both Columella and Pliny contribute items of importance. From these sources, which are set out in full, much information can be obtained concerning the different types of implement in use, and the different methods prevailing in different areas. Palladius gives little information on manual harvesting of grains, apart from an estimate of the man-hours required. His valuable account of the mechanical harvester used in Gaul is discussed in detail s.v. 'vallus' (pp. 157 ff.).

2. *The problem of the f. stramentaria*

Cato 10. 3 (the inventory for the oliveyard):

8 mowing scythes	*falces faenarias* VIII
5 reaping sickles	*stramentarias* V

The term *stramentarius* applied to the *falx* is not found elsewhere. Its meaning, 'straw-cutting', may imply that in Cato's day the common method was to cut down the whole plant, including the straw, using the straw for litter (*stramentum* being the ordinary term for the litter used in the cattle-stalls, and for beds made of straw—e.g. Columella 6. 3. 1; Plautus, *Truc.* 278, etc.). In some areas the heads of grain were reaped separately, and the straw was cut in a subsequent operation, as in Varro's second method (see below). The *f. stramentaria* might thus have been a type of sickle specially designed for this task; but Cato does not mention a reaping sickle, and this leads to the reasonable conclusion that *f. stramentaria* and *f. messoria* are identical. J. le Gall offers a different explanation of the term, assuming that *f. stramentaria* was 'the implement used to cut the part of the straw left in the field after the harvest' (*art. cit.* p. 63); so also Thielscher, *Belehrung*, 249. This surely involves the assumption that in Cato's system the heads alone were reaped, presumably with the comb (*pecten*) or 'divers' (*mergae*) (for these implements see pp. 110 ff.). The use of *mergae* was sufficiently common in Cato's day for his contemporary Plautus to employ the term proverbially (see passage (*g*), p. 111). Le Gall later (*loc. cit.*) cautiously accepts the identification of *f. stramentaria* with *f. messoria*; but his first explanation should not be lightly rejected. If heading

[1] *R-E*, s.v. 'Sichel', II A. 2, cols. 2190–3. See also V. G. Childe, 'The balanced sickle', *Aspects of Archaeology in Britain and Beyond*, essays presented to O. G. S. Crawford, ed. by W. F. Grimes (London, 1951), pp. 39–48.

was the normal method in Cato's time, this may have been due to inadequate technique in the manufacture of sickles. By the time of Varro, more than a century later, a greater variety of methods was available.

3. *Varro's account of harvesting methods* (RR I. 50. 1)

'There are three ways of harvesting corn. One way, that found in Umbria, is to cut the straw down with the sickle close to the ground, laying each sheaf, as it is cut, on the field. When a good number of sheaves has been made up, they are gone over again, and the ears are cut off from the straw, sheaf by sheaf. In the second method, used for instance in Picenum, a curved piece of wood, with a small iron saw at the end, is used. This grasps a bundle of ears, cuts them off, and leaves the stalks standing in the field to be subsequently cut close to the ground. The third method, adopted mainly in the neighbourhood of Rome, and in most other places, is to cut the stalk, the top of which is held with the left hand, midway down...That part of the stalk which is below the hand remains attached to the ground, and is cut later, while the part which is attached to the ear is carried off to the threshing-floor in baskets': frumenti tria genera sunt messionis, unum, ut in Umbria, ubi falce secundum terram succidunt stramentum et manipulum, ut quemque subsicuerunt, ponunt in terra. ubi eos fecerunt multos, iterum eos percensent ac de singulis secant inter spicas et stramentum ... altero modo metunt, ut in Piceno, ubi ligneum habent incurvum bacillum, in quo sit extremo serrula ferrea. haec cum comprenderit fascem spicarum, desecat et stramenta stantia in segete relinquit, ut postea subsecentur. tertio modo metitur, ut sub urbe Roma et locis plerisque, ut stramentum medium subsecent, quod manu sinistra summum prendunt; a quo medio messem dictam puto. infra manum stramentum cum terra haeret, postea subsecatur; contra quod cum spica stramentum haeret, corbibus in aream defertur.

4. *Columella's account of harvesting methods* (2. 20. 3)

'There are, furthermore, several methods of reaping: many cut the straw in the middle with the *spitted sickle*; these are either *bill-shaped* or *toothed*; many gather the heads only with "*divers*", and others with *combs* ...': sunt autem metendi genera complura. multi *falcibus veruculatis* atque iis vel *rostratis* vel *denticulatis* medium culmum secant, multi mergis, alii pectinibus spicam ipsam legunt ...

5. *Pliny's account* (18. 296) (on harvesting grain—after a short account of the mechanical harvester, the 'vallus')

'Elsewhere the stalks are cut through with the *sickle* and the ear is torn off between two "divers". In some places the stalks are cut off at the root, in others they are plucked out, roots and all; those who employ this last-named method explain that in the course of it they get the land broken, although in fact they are drawing the fatness out of it': stipulae alibi mediae *falce* praeciduntur, atque inter duas mergites spica destringitur. alibi ab radice caeduntur, alibi cum radice evelluntur: quique id faciunt proscindi ab se obiter agrum interpretantur, cum extrahant sucum.

6. *Design*

The sickle, the oldest of all reaping implements,[1] consists of a smooth curved blade, equipped with a smooth or serrated cutting edge, attached to a short handle, which lies in the same plane as the blade. The curvature of the blade, as known from numerous examples surviving from antiquity, as well as from a great variety of types on monuments, varies from a shallow arc to a semi-ellipse, and the set of the handle also varies considerably. The design of the implement has been the subject of several valuable studies, that of A. Steensberg (*op. cit.*) being the most important. The type known as the 'balanced' sickle, in which the organization of blade and haft is so contrived that when the implement is grasped there is a nice balance of weight between the fore and aft sections of the blade, represents a notable advance in design. The implement is now much better suited to the natural movement of the wrist, and there is a great reduction in fatigue (see the accompanying line-drawing). This was almost certainly a Roman invention.[2]

Fig. 52. Falx messoria

7. *Function and operational technique*

Although both scythe (*f. faenaria*) and sickle (*f. messoria*) are equipped with curved blades their actions are very dissimilar. Whereas the scythe cuts a swathe of standing grass at ground level with a sideways sweep, the sickle is used with a sawing stroke, the sheaf of grain being grasped with the reaper's left hand, while he draws the sickle towards him with his right. Failure to understand this difference has led many translators and commentators astray, particularly in dealing with the passage from Columella (2. 20. 3) which contains the only surviving reference to the implement known as the *falx veruculata* (see below s.v.). The action of the sickle depends upon the curvature of the blade, varying from a semi-circular to an almost straight pulling movement (see Figs. 52–4).

Fig. 53. Falx messoria

8. *Smooth and serrated types of falx messoria*

Fig. 54. Falx messoria (Italian)

The latter type is the older. Both types are still in use today in many Mediterranean countries, as well as in parts of the Middle East and Africa. It is well known that the smooth edge of the scythe and the plain sickle works most effectively when the dew is on the standing crop, since the edge will then bite into the straw and not slide along the surface. Studies of the present distribution of the two types show the serrated sickle predominating in the drier areas of the Mediterranean and in the sub-Saharan regions, where the stalks tend to be drier and tougher.[3]

[1] The earliest surviving examples, of bone with flint teeth inserted, strongly suggest an origin from the jawbone of an animal (*HT*, I, figs. 329, 356).
[2] Childe, *art. cit.* (p. 78, n. 1); Steensberg, pp. 209 ff.   [3] Hopfen, *FIATR*, p. 98.

9. *Different reaping methods*

Varro mentions three methods. Columella says that there are numerous methods, but gives only a cursory account of the matter, and in fact mentions only one method employing the *falx*, the 'middle-cut method'. This is the only method mentioned by Pliny. From a careful examination of the three passages cited it appears that we are dealing with three distinct varieties of implement, and the task of identification is not made any easier by the indiscriminate use of the term *falx*, e.g. by Varro (*loc. cit.*).

(1) The ordinary sickle (*f. messoria*), often referred to simply as *falx* (e.g Varro, *RR* i. 50. 1).

(2) 'A curved wooden handle with a small iron saw attached to the end' (Varro, *loc. cit.*); not mentioned elsewhere.

(3) The *falx veruculata*, a sickle equipped with small spits or spikes, widely used, according to Columella (2. 20. 3), but not mentioned elsewhere.

There are no difficulties with the first method; Varro's account is perfectly clear. The operator applies the sickle near the base of the plants, grasping a bundle (*manipulus*) in the left hand, and drawing the sickle towards him in a sawing movement from the curve adjoining the handle right through to the point. Each bundle as it is cut is laid on the ground to await a second operation which removes the heads of grain; these are then taken away for threshing.

The second method is the reverse of the first: The corn is to be cut as close to the ears as possible, leaving the straw to be cut in a second operation. Since the stalks taper towards the head of the plant, the task of making a clean and efficient cut presents a problem which cannot be met by the use of the ordinary sickle. If the cut is made either close to the ground or half way up, the stalks will not bend over as they are being cut, but if the cut is made near the top, they will tend to flop over, with the ragged ends hanging, and some loss of grain. In order to overcome this difficulty, an implement of a different design was used. Varro's description of this implement, however, is not sufficiently precise to make identification certain, but the description is consistent with a representation on an Egyptian painting, illustrated by Rich (*Dict. Ant.* s.v. 'falx denticulata'; see the accompanying illustration). With this implement the reaper worked upwards, pushing the bunch into the narrowing gap between the bent handle and the curved saw-blade. The narrow angle between blade and handle would keep the stalks firm during the cutting process, and easily release the heads. Against this proposed identification it may be argued that no implement answering to Varro's description appears to have been

Fig. 55. Serrula ferrea

found on any Roman site. I do not see any force in this objection: complete implements made wholly or, as in this case, partially of wood, do not survive except under the specially favourable conditions obtaining in Egypt and similar areas.

With the third method we are confronted with several difficulties. The major problem is the meaning of the term 'veruculatae' in Columella's account (*loc. cit.*). (1) The adjective is unique; (2) the word *veru* means a spit for roasting meat: it is also used in poetry with the meaning 'dart' or 'javelin': *veruculum* has the ordinary diminutive formation, and means a small spit. The termination -*atus* normally implies 'fitted with' or 'equipped with', so that 'veruculatus' should mean 'equipped with a short spit or spits'. Most editors and commentators seem to regard the problem as insoluble. Ash,[1] following some earlier commentators, translates *f. veruculatae* as 'cradle-scythes'. It has already been pointed out (above, p. 80) that the scythe has a sideways sweeping action, and that it cuts off the grass at ground-level. Anyone who has used a scythe will know that it is impossible to cut the stalks at middle height with it. Furthermore, Columella expressly states that these *falces* are either toothed or bill-shaped; a toothed scythe would indeed be a fantastic implement! In any case, the cradle-scythe is post-classical; it is an adaptation of the mowing-scythe to grain-cutting by the provision of a cradle into which the cut sheaves are collected after each stroke, to be picked up and stacked with greater ease. Such devices, which range from a simple twig or wire bow attached to the handle to a complete cradle, are only found where crops taller than 30 cm in height are to be reaped, and are clearly anachronistic here.[2] Del Pelo Pardi[3] regarded the implement as a long-handled type of special design and sought to identify it with a bill-shaped implement which appears in the hands of a reaper in an illuminated manuscript of the fourteenth century now in the British Museum.[4] This latter implement is undoubtedly a scythe. In a recent discussion of the problem Le Gall[5] returns to the notion that the *f. veruculata* must have differed from the ordinary sickle in having a longer handle, but admits that this is no more than a hypothesis. The monumental evidence cited by him suggests that the implements

[1] Columella, *De Re Rustica*, Loeb Library, ed. and transl. by H. B. Ash, 1 (London, 1948), 217. Ash offers no comment.

[2] For the design of the cradle-scythe, see Hopfen, p. 105. This is probably the implement which J. M. Gesner had in mind when compiling the following note to Colum. 2. 20. 3: '*falces veruculatae* are scythes fitted with a small spit or rod, commonly wielded not only by haymakers, but also by reapers of corn or of any short-stemmed plant': vericulatas falces esse vericulo illo vel hastili munitas, quibus vulgo utuntur non foeniseces modo, sed avenae etiam, et brevioris cuiuscumque culmi messores.

[3] *Attrezzi*, pp. 11–12.

[4] British Museum, Royal 15 E II, p. 247 v. (reproduced as Plate 1).

[5] Le Gall, p. 62.

depicted are scythes, not sickles, and are therefore inadmissible as evidence in support of his view. It is evident, however, that the two varieties of *f. veruculata* were widely used in Columella's time (2. 20. 3, p. 79), yet they are mentioned by no other authority. In the absence of a description of the implement identification is clearly impossible. Two possible solutions are presented here: both must be regarded as speculative. The first is based on a comment by J. M. Gesner on Columella 2. 20. 3, in which he says that reapers in eighteenth-century Germany used an attachment to the sickle in the form of a little rake or comb, which enabled him to lay the sheaves on the ground in an orderly manner. Unfortunately Gesner gives no further information about this modified sickle, but an implement answering to Gesner's account has been reported from the United States.[1] The second suggestion is that the *falx veruculata* may have been a sickle modified by drawing the tip out to form a spit, which might be either straight like a tooth or notched to form a beak. A sickle equipped with such a point would have the advantage of making insertion of the implement into the standing crop easier. The annexed illustrations are taken from a catalogue of English reaping hooks of the late nineteenth century, depicting a sickle with a beaked tip, known to farmers as the 'Pembroke reaping hook', and from a La Tène sickle in the British Museum. The reason for this improved sickle is clear; the 'middle-cut' method is more economical in time than heading or full-length cutting, and the improved implement would speed up the process of getting the corn to the threshing-floor.[2] The problem is fully discussed in Appendix E, pp. 207 f.

Fig. 56. Falx veruculata rostrata? (Welsh)

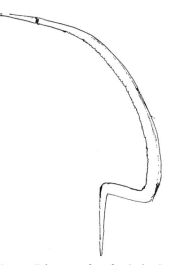

Fig. 57. Falx veruculata denticulata? (La Tène)

10. *Regional distribution and variation in design*

Regional variations in the design of a given implement are common in all countries and at all periods before the modern development of standardized implements and methods. They are determined by varying local requirements and techniques, and by local or even

[1] Private communication from Mrs J. G. Hawthorne, Chicago. That a similar attachment to the sickle was in use in eighteenth-century Germany is evident from a further note by Gesner on Colum. 2. 20. 3 (see p. 82, n. 2, above): 'In the corn harvest, they also have a little rake or comb attached to the sickle, with the help of which they lay down the stalks in so orderly a manner that it looks as if they had gathered up the bundles with their hands and laid them down': qui in frumentacia messe praeterea rastellum quoddam sive pectinem adiunctum habent falci, cuius ope ita sternunt ordinate culmos, quasi manu comprehensos manipulos deposuissent.

[2] Such an implement would probably have been needed where there was considerable 'tillering', that is, a bushing-out of the wheat-plant from the base, producing numerous sideshoots. On this phenomenon see my article, 'Wheat farming in Roman times', *Antiquity*, XXXVII (1963), 207 ff.

individual preferences; where the smith is part of the local scene, implements are commonly 'made to measure'. The regional variations in reaping tools mentioned in our authorities are clearly related to the uses to which the material reaped is to be put. Pliny gives valuable evidence on the point. At 18. 297 he follows up his account of different methods of reaping as follows: 'In areas where they thatch their houses with straw, they keep the straw as long as possible, but where there is a shortage of hay, they require straw for litter.' The commonest method, that of cutting the straw half way up, makes it possible to use the threshed straw for bedding animals and the remainder to supplement the limited grazing available for stock. The regional variations in method reported by Pliny in the previous chapter (q.v.) are consistent with this analysis; in Italy the supply of material for grazing decreases sharply as you go south. As far north as Picenum and Umbria, where the first and second methods were in vogue, natural and artificial fodder would be fairly plentiful. Around Rome and further south stubble grazing is a valuable asset in the struggle to provide sufficient fodder for cattle all the year round; hence the prevalence of the third, or middle-cut, method in these areas.

11. *Monuments*

(*a*) *Extant representations.* Harvesting scenes showing the use of the sickle are common on surviving monuments; among the more important are Trajan's Column in Rome (Cichorius, *Traianssäule*, Taf. LXXXI, 291–2— replica of the whole monument in the Victoria and Albert Museum, London); a stele from Maktar, Tunisia, now in Tunis (Musée du Bardo: Merlin–Poinssot, *Guide du Musée Alaoui*, 4ᵉ éd. pl. XLVII); two sarcophagi in the Lateran Museum, Rome (Benndorf–Schoene, *Lateran. Mus.* no. 488; H. Stern, *Calendrier*, pl. XLIX, 5; G. M. A. Hanfmann, *The Season Sarcophagus*, II, 184, no. 539; Le Gall, pl. VII, no. 2); the sarcophagus of Junius Bassus in the Grotte Vaticane beneath St Peter's, Rome (Stern, *Calendrier*, pl. XLIX, no. 4; Hanfmann, *Season Sarcophagus*, no. 540; Le Gall, pl. VII, no. 3). The sickle is also familiar as the stock attribute of figures personifying Summer in the farmer's pictorial calendars which survive in large numbers; notable items in Hanfmann's exhaustive treatment are fig. 90, no. 96 (Summer in a Pompeian painting); fig. 93, no. 127 (Winter in a mosaic from Aumale, Algeria); fig. 105, no. 16 (Summer with balanced sickle from Hadrian's Villa at Tivoli). The above examples, which between them cover a span of three centuries (first to fourth A.D.), display the same pattern, but with variations in size and curvature. Two good examples of the smaller reaping sickle, as well as grape-knives (*falcula vineatica*) and billhooks occur among the contents of a cutler's shop depicted on a funerary bas-relief now

in the Vatican Museum, Rome, easily accessible in *Histoire Générale des Techniques*, t. 1 (Paris, 1962), pl. 17, facing p. 240.

(*b*) *Extant specimens.* Fairly large numbers have survived. The various shapes are well represented in Petrie's selection (pl. 54—mostly from the Museo Nazionale, Naples). The Naples collection includes two large specimens (no catalogue numbers): (*a*) semi-elliptical blade, with chord of 40 cm, blade 4½ cm wide, tapering to 4 cm, tang 7½ cm long; (*b*) open shape, with chord of 37½ cm, blade averaging 4 cm in width, tang 7 cm long. The plain open sickle is well represented in a well-preserved specimen from Boscoreale, now in Chicago (Museum of Natural History, inv. no. 26164), illustrated Plate 7 (*b*). For Saalburg examples see Jacobi, *Römerkastell*, fig. 69, 7, and Taf. xxxv, 2.

12. *Survival*

(*a*) *Of the implement.* (i) The reaping sickle is still widely used for cutting small quantities of grain for fodder, even in areas where the grain-crop is harvested by means of reaper-binders or combines; (ii) in under-developed countries, especially in Africa and Asia, the sickle is commonly used for reaping small-grain cereals such as millet.

(*b*) *Of the name. Falx* survives in various forms in most Romance languages: note especially Fr. faux (from *falx*) = *f. faenaria*; faucille (from *falcula*) = *f. messoria*.

BILLHOOKS AND VINE-DRESSER'S KNIVES

1. *General aspects of design and function*

The eight implements belonging to these two sub-groups of the *falx* family (2) and (3), stand midway in design between the sickles (1) and the scythes (4). In their operation they differ from both these groups of implements in the fact that their action is neither that of sawing, as with the sickle, nor of sweeping at ground level, as with the scythe, but is a striking and cutting action. They are here classified generally as billhooks, the generic term in English for a number of knives used for lopping and pruning trees, and for cutting saplings, willow-shoots and the like. The term 'billhook' indicates that the blades are 'hooked' (i.e. curved) in profile and that in addition they have the characteristic projection at the top of the curved blade, known as the 'beak' (Lat. *rostrum*, a bird's beak). This type of implement consists basically of a long flat blade with a single cutting edge, curved outwards at the end to form a right angle, and ending in a point. The hook grips and holds the branch which is to be lopped or pruned, while

Fig. 58.
Falx arboraria

the knife-blade makes the cut. The upper section of the blade is usually convex in form, so as to provide greater strength behind the striking portion, which thus presents the appearance of a bird's bill. Surviving specimens show great variety both in the angle of the hook (from 90° to almost 180°), in the proportionate lengths of the lower and upper sections, and in the curvature of the blade.[1] Petrie, *TW*, 46–7, divides the billhooks into two families, those of large curvature and a gathering-in shape like that of the sickle, which are designed to catch and lop branches which are out of reach, and the straighter types, which are used mainly for cutting out thorns and brambles, or for cutting saplings and brushwood. The class includes a considerable variety of weights and sizes, as well as differences in design to suit particular requirements.

2. *The billhooks*

The variety of types reflects two characteristic features of the agricultural scene. There is first the importance of the foliage of trees and shrubs as animal fodder; secondly, there is the economic importance of the cultivation of reeds and osiers as well as of suitable trees in maintaining a regular supply of fencing-poles, vine-props, hurdles and so forth. Hence the specialized types of billhooks, such as *f. ruscaria* and *f. sirpicula*; hence also the large numbers of surviving specimens of this class (see Appendix E).

6. Falx arboraria (Cato; Varro, *LL*) = Falx putatoria (Digest; Palladius), *billhook*

Fig. 59.
Falx arboraria

(*a*) Varro, *LL* 5. 137. 'From a certain resemblance to these (i.e. sickles) are named others, the *falces fenariae* "mowing scythes" and *falces arborariae* "tree-pruning billhooks", of obvious origin . . .': a quadam similitudine harum aliae, ut quod apertum unde, *falces faenariae et arbor⟨ar⟩iae*★ . . . (★ arboriae F[v]: arboreae GHV p.a.)

(*b*) Cato 10. 3 (for the oliveyard). '5 tree-pruning billhooks': falces arborarias v.

(*c*) Cato 11. 4 (for the vineyard). '3 tree-pruning billhooks': falces arborarias III.

(*d*) Digest 33. 7. 8 (implements which must go with the estate). 'Pruning hooks': falces putatoriae.

(*e*) Pallad. 1. 43. 1 (general farm inventory). '. . . *pruning hooks* which we are to use for trees and vines':[2] . . . *falces putatorias*, quibus in arbore utamur et vite.

[1] See the reproductions in Petrie, *TW*, pls. 56, 57, 59.

DISCUSSION

1. *Design*

In Cato's account the *f. arboraria* appears after the scythe and the sickle in the oliveyard list, and after *f. sirpicula* (the reed-cutter), and *f. silvatica* (Cato's name for the *f. vinitoria* or vine-dresser's knife) in his vineyard list. The implement is thus evidently the common billhook used for lopping branches of trees. The heavier versions of the implement were used by foresters, the lighter types for pruning in the orchard. In Cato's system these would be in demand for pruning and shaping the supporting trees in the method of vine-growing known as *arbustum*.[1]

Fig. 60.
Falx arboraria

2. *Operational technique*

The oblique cut, designed to avoid loss of sap and damage to the growing tree, is clearly described by Columella (4. 25) in connection with the vine-dresser's knife (*f. vinitoria*), which is merely a highly elaborated version of the billhook. For a detailed account of the lopping and pruning operations required in order to mould the supporting tree to the desired shape and size see Columella 6. 6. 12–17. In this passage, as in numerous other discussions of pruning, the term 'falx' is used without qualification several times, and the even less precise term 'ferrum' (i.e. the 'iron') frequently; in all cases the implement referred to is the same.

Fig. 61.
Falx arboraria

3. *Monuments*

(*a*) *Extant representations.* The long-bladed billhook is commonly associated with the agricultural deity Saturnus (see the well-known fresco from Pompeii).[2]

(*b*) *Extant specimens.* The type is very well represented in the museum collections. A fine specimen found at Boscoreale, near Pompeii (Petrie, pl. 57, no. 48) has a recurved blade and a shortish bill, the handle being socketed into the blade; the collection at Saint-Germain contains a fine example of the hedge-bill, with a long socket and handle, and a projection at the back for withdrawing the branch after cutting (Reinach, *Cat. Ill.* fig. 273, no. 15894 A; cf. 15894 B, which has the wider blade and shorter bill for thicker branches).

Fig. 62.
Falx arboraria

[1] *Arbustum*: this system, in which the young vine is 'married' to a supporting tree to form trellises, was the normal method in Campania in Cato's day (*De Agri Cultura* 1. 7), and is still practised in parts of Italy. Vines trained in this way produce large quantities of wine of inferior quality. Columella (3. 2. 9) regards it as inferior to other systems, while Pliny does not even mention it in his list of recommended methods (17. 164).

[2] Reproduced by Le Gall, pl. 6, no. 5.

Fig. 63.
Falx arboraria

4. *Survival*

(*a*) *Of the implement.* 'The *falx arboraria* is the tool still generally used by woodcutters and hedgers, and is still made on the identical pattern of ancient examples discovered at Pompeii' (Del Pelo Pardi, *Attrezzi*, 17).

(*b*) *Of the name.* It. 'podetto', 'podettino', dialect forms, clearly derive from 'putare', 'to prune'. A number of pruning-hooks of fine workmanship and elegant curvature bearing these names are featured in a work on agriculture by Agostino Gallo of Brescia, dated 1775.[1]

7. **Falx lumaria** (Varro), *thorn-cutter*

(*a*) Varro, *LL* 5. 137. '*Thorn-cutters* are billhooks with which they cut thorn-thickets, that is, when thorns creep over the fields; they are called "lumecta" because the farmers "loosen" (*solvunt*), that is "free" them (*luunt*) from the ground': *lumariae* sunt quibus secant lumecta, id est cum in agris serpunt spinae; quas quod ab terra agricolae solvunt, id est luunt, lumecta.

(*b*) Paul. Fest. 120, s.v. 'luma'. 'A kind of weed or rather thorn': genus herbae vel potius spinae.

DISCUSSION

The *f. lumaria*, which is mentioned only by Varro (*loc. cit.*) is evidently a special form of billhook designed for the eradication of the weed called *luma*. The etymology of the word is much disputed; Walde–Hofmann (s.v. 'luma') mention seven proposed derivations, none of them conclusive. Bücheler (*Kl. Schr.* 3. 51, quoting *Gloss. Philox.*, takes it to be a kind of wild mint. Varro's derivation is pure folk-etymology. Low-growing, spiny weeds of this kind spread prolifically in dry climates (cf. the 'thorns' which grew up and choked the wheat in the parable of the Sower (Mark iv. 7), identified as *carduus arvensis* or 'corn-thistle'). In the absence of other evidence nothing can be stated about the design of the implement. Le Gall[2] notes that *f. ruscaria*, which seems to be a related type of billhook, is mentioned only by Cato, and suggests that the two implements may be identical.

8. **Falcula ruscaria** (Cato), Falx rustaria (Varro), *broom-cutter*

Mentioned only by Cato in the vineyard inventory (11. 4), and repeated in slightly different form by Varro (*RR* 1. 22. 5). The plant 'ruscus' from which the implement takes its name is *oxymyrsine* or *ruscus aculeatus*,

---

[1] Reproduced by Del Pelo Pardi, *Attrezzi*, pp. 16–17, fig. 2.
[2] Le Gall, pp. 58–9.

commonly known as 'butcher's broom'.[1] It is an evergreen perennial, with tough leaf-like branchlets growing from strong erect stems. Bunches of the plant were commonly bound together to make stout besoms used by butchers for sweeping their floors—hence the English name. Now it is clear from Vergil (*G.* 2. 415 ff.) that butcher's broom, like the reeds (*harundo*) and the willows (*salix*) mentioned by Vergil in the following lines, were of importance to the cultivator of the vine. Stiff stems such as are produced by this plant are mentioned by Columella (4. 12. 1), in a discussion of the various methods of propping the young vine, when he refers to 'brier canes' (*de vepribus hastilia*) as suitable for this purpose 'where local conditions permit' (*si regionis conditio permittit*). *Vepris* is a generic term for this type of plant. *Ruscus* is a shade-loving plant, and would not be generally available in Italy, hence the reference to local conditions. It is certainly not a weed and was evidently cultivated in copses, just as the reed and the osier were cultivated for cutting.

Fig. 64.
Falx ruscaria (?)

Design

A hedge-cutting type of billhook would be required, i.e. one with a short bill and a straight blade. Good surviving examples of the type abound in the Saint-Germain collection; most of Petrie's examples are of northern provenance (*op. cit.* pl. 57, nos. 41, 42).

9. Falx sirpicula, *reed cutter*

Varro, *LL* 5. 137. '*Reed-cutters* take their name from "sirpare" "to plait with reeds", that is, "alligare" "to fasten", "tie up" ... They use them in the vineyard for tying up bundles of fuel, cut stakes and kindling': *falces sirpiculae* vocatae ab sirpando, id est ab alligando ... Utuntur in vinea alligando fasces, incisos fustes, faculas.

Not in Isidore; not in Palladius' list.

Cato 11. 4. 5. '5 *reed-cutters*': *falces sirpiculas* v.

DISCUSSION

The better form is *scirpicula*, from *scirpus*, a reed. The text of Varro is not altogether clear; J. Collart[2] thinks that Varro is referring to three successive tasks mentioned by Vergil, two of them in connection with the cultivation of the vine: (1) after the pruning of the vines the prunings are collected in

Fig. 65.
Falx sirpicula (?)

---

[1] Ernout–Meillet, *op. cit.* (2nd ed.), 1030, s.v. 'ruscus'. Cf. G. Bonnier, *Flore complète illustrée en couleurs de France, Suisse et Belgique*, t. x, 99, no. 2668 (*ruscus aculeatus*), and pl. 596, no. 2668; J. André, *Lexique des termes de botanique romaine*, Études et commentaires XXIII (1956), s.v. 'ruscus'.
[2] Varro, *LL* v, ed. J. Collart (Paris, 1954), p. 232, n. 4.

bundles for fuel (*G.* 2. 408–9); (2) the vine-dresser then cuts stakes for making vine-props (*G.* 2. 409); (3) farmers cut wood for making torches (*Ecl.* 8. 29). The reed-bed, like the osier- and willow-beds, was an important feature of the farm. Baskets made of these materials provide the farmer with a wide range of containers for many different purposes. Cato (11. 4–5) mentions four different types, including forty planting-baskets (*quala sataria*) for a vineyard of only 66 acres (see Rich, *Dict. Ant.* s.v. 'corbis', 'qualus', 'scirpea', 'colum').[1]

Design

No information is available, but the task would call for a medium-sized billhook with an almost straight blade, of the type illustrated above (Fig. 65), from Bretzenheim, near Mainz, West Germany (Petrie, pl. 56, no. 25).

10. Falcicula brevissima tribulata (Pallad.), *bracken-cutter*

Pallad. 1. 43. 2 (inventory of equipment). 'Also *little* short-handled *sickles* (?), fitted with teeth (?), which we commonly use for cutting away bracken': item *falciculas* brevissimas tribulatas*, quibus filicem solemus abscindere. (* tubulatas *al.*)

Not mentioned elsewhere, except by Arnobius (see below).

Fig. 66. Falcicula
brevissima
tribulata (?)

DISCUSSION

Both *falcula* and *falcicula* occur as diminutive forms of *falx*. Falcula occurs twice (Cato 11. 4; Columella 12. 18. 2) with the meaning 'grape-cutting knife' (below, p. 96, s.v. 'falcula viniatica'); *falcicula* only here and in Arnobius (6. 209). Either of these diminutives, if unqualified, could refer either to a billhook or a sickle. The adjective 'brevissima' seems to refer to the length of the handle, since *falcicula* appears to imply a very small blade. The other qualifying word 'tribulata' should have the meaning 'fitted with' a *tribulum* (cf. 'dentatus' = 'fitted with teeth'). The *tribulum* or threshing-sledge was a heavy board fitted on its underside with rows of flints or metal teeth, which was dragged over the straw by animals to separate the heads of grain (see 'tribulum', pp. 152 ff.). It seems reasonable to suppose that the implement was fitted with teeth. In that case it will have been a sickle, not a scythe or billhook. M. G. Bruno (*Lessico*, s.v. 'falx', no. 189) refers to the alternative reading 'tubulatas', and suggests that the implement was in some way hollowed out like a pipe (*tubus*). But it is difficult to see what precisely is meant by the application of such a term to a *falx*; it could scarcely refer to tubular construction! Le

[1] On the economic importance of the 'scirpus' see Pliny 16. 178.

Gall (*art. cit.* 69, n. 2) states that it is impossible to determine the meaning of 'tribulatus', which occurs nowhere else. It should mean 'equipped with sharp points' (cf. 'acuminatus in modum tribuli'—Forc. s.v.). In the absence of clear evidence, one might perhaps suggest that the teeth of this implement were more widely spaced and more deeply cut than those of the serrated sickle, thus giving some resemblance to the teeth of a *tribulum* (for the latter see Fig. 115, p. 152). Much less satisfactory is the suggestion that *tribulatus* may refer to a hook for pulling out the bracken; bracken cannot be pulled out in this way.

11. Falcastrum (-i, n.) (Isid.†) = Runco (-onis, m.) (Pallad.†), *bramble-cutter*

Not in Varro, *LL.* Only occurs in a single passage in Isidore.

Fig. 67. Falcastrum

(*a*) Isid. 20. 14. 5. 'The *bramble-cutter* is so called from its resemblance to the scythe. It is a curved iron implement with a long handle, for cutting down dense brambles. They are also known as "grubbers" from their action of grubbing': *falcastrum a similitudine falcis vocatum. est autem ferramentum curvum cum manubrio longo ad densitatem veprium succidendam. hi et runcones dicti, quibus vepres secantur, a runcando dicti.*

(*b*) *Corp. Gloss.* s.v. 'falcastrum'. *Falcastrum* uuidubil (*AS*) v 361. 40. Runco a similitudine falcis v 568. 48. V. harpis, runcones. Cf. Isid. 20. 14. 5. Runcones ⟨a⟩ [t]runcando id est [sunt] falcastra v 578. 7.

(*c*) Pallad. 1. 43. 3 (farm inventory). '*Grubbers*, with which we attack the bramble-thickets': *runcones, quibus vepreta persequimur.*

DISCUSSION

1. *Design*

The terms *falcastrum* and *runco* are synonymous. Rich is perhaps right (*Dict. Ant.* s.v. 'falcastrum'), in supposing *falcastrum* to have been 'a provincial term in use among the labouring population'. The rare and late occurrence of both terms implies that the implement was a specialized form of *falx* invented in later times. But to which category of *falx* does it belong? Rich is certainly in error in describing the implement as a long-handled sickle. Thielscher, *Belehrung,* 215, says the *falcastrum* was a large sickle, too big for reaping, and that it was used for weeding corn during the growing period. He identifies it with the large hooks found at Lauriacum, near Enns in Upper Austria (Abb. 1), and even more strangely with the implement displayed on the well-known weeding scene in the Peterborough Psalter, now in Brussels (Abb. 2). The *falcastrum* or *runco* is much more likely to have been a long-handled billhook, with a crescent-shaped blade, which would give it the appearance of a bird's beak—that is if we assume the word to be connected with the root which appears in the

Greek ῥύγχος, a bird's bill. It is not certain, however, whether the allusion is to the shape of the blade or to the manner in which it was used, perhaps like a fowl pecking or rooting up the ground. But Isidore's specific reference to 'cutting down' (*succidere*) seems decisive against this interpretation (see further below, section 2). Le Gall[1] presumes that it had a scythe-like blade, resembling the French gardener's billhook, which is known as a 'croissant', or 'crescent'. The brief Glossary references are late, and give no clue.

2. *Operational technique*

Brambles can be cut down ('succidere'—Isid.) with a crescent-shaped blade and with a sweeping action. But the word 'runcare' (= to 'weed') seems to have generally the meaning to 'root up' rather than to 'cut down' (see, for example, LS s.v. 'runcare'). There is also the related word 'runcina' (= a 'plane'), which is derived, according to Varro (*LL* 6. 96) from the Greek ῥυκάνη', meaning a 'plane'. There is a good deal of confusion in the commentaries on tools and operations concerned with the removal and eradication of weeds, thorns, briers and so on. This arises from imprecise language, as well as ignorance of the problems involved. The terms 'weeding-hook' and 'grubbing-hoe' (LS s.v. 'runco') are both inappropriate here. Weeding, in the sense of removing unwanted growth among cereals or garden plants, was done by hand in Roman times, as it still is done in many parts of the Mediterranean region.[2] It has been suggested that weeding in this sense was carried out by means of an implement known as a 'runca', similar in design to the Italian 'falciolo'. But the following passage from Palladius (4. 9. 7–8) is decisive against this commonly held opinion. Discussing the cultivation of the cucumber (*cucumeris*) he says: 'they have a partiality for weeds, and therefore need neither the hoe nor weeding'. As for hoeing, in the sense of tilling the surface between the rows of a growing crop, this was carried out as a necessary routine with implements of an entirely different design from those discussed in this section (see the discussion s.v. 'sarculum', above, pp. 45 f.). All the available evidence thus points to the view that the *falcastrum* or *runco* was an implement with a scythe-like blade, used for cutting down, not for uprooting.

3. *Monuments*

(*a*) *Extant representations.* Two good examples are reported: (1) a bronze model from the Villa Pisanella, near Pompeii, now in the National Museum at Naples (*Mon. Acad. Lincei*, VII, 439, fig. 39); the blade has a pronounced

---

[1] Le Gall, p. 59.
[2] I have seen hand-weeding by gangs, chiefly of women, but sometimes of whole families, in Sicily and Tunisia.

backward sweep, but otherwise resembles the *f. arboraria* (above, Figs. 59–63 (the model is reproduced by H. Thédenat (Daremberg–Saglio, s.v. 'runco', fig. 5967)); (2) a sculptured example in the hand of a conventional figure representing Summer from Ostia, now in the church of S. Paolo alle Tre Fontane, Rome (Hanfmann, *The Season Sarcophagus*, fig. 114, no. 151). This example has a crescent-shaped blade.

(*b*) *Extant specimens.* I have not been able to trace any recognizable specimens in any of the major collections. P. Thielscher (*Des Marcus Cato Belehrung über die Landwirtschaft*, Berlin, 1963, p. 215) identifies *runco* with a *falx* found at Lauriacum (Lorch, an important Roman station near Enns in Upper Austria), now in the Museum at Enns (*op. cit.* Abb. 1), and with an implement depicted on the Peterborough Psalter in Brussels, where it is used for cutting off weeds in the corn with the aid of a stick (Abb. 2). I do not agree that his *falx* is necessarily a *runco*; the *f. messoria* can be used for all sorts of tasks apart from that of reaping corn. It is more likely that some of the short-bladed implements labelled 'scythes' are really brush-cutters for clearing brambles. The Italian derivatives of *runco* are all hooks, not grubbing implements (see below, under 'Survival').

4. *Survival*

(*a*) *Of the implement.* ? Fr. 'croissant', a crescent-shaped billhook with a long handle, used by gardeners for lopping high branches. There is a good illustration in *Larousse du XXᵉ siècle*, s.v. 'croissant'.

(*b*) *Of the name.* (1) *falcastrum* survives unchanged: It. 'falcastro' (m.), a billhook. (2) It. 'ronca' (f.), 'roncola' (f.), a pruning-hook; 'roncone' (m.), a sickle; 'ronchetta' (f.), 'ronchetto' (m.), a vine-dresser's knife; 'roncinato' (adj.), hooked (in shape).

Fig. 68. Falcastrum (French)

12. **Falx vinitoria** (Colum.) = Falx silvatica (Cato), Falx a tergo acuta atque lunata (Pallad.), *the vine-dresser's knife*

(*a*) Not in Varro, *LL.*

(*b*) Isid. 20. 14. 4 (*falcis* generically to denote various forms of pruning-hook, including *f. arboraria* and *f. vinitoria*). 'The *pruning-knife* is what is used for pruning trees and vines': *falcis* est quo arbores putantur et vites.
    Note: Falx alone is common in the sense of *f. vinitoria* (e.g. Colum. 4. 6. 5; 4. 7. 2; 4. 9. 1, etc.). See further Appendix E, p. 205 (on meanings of *falx*).

(*c*) Cato 11. 4 (vineyard inventory). 'Six *pruning-knives*': *falces silvaticas* VI.

(*d*) Colum. 4. 25 (a complete description of the design and functions of the various parts of the *f. vinitoria*). 'Now the shape of the *vine-dresser's knife* is so designed that the part next to the haft, which has a straight edge, is called the *culter* or "knife" because of the similarity. The part that is curved is

Fig. 69. Falx vinitoria

called the *sinus* or "bend"; that which runs on from the curve is the *scalprum* or "paring-edge"; the hook which comes next is called the *rostrum* or "beak", and the figure of the half-moon above it is called the *securis* or "hatchet"; and the spike-shaped part which projects straight forward from it is called the *mucro* or "point". Each of these parts performs its own special task, if only the vine-dresser is skilful in using them. For when he is to cut something with a thrust of the hand away from him, he uses the *culter*; when he is to draw it towards him, he uses the *sinus*; when he wishes to smooth something, he uses the *scalprum*, or, to hollow it out, the *rostrum*; when he is to cut something with a blow, he uses the *securis*; and when he wants to clear away something in a narrow place, he makes use of the *mucro*. But the greater part of the work in a vineyard must be done by drawing the knife toward you rather than by hacking; for the wound which is made in this way is smoothed with one impression, since the pruner first puts the knife in position and so cuts off what he has intended to cut. One who attacks the vine by chopping, if he misses his aim, as often happens, wounds the stock with many blows. Therefore that pruning is safer and more advantageous which, as I have said, is accomplished by the drawing of the *knife* and not by striking': est autem sic disposita *vinitoriae falcis* figura, ut capulo pars proxima, quae rectam gerit aciem, culter ob similitudinem nominetur; quae flectitur, sinus; quae a flexu procurrit, scalprum; quae deinde adunca est, rostrum appellatur; cui superposita semiformis lunae species securis dicitur; eiusque velut apex pronus imminens mucro vocatur. harum partium quaeque suis muneribus fungitur, si modo vinitor gnarus est iis utendi. nam cum in adversum pressa manu desecare quid debet, cultro utitur; cum retrahere, sinu; cum adlevare, scalpro; cum incavare, rostro; cum ictu caedere, securi; cum in angusto aliquid expurgare, mucrone. maior autem pars operis in vinea ductim potius quam caesim facienda est; nam ea plaga quae sic efficitur, uno vestigio adlevatur, prius enim putator applicat ferrum, atque ita quae destinavit praecidit. qui caesim vitem petit, si frustratus est, quod saepe evenit, pluribus ictibus stirpem vulnerat. tutior igitur et utilior putatio est, quae, ut rettuli, ductu *falcis* non ictu conficitur.

DISCUSSION

1. *The vine-dresser's knife*

Columella (4. 25) has given the classic description of this beautifully designed implement, developed from the simple billhook, which has remained virtually unchanged to this day.

The six parts of the implement are clearly shown in the attached illustration (from E. de St-Denis, 'falx vinitoria', *Rev. Arch.* XLI, 1953, 173, fig. 3). The implement is in fact a refinement, for specialized purposes, of the ordinary billhook (*f. arboraria, f. putatoria*), which has four of the six parts, viz. the knife (*culter*), the bend (*sinus*), the paring-edge (*scalprum*) and the beak (*rostrum*); see s.v. 'f. arboraria', above, p. 87, Fig. 60). The six parts of the implement are:

(i) the straight-edged knife (*culter*), used when the operator has to cut something with a thrust of the hand away from him (*resecare*);

Fig. 70. Falx vinitoria. 1, Culter; 2, sinus; 3, scalprum; 4, rostrum; 5, ecuris; 6, mucro

(ii) the bend (*sinus*), used when he needs to draw the branch or shoot towards him (*retrahere*); the bend will partially enclose the shoot and prevent the implement from slipping;

(iii) the paring-edge (*scalprum*), used when he wishes to smooth a rough surface or remove some bark;

(iv) the beak (*rostrum*), used for hollowing out a portion of a branch;

(v) the hatchet (*securis*), which makes a safe, clean cut in pruning, where conditions allow of cutting off a useless branch or shoot by striking;

(vi) the spike (*mucro*), used for clearing away dead wood, etc., when working in a confined space.

Thus each separate part of this multi-purpose implement has its own particular function, 'provided the vine-dresser understands their use' (*si modo vinitor gnarus est iis utendi*—Columella 4. 25. 1); or again: 'and he should know what part of the pruning-knife is to be used in each operation; for I have learnt that a great many people ruin their vineyards through ignorance on this point' (*nec ignoret in quaque re, qua parte falcis utendum sit: nam plurimos per hanc inscitiam vastare vineta comperi*—ibid. 4. 24. 22).

2. *Palladius' implement*

Palladius 1. 43. 2 (inventory of implements): '*pruning-knives* which are sharp and lunate at the back': '*falces* a tergo acutas atque lunatas'. This reference is usually either ignored by commentators or abandoned as an insoluble problem. Yet it is difficult to resist the conclusion that the distinguishing marks of the implement ('sharp-edged and lunate at the back') refer to the peculiar shape of the 'hatchet' or *securis* of the implement described in detail by Columella (see below). Against this identification it may be argued that Palladius has already mentioned the vine-dresser's knife when referring to the *f. putatoria* or billhook, 'which we are to use for trees and vines' (1. 43. 1). But there is ample evidence for the use of the simple billhook in the pruning of vines. In fact both billhook and vine-dresser's knife are found being used together (e.g. in the painting by Brill representing the month of March reproduced by Del Pelo Pardi, *Attrezzi*, 18, fig. 23). The passage from Isidore, like the Glossary references (see above, p. 73) is vague and uninformative, making no distinction between the vine-dresser's knife and the ordinary billhook.

3. *Monuments*

(*a*) *Extant representations*. The best-known representation of the implement described by Columella is contained in an ancient MS of the author, which is frequently reproduced in modern works (see R. Billiard, *La Vigne*, 349; E. de St-Denis, 'falx vinitoria', *Rev. Arch.* XLI, 1953, fig. 1,

Fig. 71.
Falx vinitoria

Fig. 72.
Falx vinitoria
(Italian)

Fig. 73.
Falx vinitoria

p. 170; Le Gall, pl. VI, 1—see Fig. 69, p. 93). A simpler version, lacking the spike, and with a straight-edged back-axe in place of the lunate one, is common on monuments (e.g. Le Gall, pl. VI, 2, from the tomb of a Gallo-Roman vine-dresser now in the museum at Nîmes, S.E. France—see Fig. 71). This simpler version recurs frequently in the medieval period: a fine example appears in the hands of a vine-dresser on one of the miniatures of the Codex Virgilianus which at one time belonged to the Italian poet Petrarch (†1374). The implement has the typical broad blade and back-axe, but no point (Del Pelo Pardi, 14, fig. 19, who describes the implement as identical in shape to that used today; see also P. Brandt, *Schaffende Arbeit und Bildende Kunst*, Leipzig, 1928, II, 50, Abb. 46).

(*b*) *Extant specimens.* The Landesmuseum at Trier, West Germany, contains a fine collection. Many specimens are reproduced by S. Loeschke, *Denkmäler vom Weinbau . . .* (Trier, 1933), p. 13, Abb. 11, nos. 1, 2—see also De St-Denis, *art. cit.* fig. 3, p. 173 (a Gallo-Roman specimen now in the museum at Chalon-sur-Saône: inv. no. 7. 12. 1666). There are several excellent specimens in the collection found on the premises of a *faber ferrarius* at Pompeii, now in the Vatican Museum, Rome.

4. Survival

(*a*) *Of the implement.* Before the invention of the secateur or pruning-shears by Bertrand de Molleville (1744–1818) all pruning was done with the *falx* (= Fr. 'serpette', It. 'pennato', 'falcetto').

(*b*) *Of the name.* It. 'falcetto' (m.), the pruning-knife. Serpette is the standard term in French for the pruning-knife; 'faux' is the scythe. R. Dion (*Histoire de la vigne et du vin en France des origines au xixe siècle*, Paris, 1959), claims the occurrence of a local dialect form of 'falx' in the historic Médoc region as evidence of an early date for the establishment of the vine in that area.

13. **Falcula vineatica** (Cato), Falcula (Colum.), *grape-knife*

Not in Varro, *LL*; not in Isidore; not in Palladius' list.

Fig. 74.
Falcula vineatica

(*a*) Cato 11. 4 (vineyard inventory). 'Forty *grape-knives*': *falculas vineaticas* XL.

(*b*) Varro, *RR* I. 22. 5 (Stolo, citing Cato's inventory). 'Thus the same author says that forty *grape-knives* will be needed . . .': nam dicuntur ab eodem scriptore vineaticae opus esse XL . . .

(*c*) Colum. 12. 18. 2 (on preparations for the vintage). 'Also as many *small sickles* and iron hooks as possible must be procured and sharpened, so that the grape-picker may not strip off the clusters with his hand, which causes much of the fruit to fall to the ground and the grapes to be scattered': nec minus *falculae* et ungues ferrei quam plurimi parandi et exacuendi sunt, ne vindemitor manu destringat uvas, et non minima fructus portio dispersis acinis in terram dilabatur.

1. *Discussion*

This is the ordinary grape-knife; as the diminutive form (*falcula*) indicates, it is a small sickle, which must be specially sharpened (Columella (*c*)) so as to make a clean cut through the tough stem, and avoid damaging the vine. Picking by hand is rightly condemned, but the corollary, as Columella points out, is to provide a sufficient supply of knives; hence Cato's specific requirement of forty for a vineyard of one hundred *iugera* (*a*). Speed is essential to the operation and all available labour must be laid on. Elsewhere (11. 1. 20) Columella stresses the need to supply a double quantity of the commoner implements, since the cost of additional tools is as nothing compared with the loss suffered when a labourer stands idle for lack of an implement which has been broken or mislaid. The omission of this item from later lists of implements may possibly reflect a decline in standards. The clusters can be plucked by hand, but at the risk of loss. Columella's 'iron hooks' (*ungues ferrei*) are not mentioned elsewhere; and the casual nature of the reference suggests that both small sickles and hooks were normally used for another purpose. Small sickles were used for reaping millet and other similar crops, and the iron hooks were probably small pruning-hooks and brush-cutters. In modern viticulture the grape-knife has been to some extent superseded by the secateur, which is specially designed for making a clean cut, but the French 'serpette à vendanger' (see Le Gall, *art. cit.* 58) is essentially the same implement as that referred to here.

2. *Monuments*

(*a*) *Extant representations.* Few examples are reported; two excellent examples are illustrated in the collection of the Landesmuseum at Trier, West Germany: the first is sickle-shaped, the second resembles a billhook. Both are from the same column-drum in the museum at Speyer (Loeschke, *Denkmäler*, Abb. 13 *a* and 13 *b*, p. 17). The billhook type is also displayed on a mosaic pavement depicting vintage scenes found at Cherchel, Algeria (first reported by J. Lassus in *Libyca*, VII, 1959, fig. 34, p. 263).

(*b*) *Extant examples.* (1) Trier, Prov. Mus. no. 07, 99; length 11·5 cm, with sickle-shaped blade and curved handle (from Nattenheim). (2) Frankfurt, Hist. Mus. no. X. 2299; length 13 cm, with hook and straight handle (from Heddernheim) (= Fig. 75).

Fig. 75.
Falcula vineatica

3. *Survival*

(*a*) *Of the implement.* Fr. 'serpette à vendanger' of similar design to (*b*)(2) above.

(*b*) *Of the name.* Fr. 'faucille' (f.), sickle (with loss of diminutive meaning).

14. Falx faenaria, *scythe*

Fig. 76. Falx faenaria

(*a*) Varro, *LL* 5. 137. 'From a certain resemblance to these (i.e. sickles) there are others, including the *mowing scythes* and tree-lopping billhooks, of obvious origin . . .': a quadam similitudine harum (i.e. falcium) aliae, ut quod apertum unde, *falces faenariae* et arborariae . . .

(*b*) Cato 10. 3 (oliveyard inventory). '8 scythes': falces fenarias VIII.

(*c*) Varro, *RR* 1. 49. 1 (on harvesting hay). 'First the grass on the meadows should be cut close with the *scythe* when it has stopped growing and is beginning to dry from the heat . . .': primum de pratis summissis herba, cum crescere desiit et aestu arescit, subsecari *falcibus* debet . . . (Colum. 2. 18 (on haymaking) makes no mention of the implement used in the process. Elsewhere in Colum. *falx* alone often = *f. faenaria*, as in Varro, *RR* 1. 49. 1.)

(*d*) Pliny 18. 261 (on the mowing of meadows—a comprehensive treatment of the topic). 'Of the *scythe* itself there are two types: the Italian scythe is shorter, and may also be used even among brambles; the type used on the large estates in Gaul is larger; in fact they economize by cutting through the stalks at middle height and missing the shorter ones. The Italian mower cuts with the right hand only': *falcium* ipsarum duo genera: Italicum brevius ac vel inter vepres quoque tractabile, Galliarum latifundiis maiores* compendio quippe medias caedunt herbas brevioresque praetereunt. Italus faenisex dextra una manu secat. (* *Sic? Mayhoff*: latifundia a maioribus *codd.*)

DISCUSSION

1. *General observations*

In spite of minor modifications and variations in the design of the blade, and major improvements in the shape and set of the handle, the mowing scythe, like the sickle, has retained its essential pattern over the centuries. With the sickle, it is the agricultural implement most frequently represented in works of art of all periods down to the present day. In ancient Italy it was first the attribute of Saturn, god of agriculture, and then, by an erroneous identification, it became the emblem of Time, the Destroyer. On Saturn the scythe-bearer see Macrobius, *Saturae* 1. 7–8.

2. *Scythes and sickles confused*

Confusion between the scythe (*f. faenaria*) and the sickle (*f. messoria*). The two implements are frequently confused by editors and translators. The main reason for this is that both technical and non-technical writers frequently employ *falx* without an attribute with any of the three meanings *f. faenaria*, *f. messoria* and *f. vinitoria*; *falx* = *f. faenaria* is the least common, and *f.* = *f. messoria* is the most frequent of these ellipses. The lists of passages in Appendix E, p. 205, will probably be helpful; but the context normally makes the meaning perfectly clear. Thus at Varro, *RR*

1. 49. 2 (*pace Thes.* s.v. 'falx') it is surely *f. faenaria* that is meant, since the scythe is the normal implement for cutting hay. For detailed discussion see Le Gall, *op. cit.* pp. 59 ff.

3. *Design: short- and long-handled scythes*

The mowing scythe consisted of a gently curving concave blade set at right-angles to a straight handle. The length of the latter was variable; Pliny (18. 261) mentions a long-handled Gallic type, and a shorter Italian model, operated by one hand only. Sickle-blades and scythe-blades survive in considerable quantity; and it is evident that the shallow-bladed sickles represent a half-way stage between sickle and scythe.[1] Unfortunately the surviving examples of true scythe-blades of Roman origin must have required a long handle; furthermore, the passage cited above from Pliny is our sole literary reference for the shorter type, and he gives no description of the implement, beyond the important statement that it was operated by one hand. The use of a short or long handle for cutting grass or hay is obviously dictated by the height of the grass: poor crops of hay and fodder grass are still reaped with the sickle. The design of the shorter scythe is uncertain; but a single-handed implement of this type, well known in medieval Europe and still used in Belgium and the Netherlands and neighbouring areas,[2] may well be a survivor of the type referred to by Pliny. The medieval type consists of a shallow-curved scythe blade attached to a short stout handle which is bent backwards at the top away from the line of the blade, to form a short hand-grip (see Fig. 77). The surviving version of this implement, known as the 'scythette', is very similar in design, and has a similar but improved hand-grip, shaped like a horse's hoof (see Fig. 78). If this suggested identification is correct (there is of course no means of proving it at present), its design would fit the limited information provided by Pliny: it is a single-handed implement, and it is suitable for cutting brambles as well as hay.

Fig. 77. Falx faenaria (medieval French)

Fig. 78. Falx faenaria

The long-handled type presents no problems of identification; it is well known from numerous representations on monuments of many kinds; it is the common attribute of Saturnus, bringer of agriculture to Italy; and later, in its most familiar form, became associated with Time, the Destroyer. The literary sources give no information about the length or the shape of the handle: on most of the monuments it is long and straight, with no hand-grips. Now the action of the scythe, as we have seen (above, p. 80), is a forward sweeping action, the line of cutting being an arc. The bar-handle, which made its first appearance in the twelfth century A.D.,[3]

[1] See the various types reproduced by Petrie, pls. 54, 55.
[2] Discussed and illustrated under the name 'scythette' by Hopfen, p. 100, fig. 72.
[3] Jope, *HT*, II, 95, fig. 62 (= London, British Museum, Cotton MS. Jul. A VI, fol. 6).

enabled the mower to increase the size of the cut by swinging the body with the full stretch of the arms. Without the help of the bar-handle, the swing is much restricted. The backward-curving handle which appears on a monument of the late eighth century[1] will have served to increase the size of the cut. Straight-handled scythes are still used by farmers in the U.S.S.R. and in the Iran/Iraq border region.

4. *Operational technique*

The scythe is not an easy implement to operate. It is difficult to get a clean sweep at ground-level without digging the point into the ground; and Columella (2. 17. 4), discussing the building-up of a meadow, gives precise instructions about the proper levelling of the soil and the removal of the small heaps of earth formed by the 'drag' or clod-remover (*crates*), as it turns at the end of its run 'to prevent the mower's iron blade (*ferramentum*) from striking against anything'. For this reason the sickle (*falx messoria*) was used where the ground was rough or uneven. The compound verb *subsecare*, 'to cut close', used by Varro (*loc. cit.*) correctly emphasizes the technique of cutting with this implement: the curved blade sweeps along the ground through an arc, slicing the grass close to the ground. It is easy to see that humps or ridges would cause the point of the blade to stick in the ground, while small stones left by the 'drag' could easily damage the cutting edge.

There is a peculiar difficulty in the passage from Pliny in which reference is made to the two varieties of scythe (*HN* 18. 261—passage (*d*), p. 98). The text is obviously corrupt: as corrected, with some reserve, by Rackham, the Loeb editor, the sense is that the long-handled Gallic scythes (*maiores*) effected an economy in the use of labour 'since they cut the stalks half-way down and leave the shorter ones'. This operation is not possible with the scythe! I conclude that Pliny has transferred to his account of haymaking what Columella had said (*RR* 2. 20. 3) about the use of the *falx veruculata* for cutting corn (see pp. 79 f.). The actions of the two implements are quite different. H. Stern[2] has recently re-opened the question of the type of implement displayed on the panel representing the month of July on the central arch of the Porte de Mars at Reims, north-east France. Following the opinion of Le Gall (*art. cit.* p. 65) that this panel illustrates haymaking, he concludes that the implement depicted is a long-handled sickle. The strongly curved blade is unusually large, and the attitude of the right-hand figure, who is at work, while one of his companions is sharpening his blade, and the other rests on the implement, strongly suggests that it was worked

[1] Reproduced by Le Gall, pl. x, no. 5 (from a Carolingian MS now in Salzburg).
[2] H. Stern, 'Le cycle des mois de la Porte de Mars à Reims', in Hommages à Albert Grenier, *Coll. Latomus* (1962), t. III, 1441–6.

with both hands, and with a sweeping action similar to that of the true scythe (*art. cit.* p. 443). If this identification is correct, we have here in Gaul an implement intermediate between the sickle and the scythe in use from the third quarter of the first century A.D. (Pliny died in A.D. 79). No apology is made for the lengthy treatment of the mowing scythe. The fundamental distinction between scythes and sickles is frequently obscured by translators and commentators, even to the point of making nonsense of a perfectly intelligible text.[1]

5. *Monuments*

(*a*) *Extant representations*. Le Gall (*art. cit.* p. 65) has pointed out that the only surviving classical monument depicting the scythe is on an arch of the Porte de Mars at Reims, north-east France. For the interpretation of this monument we are still dependent on the drawings made in the eighteenth century by M. S. Bence (A. de Laborde, *Les monuments de la France*, Paris, 1816, pl. CXIII; Le Gall, pl. VII, 4; H. Stern, *Le Calendrier de 354, Étude sur sa texte et ses illustrations*, pl. XXXVIII, 4, Paris, 1953). The implement as drawn by Bence has a large semicircular blade, and a long, straight handle, and is more like a *falcastrum* (q.v.) than a scythe. The blades of all the early medieval representations (e.g. Le Gall, pl. VIII, 4; pl. IX, 2 and 4) closely resemble the surviving blades at Saint Germain-en-Laye (see below).

(*b*) *Extant specimens*. A good collection of surviving scythe-blades is to be found in Petrie, pl. 54. The small collection at Saint-Germain-en-Laye contains two mutilated scythe-blades of the long-handled type (Reinach, *Cat. Ill.* fig. 278, nos. 15888 (see Fig. 79) and 29036), both of which have a reinforcing metal strip along the upper edge, and two with shorter, wider blades which fit the shape of the short-handled scythes depicted on some medieval manuscripts (Reinach, *Cat. Ill.* fig. 278, nos. 1481 (see Fig. 80), and 10190).[2]

Fig. 79. Falx faenaria

Fig. 80. Falx faenaria

Del Pelo Pardi (*Attrezzi*, 7–9, figs. 7–14) has drawings of various types of scythe-blade, and also reproduces the British Museum MS of the fourteenth century (BM Royal 15 E II, fo. 247 v.—see Frontispiece), and a sixteenth-century painting of Christ, now in the Cathedral at Biella, near Novara, north-west Italy, depicting the Saviour surrounded by a remarkable array of implements. Each of these latter paintings contains a representation of the same short-handled single-handed scythe.

[1] Pliny, *Natural History*, ed. H. Rackham (Loeb Classical Library, London, 1950), v, p. 355. The term 'falx', standing alone, may be used in several different senses (see Appendix E, p. 205, 'On the various meanings of "falx"').
[2] On the exceptionally long scythe-blades from Great Chesterford, Cambridge, see Appendix E, pp. 208 f., and Plate 9 (*a*).

The Saalburg museum contains a fine specimen of the long-handled scythe (*Saalburgjahrb.* IV, 1913, Taf. 14, no. 7).

6. *Survival*

(*a*) *Of the implements.* (1) The long-handled scythe. Le Gall (*art. cit.* pp. 68–9) declares that one might well conclude that the scythe is one of the numerous inventions for which Rome was indebted to the Gauls, were it not for the gap of several centuries which separates the text of Pliny from the MS from Salzburg, Austria, now in the library of Vienne, S.E. France, which contains the earliest known representation of the scythe. The author has surely overlooked the long-handled scythe which appears in the hands of 'Father Time' on monuments of the middle and later Roman Empire; Smith (*Dict. Ant.* 3rd ed. 1902, s.v. 'falx'), depicts three cameos with Kronos (Saturn) as subject, which clearly illustrate a stage in the adaptation of the symbol of Kronos/Saturn to those of Father Time and his scythe. The earlier representations show him armed with a *falx arboraria* or billhook (e.g. Le Gall, *art. cit.* pl. VI, 5 (from Pompeii)), while the later types show him with the *falx faenaria* or mowing scythe.

(2) The short-handled scythe. The scythette has been established for many centuries in north-west Europe (above, p. 99), and may reasonably be regarded as having originated with Pliny's 'Italian' scythe. Billiard (*L'Agriculture*, p. 130) describes the method of cutting with this type of short-handled scythe, a type still employed by Belgian farmers. The local name for the implement is 'sape' (a Flemish dialect form). A hook is used in the left hand, as depicted in the British Museum miniature (see Plate 1).

(*b*) *Of the name.* Fr. 'faux' (f.), the scythe; the diminutive form 'faucille', from *falcula*, is reserved for the sickle (see Le Gall, *art. cit.* p. 60). It. 'falce' (f.), (1) sickle, (2) scythe, preserving the confusion arising from the use of the same term 'falx' in the ancient authorities to denote either 'scythe' or 'sickle'. The specific term 'falce fienaia' (= *f. faenaria*) is also used in Italian to denote the mowing-scythe.

7. *Development and survival of the long-handled scythe*

The straight, long-handled type continued to be used until the invention of the bar-handled scythe in the twelfth century. The development in design represented by the Gallic scythe raises a question of importance in agricultural economics. Two factors probably influenced the change in design: first, the improvements in animal husbandry which are known to have taken place in imperial Roman times[1] created an increased demand for

---

[1] Varro devoted the whole of his second book *De Re Rustica* to stock-raising. For the range of cattle-breeds see Colum. 6. 1. 1–3; on horse-breeding Colum. 6. 27. 1 and Pliny 8. 162.

fodder, and consequently for easier methods of cutting fodder crops; under the same head should be noted the effect of the stalling of animals and the increased demand for leaf-cutting tools with a view to extending the supplies of animal feed throughout the agricultural year (see the sections on 'falx messoria', pp. 83 ff., and other specialized varieties of *falx*); secondly, the change in farm organization from fields haphazardly interspersed with bush to larger open fields and properly managed meadows (see, for example, Columella 2. 16–17; Pliny 18. 258 ff.) favoured the development of the long-handled scythe. Most of the relatively small number of genuine advances in technique occurred on the large estates in Gaul (see pp. 157 ff. v.s. 'vallus'). Shortage of seasonal labour for harvesting operations must also have been a factor of some importance.[1]

---

[1] References to labour shortages are infrequent but significant, e.g. Colum. 4. 6. 2 (in the vineyard), Varro, *RR* 1. 53 (for gleaning), and Pliny 18. 300 (threshing method governed by size of harvest and scarcity of labour).

4

FORKS

I. FVRCA   2. FVRCILLA   3. FERREA (?furca)   4. PASTINVM
5. ACVS   6. MERGAE   7. PECTEN

'Furca' is the generic term for the common two- or three-pronged fork
(cf. Ital. 'tridente', a hayfork, pitchfork), used mainly for stacking hay,
corn and straw. The diminutive 'furcilla' was often used, as in modern
Italian, with no difference in meaning (e.g. Varro, *RR* 1. 49. 1—below, s.v.
'furcilla'). The only other implement of this type known to have been
used in agriculture was the *pastinum*, an iron implement with two prongs,
used for planting vines in the nursery, and for similar tasks in the kitchen
garden. It has already been pointed out (above, p. 17) that the large multi-
tined fork of north-west Europe found no place in the equipment of the
Roman farmer. For an implement which combined the action of a fork with
that of a spade see the discussion s.v. 'pala lignea' (above, pp. 31 ff.).

1. **Furca** (-ae, f.), *fork*, (rare) *pitchfork*

Fig. 81. Furca
(ancient Egyptian)

(*a*) Not in Varro, *LL*; not in Isidore; not in Palladius' list.

(*b*) *Corp. Gloss.* s.v. 'furca'. *Furca* δίκρανος II 277. 42. τύρχη II 461. 10. vaergrod
(vel uueargrod) *AS* v 360. 25. supplicii genus, etc. . . . v 204. 2. genus ligni
bicipitis v 297. 18. duplex fustis II 580. 55. Cf. τύρχη διόδους ξυλίνη *Edict.
Diocl.* 15. 47.

(*c*) Verg. *G.* 1. 264–5 (work to be done in bad weather).
'Some sharpen stakes and *two-pronged forks*,
and prepare ties of purple willow for the bending vine':
exacuunt alii vallos *furcasque bicornis*
atque Amerina parant lentae retinacula viti.

(*d*) Hor. *Ep.* 1. 10. 24. 'Drive nature out with a *pitchfork*, yet she will always
return . . .': naturam expelles *furca*, tamen usque recurret . . .

DISCUSSION OF FVRCA (= PITCHFORK)

Furca with the meaning 'pitchfork' is rare, the diminutive *furcilla* being
the common form. The Greek word δίκρανος (adj.) means 'two-headed',
and is also used as a substantive, meaning 'pitchfork' (LSJ). Τύρχη is
a late form, derived from the same root as *furca*.

1. *Design and functions*

The oldest surviving specimens of the pitchfork (e.g. Petrie, pl. 67, no. 41, from an Egyptian tomb of the Vth Dynasty), have obviously been cut from a naturally forking branch. The same primitive type may still be seen in South Italy today, whereas in the more advanced northern districts it has been superseded by a manufactured product fitted with prongs of uniform size (see below, under 'Survival').

The *furca* was a multi-purpose implement, being employed in hay-making, stacking, loading manure or compost, laying out bedding in the cattle-stalls, spreading the straw for threshing, etc. Its absence from the inventories of farm equipment (*instrumentum fundi*) is doubtless due to the fact that, since forks could be cut without trouble, they were no more part of an inventory than stakes.

2. *Monuments*

(*a*) *Extant representations.* Haymaking scenes, which were very popular both in Egyptian and medieval art, often include stacking as well as cutting operations, but the only sculptured representation of haymaking surviving from classical times, that from the Porte de Mars at Reims (see p. 100), is confined to the actual harvesting.

(*b*) *Extant specimens.* As in the case of other wooden implements, the only surviving specimens of *furcae* and *furcillae* are those found in Egypt.

3. *Survival*

(*a*) *Of the implement.* Jaberg–Jud, *op. cit.* Karte 1485, no. 2 (manufactured three-pronged type from North Italy (see Fig. 82).

(*b*) *Of the name.* Fr. 'fourche' (f.), 'fourche-bidente' (f.), hayfork (with two prongs). It. 'forca' (f.), pitchfork; 'forca da paglia' (f.), hayfork; the common form of the latter is three-pronged and called 'tridente'.

2. **Furcilla** (-ae, f.), *hayfork, vine-prop*

(*a*) Not in Varro, *LL.*

(*b*) Isid. 20. 14. 11. '*Furcillae* "forks" are so called because they are used for "stirring" (*cillere*), that is for shifting the corn': *furcillae* dictae ab eo quod ⋆celluntur, id est moventur. (⋆ *celluntur* makes no sense; no such verb occurs elsewhere. Immediately after the above passage Isidore correctly derives 'oscillare' to 'swing' from 'cillere' to 'put in motion'; if *cilluntur* is the correct reading, the etymology is of course wrong.)

(*c*) *Corp. Gloss.* s.v. 'furcilla'. *Furcilla* δίκρανον III 196. 1. δίχαλον (cf. Hesych. δίχαλον ζυγόν) III 449. 51. δίχαλλον III 477. 39 . . .

Fig. 82. Furcilla
(Italian)

(*d*) Varro, *RR* 1. 49. 1 (after haymaking). 'The grass should be turned over with *forks* until it completely dries out': herba, quoad dearescat, *furcillis* versari debet.

(*e*) Colum. 2. 10. 13 (on threshing with flails or forks). 'Have a moderate number of loose sheaves brought together at one end of the threshing-floor, and let three or four men push them along with their feet . . . and beat them with flails or *forks*': modicus fasciolorum numerus resolutus in extrema parte areae *colligetur, quem tres vel quattuor homines promoveant pedibus et baculis *furcillisve* contundant. (*Lundstr.*: collocetur R aliquot.)

(*f*) Varro, *RR* 1. 8. 6 (on the most economical method of supporting vines). 'There are two types of these (vineyards) . . . in the other type only those branches are raised from the ground which give promise of producing fruit. These are propped on *forked sticks* about two feet long . . .': huius (vineti) genera duo . . . alterum genus vineti, ubi ea modo removetur a terra vitis, quae ostendit se adferre uvam. sub eam . . . subiciuntur circiter bipedales . . . *furcillae* . . .

(*g*) Pliny 14. 32 (on a certain prolific variety of wine-grape). 'These vines must be supported on *forked props*; otherwise they cannot support the weight of their abundant vintage': *furcas* subdere iis necessarium; alioqui ubertatem suam non tolerant.

DISCUSSION

1. *Various meanings of the term 'furcilla'*

The diminutive of *furca* was used to denote two different items:

(*a*) like *furca*, a fork for turning over the hay while it was drying in the field (passage (*d*)); this wooden pitchfork could also be used instead of a plain flail (*fustis*) for threshing corn (passage (*e*));

(*b*) a fork-shaped vine-prop made of wood (passages (*f*) and (*g*)), *furca* being very rare in this sense. Varro lays down that these supports should be about two feet long. Columella and Palladius do not favour this system of training vines, and neither mentions the term. In neither of these uses is the force of the diminutive felt. Not an implement, but included here for reference.

Fig. 83. Furcilla

2. *Monuments*

See above, s.v. 'furca', p. 105.

3. *Survivals*

(*a*) *Of the implement.* See above, s.v. 'furca'.

(*b*) *Of the name.* It. 'forcella' (f.), a forked stick. Fr. 'fourchette' (f.), fork.

3. **Ferrea** (scil. furca), *iron fork*

Under this heading three distinct varieties of fork are involved:

(i) a light, two-pronged fork, used in vineyards, orchards and gardens;

(ii) a fairly large, three-pronged fork, identical in pattern with the English four-pronged digging-fork, except for the number of prongs;

(iii) a pitchfork or hayfork, of the same design as the common wooden pitchfork described above (pp. 104 f.), but fitted with iron prongs.

I. THE LIGHT, TWO-PRONGED TYPE

(*a*) Not in Varro, *LL*; not in Isidore; not in Palladius' list.

(*b*) Cato 10. 3 (oliveyard inventory). '8 iron forks': ferreas VIII.

(*c*) Cato 11. 4 (vineyard inventory). '10 iron forks': ferreas X (cf. Varro, *RR* 1. 22. 3).

1. *Identification of the implement*

The identification of this implement has already been fully discussed in the section on spades (above, p. 25). The choice of implement lies between the categories of spade and fork. Since the literary evidence is so inconclusive, it seemed appropriate to discuss the term 'ferrea' under both headings. The chief argument in favour of identifying the implement as a fork is the discovery, in at least one area known for the intensive cultivation of vines and orchard trees, namely the estate of Herennius Florus at Boscoreale on the slopes of Mount Vesuvius, of forks made of iron. Such light, two-pronged types would be very suitable for work in plantations or vine-nurseries. The term 'ferrea' does not occur in the later writers, and it is perhaps not unreasonable to infer that *ferrea* and *pastinum* are earlier and later names for the same implement (see below, pp. 109 f.). A further point that seems to tip the balance in the same direction is that Cato's inventories already include quite enough digging implements (six spades and two drag-hoes), without the addition of ten spades of a different type. Furthermore, the vineyard already has a force of ten labourers; if the *ferrea* were a spade, it must, by reason of its abbreviated name, have been heavier, and therefore more expensive, than the *pala*, and it is difficult to think of any operation in the vineyard that would warrant the all-out deployment of the entire labour-force on a digging operation, at the expense of other necessary work. Large quantities of implements have to be provided for the harvest and the vintage, when either the weather conditions, or the rapid maturing of the crop, make speed imperative; but

digging over ground for the planting of vines does not fall into this category. The weight of the evidence thus favours the identification of *ferrea* as a fork.

2. *Monuments*

(*a*) *Extant representations.* I know of no identifiable representations.

(*b*) *Extant specimens.* The two surviving forks from Boscoreale (Chicago, Mus. Nat. Hist. nos. 26160 and 26161) are very different in design and weight; the tines are of the same length, but those of 26160 are twice as thick as those of 26161, and much more closely set. Vineyard soils vary enormously in texture; and the implements are obviously designed for cultivating very different kinds of soil. Although Columella does not mention forks in his lengthy treatment of preparation and cultivation of soils for vines in *De Arb.* 1–6, the kind of careful cultivation after planting prescribed (e.g. *De Arb.* 5. 3 and 6. 2) could best be carried out with forks of this type.

3. *Survival*

(*a*) *Of the implement.* Modern planting or tilling forks are of three prongs, but otherwise not dissimilar in design to the Chicago specimens.

(*b*) *Of the name.* See above, s.v. 'furca', p. 105.

Fig. 84. Furca ferrea

2. THE LARGE, THREE–PRONGED TYPE

There is no literary evidence for a large three-pronged fork. In the Saint-Germain collection, there are three large iron forks (Reinach, *Cat. Ill.* Fig. 278, nos. 29020, 29020 A and 29023). No. 29020 has three prongs, and the tang which fits into the handle is set at an angle of approx. 120° to the prongs; it is evidently a lifting fork for lifting and spreading bedding or manure, and very closely resembles the modern fork of this type as used in northern Europe. No. 29023 (=Fig. 84) is clearly a pitchfork (see section 3). No. 29020 A (=Fig. 85) has three strong tines each 20 cm in length, and a long socket 30 cm in length and it closely resembles the northern digging fork in size and shape. Its appearance in the Compiègne collection from north-eastern France, and its absence from the range of implements from the Mediterranean region, suggest that it developed independently as a digging and cultivating tool in the cold and wet areas of northern Europe, where it has remained an essential item in the farmer's equipment.

Fig. 85. Furca ferrea

3. THE IRON PITCHFORK

In addition to no. 29023, Rich (*Dict. Ant.* 307, s.v. 'furca') has an illustration of an ancient iron pitchfork of uncertain date, recovered from the old bank of the river Nene, near Peterborough, Northants, England. This was an area of intensive Roman settlement and the implement may possibly be Roman. Like the Compiègne specimen, which it resembles, it has two prongs which curve outwards at the fork, and close towards the points.

Fig. 86. Furca ferrea

4. Pastinum (-i, n.) (Colum.), Pastinatum (-i, n.) (Isid.), *dibble*

(*a*) Not in Varro, *LL*.

(*b*) Isid. 20. 14. 8. '*Dibble* is the name given by farmers to a two-pronged iron implement used for setting out plants': *pastinatum* vocant agricolae ferramentum bifurcum quo semina panguntur.

(*c*) Colum. 3. 18. 1 (on planting out vine-cuttings). '*Dibble* is the name given by farmers to a two-pronged implement used for setting out plants': *pastinum* autem vocant agricolae ferramentum bifurcum quo semina panguntur.

(*d*) *Corp. Gloss.* s.v. 'pastinum'. *Pastinum* βωλοστρόφιον II 260. 54 (i.e. a turning over or ploughing of the sod).

Fig. 87. Pastinum

DISCUSSION

1. *Terminology*

Columella's definition of this implement is repeated almost verbatim by Isidore, except for the change from *pastinum* to *pastinatum*. That Isidore's name is wrong is evident from the subsequent discussion in Columella, who goes on to say that the implement has given its name to the operation known as 'repastinare', that is, the process by which old vineyards were turned over with the spade a second time, the term 'pastinatum' being properly applied to a vineyard that has been restored (*restibilis*). He adds that it has lately been applied incorrectly to any ground that is stirred up in preparation for the setting of vines. Elsewhere (e.g. 3. 15. 1) he correctly applies the term *pastinatio* to the operation of preparing the ground for planting. *Pastinatum* properly means a field dug and levelled off for planting (e.g. Columella 3. 13. 7; at 13. 6 he has *pastinatum solum* with the same meaning). In Palladius *pastinum* is used frequently with the meaning *pastinatio*, the process of making the ground ready for vines, and as equivalent to *pastinatum*, i.e. the ground that has been so prepared (1. 7 and 34; 2. 10. 1 and 4). This latter meaning had evidently become standardized by the time of the Glossaries, where the verb *pastinare* has become a synonym for ploughing or cultivating in general.

Fig. 88. Pastinum

Fig. 89. Pastinum
(modern)

2. *Monuments*

(*a*) *Extant representations.* No identifiable representations have been reported.

(*b*) *Extant specimens.* The two small two-pronged forks from Pompeii, illustrated by Petrie (*TW*, pl. 67, nos. 44 and 45) are appropriate both in size and length of tines, and are probably *pastina*.

3. *Survival*

(*a*) *Of the implement.* 'An implement of the same kind, called "trivella" by the Romans, and "cruccia" by the Tuscans, is still employed for a similar purpose in Italy' (Rich, *Dict. Ant.* s.v. 'pastinum').

(*b*) *Of the name.* The name survives in certain Romance dialect forms (e.g. S. It. 'pástino' (Meyer-Lübke 6277)).

5. **Acus** (-us, f.), *needle, planting dibble*

Only used once by an agricultural writer in this special sense.

Pallad. *RR* 1. 43. 2 (inventory of farm equipment). '*Dibbles* for planting vine-shoots in dug-over ground': *acus*[1] per quas in pastinis sarmenta merguntur.

Design

The general shape is determined by the name. For planting out tender shoots gardeners use a short stick with a rounded point, with which the soil can be readily compacted around the base. This is essential if the cutting is to root. Gesner's suggested equivalent, the *subula*, is in fact a different implement, the awl, which is used for fine boring operations (Palladius 2. 14. 3).

Neither representations nor surviving specimens are known.

Fig. 90. Mergae (ancient Egyptian)

6. **Mergae** (f. pl.), *reaping-boards* [Merges (-itis, f.), *sheaf*]

(*a*) Not in Varro, *LL*; not in Isidore; not in Palladius' list.

(*b*) Fest.(Lindsay) 124. 1 s.v. 'mergae'. '[Small] *forks* used for piling up crops, so called from the birds called gulls or "divers" (*mergae*); as the gulls plunge into the sea in pursuit of the fish, so the reapers plunge them into the crops in order to be able to lift up their bundles (i.e. sheaves)': furculas quibus acervi frugum fiunt, dictas a volucribus *mergis*, quia, ut illi se in aquam mergunt, dum pisces persequuntur, sic messores eas in fruges demergunt, ut elevare possint manipulos.

[1] *h.e. subulas*, Gesner.

(c) *Corp. Gloss.* s.v. 'merga'. *Merga* est furca V 621. 9. *mergae* fustes, quibus messes colliguntur vel corvi marini V 310. 19; 373. 35.

    Note: The complete Glossary references, in which *merga* and *merges* are hopelessly confused, are omitted here.

(d) Colum. 2. 20. 3. 'Many gather the heads only with *forks*, and others with combs—an operation which is very easy in a thin crop, but very difficult in a thick one': multi *mergis*, alii pectinibus spicam ipsam legunt, idque in rara segete facillimum, in densa difficillimum est.

(e) Pliny 18. 296. 'Elsewhere the stalks are cut off at mid-height with the sickle and the ear is stripped off between two *forks*': stipulae alibi mediae falce praeciduntur atque inter duas ★*mergites* spica destringitur.

(f) Plautus, *Poenulus* 1018–19. '*Milphio:* He says he's been given spades and *forks* for sale. They're for reaping, I suppose, unless you have another idea . . .':

    MI. palas vendundas sibi ait et *mergas* datas,
    ad messim credo, nisi quidem tu aliud sapis . . .

(g) *Ibid. Rudens* 762–3. '*Daemones:* If you touch the door, I'll jolly well reap a harvest off your face with fisty *forks*':

    DA. si attigeris ostium,
    iam hercle tibi messis in ore fiet *mergis* pugneis.

(h) Verg. G. 2. 516–17. 'Earth never rests: the year overflows either with fruit, or with young lambs, or with the wheaten *sheaf* of Ceres':

    nec requies, quin aut pomis exuberet annus
    aut fetu pecorum aut Cerealis ★*mergite* culmi.

(j) Servius *ad loc.* (*Cerealis mergite culmi*); cf. *Corp. Gloss.* IV 258. 5; V 222. 18. ★'*Mergites* are bundles of stalks with the ears attached, which they embrace with the left hand as they reap': *mergites* fasces culmorum spicas habentium, quos metentes bracchiis sinistris complectuntur. (★ For the confusion of *mergae* and *merges* see below, p. 112.)

DISCUSSION

1. *Design and function*

The precise nature of this implement is not clear. Apart from the passage from Pliny (*e*), and several Glossary references, where there is obvious confusion with 'merges' a 'sheaf', there is general agreement among the literary references that it was a kind of fork. Festus (*b*) says that it was a pitchfork (*furcula*), used for loading or carrying off the sheaves after the corn was cut. This is in direct conflict with Columella (*d*), who mentions *mergae* as one of two types of implement used in the process of removing the heads of grain only; unfortunately he gives no details either of the design of these *mergae* or of the way in which they were used. This omission is in keeping with the general practice of the agricultural writers in not giving detailed descriptions of common implements. That *mergae* were familiar implements is evident from the two Plautus passages: in (*f*) it is

implied that *mergae* are as common in the cornfield as *palae* are in the garden, while the metaphorical use in (*g*) confirms this view. The etymological evidence is not conclusive, although the widely supported connection with the Greek verb ἀμέργω, 'pluck', 'pull off', seems most likely. Festus' derivation from the masculine form 'mergi', 'gulls', has been rightly rejected as folk-etymology (see Walde–Hofmann, s.v. 'mergae', 76). It is also clear from the available evidence that reaping with *mergae* means reaping with a pair of implements. It cannot have been a method similar to the English 'hook and sickle' method, in which the reaper, instead of grasping a bundle of corn with his left hand, employed a hooked rod, and thus speeded up the process of securing the bundle of corn for cutting with the sickle. Varro does not mention reaping with *mergae*, which is surprising in view of his lengthy account of three recognized methods of reaping (see pp. 79 f. above).

The passage quoted above from Pliny (*e*), usually dismissed as worthless in discussions of the problem (e.g. by Blümner),[1] nevertheless contains information of importance to the elucidation of the term 'mergae'. Pliny appears to have confused two different methods of reaping, the 'middle-cut' method (see above, s.v. 'f. messoria', pp. 77 ff.), and that employing *mergae*. His account creates further difficulties through a confusion of *mergae* with *mergites*, the plural form of 'merges', a bundle, the correct meaning of which is known from the reference in Vergil (*h*). But he does appear to be describing a distinct process, that of stripping off (*destringere*) the ears between two implements. The phrase suggests the idea of a reaper armed with a pair of these implements drawing them together from two sides so as to enclose a bundle, and then ripping the ears off with an upward movement. Further light is thrown on the problem by the following practice reported by Steensberg.[2] 'For reaping spelt (*triticum spelta*) in Georgia, USSR, the reaper uses two pieces of wood, 45 to 50 cm long, fastened together at one end with a cord . . . for breaking the ears. Here again the straws are cut in a separate process.' In the Spanish province of Asturias, where traditional methods survive in all farming operations, Vavilov[3] observed the same method for reaping spelt. Possibly Columella had similar methods in mind when he wrote of harvesting with *mergae* or *pectines*, 'combs' (q.v.). Columella (*d*) adds the significant fact that the process of gathering the heads with 'combs' (? as well as *mergae*) is very easy in a thin crop, but difficult in a thick one. It is not certain whether his last remark is intended to refer to *mergae* as well as to *pectines*, but the point is clear enough. In either case the reaper would have to move about in the

[1] H. Blümner, *Die römischen Privataltertümer* (München, 1911), III, 2, 569, n. 6.
[2] Steensberg, *op. cit.* pp. 124 ff.
[3] N. F. Vavilov, 'Studies in the origin of cultivated plants', *Journ. Appl. Bot.* XVI (1926), 2.

standing crop, removing the heads, whereas the reaper using the sickle stands in the stubble and works his way into the standing corn, and the density of the crop is irrelevant. On the assumption that the *mergae* were wooden boards, the second Plautus passage (*g*) gains significance: Daemones threatens to disfigure his opponent by using his fists as *mergae* and bringing them into violent contact with his face by an upward sweeping action from both sides.

2. *Monuments*

The illustration (Fig. 90, p. 110) is of a pair of winnowing boards from the Petrie collection of Egyptian antiquities now in University College London. They appear to represent more or less the shape required for the operation described above. No examples of *mergae* seem to have survived from Roman times.

7. **Pecten** (-inis, m.), *comb, reaping comb*

(*a*) *R-E* XIX. 1 (B. 2), col. 10 [Herzog-Hauser].

(*b*) Not in any of the inventories; in fact the term occurs only three times in an agricultural context.

(*c*) Colum. *RR* 2. 20. 3 (on various methods of harvesting grain). 'Many gather the heads only with forks, and others with *combs*, an operation which is very easy in a thin crop, but very difficult in a thick one': multi mergis, alii *pectinibus* spicam ipsam legunt, idque in rara segete facillimum, in densa difficillimum est.

(*d*) Pliny, *HN* 18. 297 (on methods of harvesting cereals). 'In the Gallic provinces they gather both varieties of millet ear by ear with a *comb* held in the hand': panicum et milium singillatim *pectine* manuali legunt Galliae.

(*e*) Ovid, *Rem. Am.* 191–2 (activities of the countryman). 'At fixed seasons he binds up the cut grass and sweeps the shorn earth with a wide-toothed *rake*':

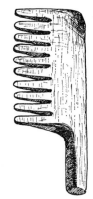

Fig. 91. Pecten (ancient Egyptian)

> temporibus certis desectas alligit herbas
> et tonsam raro *pectine* verrit humum.

DISCUSSION

1. *Design*

Pecten is the generic word for comb, most commonly of the hair-comb, also of the comb-like instrument used for holding the warp threads in a loom, and of the wooden hayrake (passage (*e*)); the technical name for this implement is *rastellus* (see s.v.). It is evident from passage (*c*) that the functions of *mergae* and *pectines* will have been somewhat alike; but the combing operation on the heads of grain was done with a single implement, and with a slight variation in the action; while the two *mergae* were brought

together so as to hold a number of stalks (above, p. 112). The reaper using the *pecten* presumably grasped a bundle of stalks with his left hand a short distance below the heads, then passed the teeth of the comb through them, and stripped them off. The illustration on p. 113 (Fig. 91) has been prepared to suggest the kind of implement required. Millet in its various forms (passage (*d*)) is a very small-grained cereal, and a comb of this type would be reasonably effective. In Egypt and in the northern areas of West Africa beyond the rain-forest, where large quantities of millet are grown, the crop is still reaped by hand, usually with a small serrated sickle (for the type see Fig. 54, p. 80), the grains being deposited in a small haversack slung over the reaper's shoulder. The reaping comb is 'wide-toothed' (passage (*e*)), as compared with an ordinary hair comb.

2. *From manual to mechanical harvesting*

According to Pliny heading by means of the *pecten* is typical of the Gallic provinces. Pliny is also our earliest authority for the existence, in the same areas, of a heading machine for grain, which is based on a comb, mounted on a wheeled frame. The transition seems a natural one, where fields were large and flat enough for mechanical operation (see further s.v. 'vallus', pp. 170 ff.).

3. *The economics of different reaping methods*

The process of stripping the ears from the straw described here is somewhat time-consuming, even by comparison with sickling. It is curious that Pliny should have begun his chapter on reaping methods (18. 296 f.) with an account of the mechanical animal-drawn 'header', concluding it with an account of this laborious method, which was also employed in Gaul. Were crops of millet so valuable in the cooler northern regions that harvesting in this tedious way was still profitable? This manual method would certainly involve less loss of grain, and time would also be saved at a later stage, since only winnowing would be required.

Three of the six methods mentioned by the Roman authorities are paralleled from different periods in the history of Egyptian agriculture. Under the Old Empire the corn was cut at knee-height (the commonest method in Italy according to Varro (*RR* 1. 50. 1), and bound into sheaves. In the Middle Empire they severed the heads (Varro's second method) and collected the grain directly into baskets or haversacks carried by the reapers. Under the New Empire the entire plants were pulled up by the roots (Pliny's fourth method (18. 296)). The economic advantage of reaping the ears separately is twofold: (*a*) the long straw may be used for thatching, and (*b*) the saving in labour in hauling and threshing is considerable. Pliny (18. 297) has a valuable comment on the economic aspects of the various

methods: 'There are also these differences: where they thatch the houses with straw, they keep it as long as possible, but where there is a shortage of hay, they require the chaff for litter.' The popular 'middle-cut' method represents a compromise solution of the economic problem in areas where the straw is not used for thatching, but where, as in the southern half of the Mediterranean, the competing claims of litter for stock, and stubble as grazing when fresh fodder is in short supply, are met in this way. This clear division between northern and southern practice is well supported by monumental and by literary evidence (see above under 'Monuments', pp. 84 f.). In addition to the evidence already cited from Gaul, both Strabo (4. 5. 5) and Diodorus (5. 21) say that in Britain only the ears were brought in from the field. This is paralleled from sixteenth-century France and late seventeenth century Germany. On the 'heading' machine, for reaping the ears only, see Section 10, pp. 157 ff.

Finally, there is evidence that cutting close to the heads with the sickle in order to preserve as much of the straw as possible was the method widely employed by enlightened farmers in the United States little more than a century ago: 'Further, by using the sickle, and cutting as high as can be ... most of the tall straw is left standing as stubble in the field, which is the cheapest, and as good a disposition as can be made of it for manuring the land, and makes a vast saving of labour in the hauling, thrashing and stacking, compared to the handling of all the greater length of straw, as usually cut by the scythe and cradle, or by a reaping machine.'[1]

4. *Monuments*

(a) *Extant representations.* A good illustration of a *pecten* in use will be found in Tylor and Griffith, *The Tomb of Paheri at El Kab*, Egypt Exploration Fund, 11th memoir, pl. III, pp. 12–14. The scene depicts reapers 'heading' a crop of flax with the *pecten*. I have been unable to find any representation of the implement in classical art.

(b) *Extant specimens.* No surviving specimens have been reported; the shape, as shown in the Egyptian example noted above, is traditional, being simply a larger version of the handled type of hair comb, and the Roman *pecten* was probably of identical shape.

5. *Survival*

Neither the implement nor the name (in this specific sense) appears to have survived.

[1] L. C. Gray, *A History of Agriculture in the Southern United States to 1860*, II (Washington, D.C., 1933), 798 (quoting Ruffin, 'Agricultural features in Virginia and South Carolina', *De Bow's Review*, XXXIII, 1857, 12). Cf. *ibid.* p. 799: 'as late as the end of the eighteenth century machines designed to thresh the ears only were still in common use in the Southern United States'.

5

SAWS

Saws in a great variety of types are known; wood-working and stone-cutting saws, as well as surgical saws, are well represented on monuments and in the museum collections.

The generic term *serra* is applied to the carpenter's and mason's implements, the diminutive *serrula* being used for the smaller types, including those used for tree-pruning.

I. Serrula (-ae, f.), *saw, pruning-saw*

> *RE* II A. 2, 1738–42, no. 1 [Hug].

(*a*) Not in Varro, *LL*.

(*b*) Isid. 20. 14. 6 (the pruning-saw). 'The *pruning-saw* is a very thin flat piece of iron which with the bite of its teeth cuts back trees or branches': *serrula est praetenuis lammina ferri dentium mordacitate resecans arbores seu ramos.*

> *Note:* The verb '*resecare*', used here in reference to trees, does not mean to fell (this was done with the axe), but to prune, being used as now where the branches were too thick to be lopped by a pruning hook, or too closely set for the billhook to make a cut (see below on 'serrula manubriata' (no. 2)).

(*c*) Colum. *De Arb.* 6. 4 (on cutting back old vines). 'You should leave the stock four inches from the roots and, if possible, cut it off with a *pruning-saw* near a knot...': quattuor digitos ab radicibus truncum relinquito, et si fieri poterit, iuxta aliquem nodum *serrula* desecato...

(*d*) Varro, *RR* 1. 50. 2 (on methods of reaping). 'There is a second method of reaping, used for example in Picenum, where they have a curved piece of wood with a small iron *saw* at the end. This grasps a bundle of ears, cuts them off, and leaves the stalks standing in the field to be cut off later': altero modo metunt, ut in Piceno, ubi ligneum habent incurvum bacillum, in quo sit extremo *serrula* ferrea. Haec cum comprehendit fascem spicarum desecat et stramenta stantia in segete relinquit, ut postea subsecuntur.

2. Serrula manubriata (= Lupus), *small pruning-saw, wolf*

(*e*) Pallad. 1. 43. 1 (inventory of agricultural implements). '"Lupi" ("wolves") are small hand saws of smaller or larger size, measuring up to 18 inches long; with these it is easy to perform operations which are impossible with an

Fig. 92. Serrula

ordinary saw, either . . . or allowing for the intercultivation of vines by lopping the branches of trees': lupos, id est serrulas manubriatas minores maioresque ad mensuram cubiti, quibus facile est, quod per serram fieri non potest . . . resecando trunco arboris, aut vitis interseri.

Fig. 93.
Serrula manubriata

DISCUSSION

1. *Identification of types*

These two items are discussed together, since the somewhat limited literary evidence suggests that they are one and the same, and that Palladius' term 'lupus' is the popular term used in his day for the pruning-saw, deriving its name from its resemblance to the fangs of a wolf. Surviving examples from the Roman period are cut to run in either direction, and the teeth thus have a closer resemblance to the sharp fangs of a wolf than those of a one-way carpenter's saw. Varro's reaping saw is fully discussed on pp. 81 f. It is included here for the sake of completeness.

2. *Design and function*

The teeth of the pruning-saw must be arranged to work in both directions because of the confined space in which the implement has to work. Modern pruning-saws are either straight or curved, the latter type being essential for the kind of pruning described by Columella (*De Arb.* 6. 4). Surviving examples of the size mentioned by Palladius have been found on Roman sites (see, for example, Reinach, *Cat. Ill.* fig. 274, no. 38146, an example from the Department of the Aisne in northern France).

Fig. 94. Serrula

The full text of Columella's discussion (*loc. cit.*) affords an excellent example of the exquisite care devoted to the skilled task of vine-pruning. In this delicate operation the small pruning-saw enables the vine-dresser to remove all superfluous wood from the stock without damage to the stock itself or to the bearing shoots. The passage from Palladius cited above appears to be corrupt, since the text as it stands makes no sense. The most reasonable solution is to assume that some phrase parallel to 'or for the intercultivation of vines', *aut vitis interseri*, has fallen out, and that Palladius is describing two important uses of the implement, the second being that of lopping off branches in a vineyard in order to establish another crop (e.g. corn) in between the rows (*interseri*). It would be natural to assume that the missing phrase referred in some way to the use of the *serrula* for vine-pruning as described earlier by Columella. Palladius is clearly referring to vines grown on supporting trees (hence 'resecando trunco arboris'), and to the removal of superfluous branches from the trees in order to keep the spaces between the rows clear for ploughing and cultivation.

3. *Monuments*

Various types of carpenter's saw occur frequently on sculptured monuments, but I have found no recognizable specimen of this rather specialized
pruning implement. The Petrie collection includes some good specimens
of saws, but few of them correspond with the requirements. This is not
surprising, since small iron implements have a poor chance of survival. The
accompanying illustrations (Figs. 92, 93 and 94) all have two-way blades,
an essential requirement either for carpentry or pruning. Fig. 92, from
Pompeii, has a concave blade, but only the haft end has survived; it is
probably a pruning-saw. Fig. 94, from the Roman fort at Newstead in
Scotland, is very small and is probably a wood-worker's tool; it has an
off-set horn handle and a straight blade. Fig. 93, from Presles-St-Audebert,
Dept. of Aisne, northern France, fits the requirements very well. Reinach,
Cat. Ill. fig. 274, includes it with several other saws, but describes it as a
'scie à guichet', a keyhole saw. But a blade of 28 cm is too long for a
keyhole saw. It is more probably a compass saw.

4. *Survivals*

Both straight- and curved-bladed types are still in general use for
pruning. The name has not survived.

6

SHEARS

Forfex (-ficis, f.), forpex (-picis, f.) *sheep-shears*

RE VI. 2, cols. 2853–6 [Mau].

This class of implement consists of a pair of blades which are set to intersect in the act of cutting, either by means of a central pivot uniting two separate blades, as in scissors, pliers, pincers or tongs, or by means of a tensioned spring joining the blades at their butt ends, and forming a unit with them. Pivoted implements of the first type have been known from about 300 B.C., and are apparently an Italian invention (Petrie, *TW*, p. 48), but the improved form of this implement, the true scissors operated independently by two fingers, dates only from the first century B.C. The spring-shears have some advantage over the scissors in performing similar operations in that only one hand is required, leaving the other hand free, as in sheep-shearing, to handle the animal and, where need arises, to explore the skin in advance of the shears, and so avoid nicking the flesh. Both types are found in Roman practice, whether as tongs, pliers, forceps or shears. In agriculture we are concerned only with *forfex* (vulg. *forpex*), used of sheep-shears, grape-cutters and so on. For the spelling and the distinction between *forceps* = tongs, pincers, etc., and *forfex* = shears, scissors, etc., see *Thes. L.L.* s.v. 'forceps'. The Glossaries are confused.

Fig. 95. Forpex

Not mentioned in the lexicographers or in the lists of implements.

(a) Calpurnius Siculus, *Ecl.* 5. 73–4 (on sheep-shearing). 'Lest the skin be damaged by the sharp *shears*': ne sit acuta *forpice* laesa cutis.

(b) Colum. 12. 14. 4 (on the vintage). 'Others, when they pick a bunch, cut off diseased grapes with *scissors*': alii, cum legerunt uvam, si qua sunt in ea vitiosa grana (grapes) *forficibus* amputant.

(c) Pliny, *HN* 15. 62 (on the vintage). 'Disease-spreading grapes being removed from the cluster with *scissors*': demptis *forfice* corruptoribus acinis ex uva.

DISCUSSION

1. *Sheep-shears*

Although there are numerous literary references to the *forfex* as an instrument for cutting the beard, the passage from Calpurnius Siculus (a), a pastoral poet of the first century A.D., is the only surviving reference to an implement that was familiar to almost every farmer. Smith (*Dict. Ant.* 2nd ed. 1902, s.v. 'forfex') cites no literary evidence, but shows a drawing of an engraved gem from the Berlin collection, in which a sheep is repre-

Fig. 96. Forpex

sented grazing beneath a symbolic pair of shears. The blades of the implement are thin and flat (see Isidore, *Etym.* 20. 13. 3), the sharpened edges being
set so as to intersect like a pair of scissors when the instrument is grasped
between the thumb and the fingers; the blades are then pressed together
against the tension of the semi-circular spring (see Fig. 96, p. 119).

2. *Grape-cutters*

Apart from the two literary references cited above, there appears to be
no surviving evidence concerning the implement. They may have been
true scissors (above, p. 119), but nothing can be stated for certain about
their design.

3. *Monuments*

(*a*) *Extant representations of the sheep-shears.* The Berlin gem appears to
be unique.

(*b*) *Extant specimens.* Petrie reproduces two specimens: (i) *TW*, pl. 58,
no. 11 (from the National Museum, Naples: inv. 718183 = Fig. 95); pl. 58,
no. 19 (from the Römisch-Germanisches Zentralmuseum, Mainz: inv.
3. 3. 5 = Fig. 96). Other examples from Roman Germany are featured in
Blümlein, *Bilder*, p. 96, Abb. 314*a*. The Saalburg museum has several
well-preserved specimens; most of these have long narrow blades (e.g.
Saalburgjahrb. XI, 1952, Taf. 12, no. 57, from Bad Neuheim); one has
shorter, wider blades and a thicker spring (*ibid.* IX, 1939, Taf. 29, no. 9).

4. *Survival*

(*a*) *Of the implement.* Sheep-shears of similar design are still in use in many
parts of the world, though now largely superseded by the modern power-
driven clipper.

(*b*) *Of the name.* It. 'forbici' (f.pl.), scissors, shears.

DESCRIPTION OF MACHINES

7

PLOUGHS

1. Aratrum (-i, m.), *the symmetrical plough*

R-E, s.v. 'Pflug' XIX. 2, cols. 1461–72 (Drachmann).
    Note: The *testimonia* are given in full, including the evidence for the parts of the plough, which are discussed in turn below. For the complete text of Servius and Schol. Dan. on Vergil, *G.* 1. 170 ff. see Appendix F, p. 212.

(a) Varro, *LL* 5. 134. 'The plough takes its name from the fact that it "works" (*arat*) the soil. Its iron (i.e. "share") (*vomer*) is so called because it enables the plough to "vomit out" (*vomere*) the earth better. The sole (*dens*) . . . because the earth is "bitten" (*mordetur*) by it. The pole which stands above the sole is called the stilt (*stiva*) because it "stands up" (*stando*), and the transverse bar upon it is called the hand-grip (*manicula*), because it is grasped in the hand (*manu*) of the ploughman. The piece which is, as it were, a pole (*temo*) between the oxen is called the yoke-beam (*bura*) from *bos*, an ox; others call it an *urvum* from its curved shape': *aratrum*, quod arat terram. eius ferrum *vomer*, quod vomit eo plus terram. *dens* quod eo mordetur terra; supra id regula quae stat, *stiva* ab stando, et in ea transversa regula *manicula*, quod manu bubulci tenetur. qui quasi temo est inter boves, bura a bubus; alii hoc a curvo *urvum* appellant.

(b) Isid. *Etym.* 20. 14. 2. 'The plough (*aratrum*) is so called from the action of ploughing (*arando*) the earth, as if from "earth-plougher" (*araterrium*). The plough-beam (*buris*) is the curved part of the plough, as if from "ox-tail" (βοὸς οὐρά), since it resembles the tail of an ox. The sole (*dentale*) is the first part of the plough; the share (*vomer*) is drawn over it as a kind of tooth (*dens*)': *aratrum* ab arando terram vocatum, quasi araterrium. *buris* est curvamentum aratri, dictum quasi βοὸς οὐρά, quod sit in similitudinem caudae bovis. *dentale* est aratri pars prima; in quo *vomer* inducitur quasi dens.

(c) Pallad. 1. 43. 1. '*Ploughs* are either *simple* or, if the open nature of the country permits, *eared*; so that with these it is possible to raise crops with a deeper[1] furrow to counteract the high water-table in winter': *aratra simplicia*, vel si plana regio permittit, *aurita*, quibus possint contra stationes humoris hiberni sata celsiore* sulco attolli.

(d) *Corp. Gloss.* s.v. 'aratrum'. *Aratrum* ἄροτρον II 18. 54; 245. 40; III 27. 32; 262. 52; 299. 68; 357. 32; 467. 26; 508. 68. Cf. II 546. 50 *ubi Keil* aratrum scribit: *at* rutrum *verum est.*

[1] *celsiore sulco*: the adjective is clearly 'proleptic', referring to the result of making the furrow deeper, which is to raise the ridge higher for planting in wet situations.

(e) *Ibid.* s.v. 'buris'. *Buris* ῥυμὸς[1] ἀρότρου II 31. 50. ἔλυμα[2] II 262. 55. curvamentum aratri V 348. 10; 404. 16. scaer[3] (*vel* scaes *AS*) II 570. 32. Burim ea pars aratri, quae inflexe sicium (*h.e.* inflexa est, cui) temo adiungitur (*ubi* sicium *del. et* temoni *scribit m 3 codicis Pal.*) V 173. 7.

(f) *Ibid.* s.v. 'dentale'. *Dentale* γύης III 262. 53. γύας ὁ τοῦ ἀρότρου II 265. 28. γύης ὕνεως καὶ ἀποτετμημένος (αποτευμενος *cod. corr.* h, *Vulc.*) τόπος τῆς ὕνιδος[4] II 43. 5. ξύλον ἐν ᾧ ἐμβάλλεται ἡ ὕνις II 378. 34. *dentalia* sules reost[5] (*AS*) V 405. 53. Dentales aures dicuntur aratri, quibus latior redditur sulcus V 285. 20; 627. 60 (cf. Serv. *Georg.* I. 172).

(g) *Ibid.* s.v. 'stiva'. *Stiva* (*vel* stiba) ἐχέτλη τοῦ ἀρότρου II 188. 47. ἐχέτλη II 321. 24; III 262. 54. manubrium aratri II 593. 58; IV 286. 42; 393. 33; V 246. 2; cod. Monac. *v. suppl.* manica aratri IV 177. 1; V 515. 51 (cf. Serv. *Georg.* I. 174) dicitur quod arator manu tenet. Virgilius (*Georg.* I. 174) 'stivaque...imos' V 152. 21; 246. 3. velut manubrium est aratri, quod manu tenet (tenens?) arator aratrum sistit ut dirigat sulcum V 246. 4.

(h) *Ibid.* s.v. 'temo'. Temo ῥυμός III 173. 62; 195. 46; 357. 35. ῥυμὸς ἁμάξης II 428. 60...temo longitudo aratri vel plaustri (*vel* plostri). Virgilius (G. I. 171): huic a stirpe pedes temo V 248. 5; 156. 32 (huic a stirpe...in octo, id est aratro), temone V 485. 49.

(j) *Ibid.* s.v. 'vomer'. Vomer ὕνις II 31. 8 (bomer); 211. 28; 462. 65; 490. 35; III 23. 41; 195. 61; 204. 55 (ynyx); 299. 69; 325. 47; 357. 81; 369. 1; 466. 65; 482. 11. vomis *et* vomer ὕνις II 514. 19; 539. 50. *vomer* vomis IV 402. 62. *vomis* vomer aratri V 519. 44. vomis et vomer dicitur *Plac.* V 103. 7. bomer scar (*vel* scaer *AS*) II 570. 20.

(k) Verg. G. I. 169–72; 174. 'From the first, in the woods an elm, bent by main force, is trained for the plough-beam (*buris*), and receives the form of the crooked plough. To the base of this is fitted a pole (*temo*), eight feet in length, and a pair of "ears" (*aures*), and a share-beam (*dentalia*) with a double back, and a stilt (*stiva*) to turn the base of the car (*currus*) from the rear':

169   continuo in silvis magna vi flexa domatur
170   in *burim* et curvi formam accipit ulmus *aratri*.
171   huic a stirpe pedes *temo* protentus in octo,
172   binae *aures*, duplici aptantur *dentalia* dorso,
*174   stivaque, quae currus a tergo torqueat imos.

(* Transposing lines 173 and 174)

Note: The commentary of Servius on this passage is cited in full in Appendix G.

(l) Varro, *RR* I. 19. 2 (ploughing difficulties). 'There are places which oxen cannot break (at first ploughing) unless they are unusually powerful, and frequently they leave the *plough* in the field with a broken *plough-beam* (*bura*)': aliam terram boves proscindere nisi magnis viribus non possunt et saepe fracta *bura* relinquunt *vomerem* in arvo.

---

[1] ῥυμός = 'pole of chariot' (LSJ). No reference in LSJ to this Gloss.
[2] ἔλυμα is the sole or share-beam, not the 'buris' for which the corresponding Greek term is γύης (see Appendix G, Terminology of the plough).
[3] 'scaer', Eng. '(plough)share'.
[4] ὕνις = *vomer*, the ploughshare.   [5] sules reost (AS) lit. the 'sole-rest'.

(*m*) Colum. 2. 4. 6–9 (when not to plough). '(Do not plough during a drought. If you plough in a drought you will have trouble. In very dry ground) the point of the plough (*dens aratri*) is rejected by the hard ground; if it does enter at some point, it does not break the soil into fine particles, but rips up huge clods . . . (these clods affect the second ploughing) because the plough-share is driven out of the furrow by the weight of the clods . . . so that . . . hard skips are left and the oxen are severely injured by the uneven strain': nam vel respuitur duritia soli *dens aratri*, vel si qua parte penetravit, non minute diffundit humum, sed vastos caespites convellit . . . quia ponderibus glaebarum . . . *vomis* a sulco repellitur, quo evenit ut . . . scamna fiant et boves iniquitate operis maxime mulcentur.

THE DESIGN OF ROMAN PLOUGHS

1. *The evidence*

It is unfortunate that the only ancient description of a Roman plough and its parts that has survived is Vergil's account (passage (*k*)). The lexicographers are concerned with the separate parts, not the whole implement, and primarily with the etymology of the parts. Of the four essential parts Varro (*a*) includes all, while Isidore (*b*) mentions only three; Vergil's account (*k*), which makes no attempt at completeness, omits the *vomer*. None of the agronomists refers to the design of ploughs, though Columella (*m*) includes valuable incidental references to some of the parts in operation, and Palladius (*c*) makes brief mention of two basic types, the 'simple' (*simplex*) plough and the plough equipped with 'ears' (*auritum*). The Glossary references to the parts of the plough are numerous, uninformative and occasionally positively misleading (e.g. s.v. 'buris' III 262. 55, where the word is wrongly equated with the Greek word ἔλυμα = sole or share-beam)—above, passages (*d*)–(*j*).

Pliny has no general description of the plough, but his account of the various types of share at 18. 170–2 is valuable, despite some textual difficulties, and it concludes with our only reference to a wheeled plough (see below, pp. 141 f., for a full discussion).

The monumental evidence is often difficult to interpret, and quite unwarrantable inferences have been drawn from it. Representations of ploughs are common enough on coins (some specimens on coins of Marius are discussed by A. S. F. Gow ('The ancient plough', *JHS*, XXXIV, 1914, 249–75, pl. XVII, nos. 11–14)); but the renderings of the parts are schematic, and details cannot be distinguished. In general, where the plough is shown in action, parts of the implement are naturally obscured either by the oxen or by the furrow, so that details of construction are often obscure. An exception is the excellent mosaic from Cherchel in Algeria, where each of the two top registers depicts a plough in action,

with all its structure clearly visible (see below, p. 138). The Vergilian plough has received too much isolated attention from scholars, many of whom were clearly ignorant of the mechanics of ploughing, and many of the resulting reconstructions are quite unworkable.[1] Some confusion has also been caused by the tendency of writers on agricultural topics to use imprecise or ambiguous terms; thus 'dentale' is variously rendered as 'sole', 'stock', 'ploughstock' and 'share-beam', while the vague term 'pole' is applied to two distinct parts, the 'temo' or 'yoke-beam' and the 'buris' or 'ploughbeam'. In the discussion that follows an orderly and consistent use of terms is maintained. The following common terms are employed:

Dentale, the sole, or share-beam; *bura, buris*, the plough-beam; *vomer, vomeris*, the plough-share or share; *temo*, the yoke-beam; *stiva*, the stilt; *manicula*, the hand-grip; *aures*, the ears; *tabula, tabellae*, the ridging board(s); *rallum*, the scraper, ploughstaff; *rotulae*, the wheels.

A comparative table of technical and common terms employed by farmers and writers on agriculture will be found in Appendix G (i).

Fig. 97. Sole-ard (Italian)

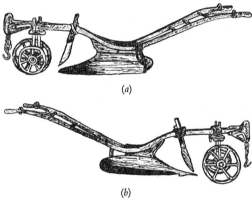

(a)

(b)

Fig. 98. Mouldboard plough (English).
(a) Land side; (b) furrow side

2. Classification of Roman ploughs

1. *Types of plough.* All ploughs belong to one or other of the two great families: the breaking plough, or 'ard' (the word is Swedish: cf. Fr. 'araire', Lat. 'aratrum'), and the turning or mouldboard plough (Fr. 'charrue', Lat. 'carruca').

Each of the two types has developed numerous varieties to suit local conditions, but the essential difference between them is as follows. The breaking plough is symmetrical in its design, and presents the same appearance when viewed from either side; when pulled through the ground it throws up soil on both sides of the dividing ploughshare (see Fig. 97). The turning plough, on the other hand, is asymmetrical. On the furrow side of the implement there is a curved mould-

---

[1] E.g. A. Dickson, *Husbandry of the Ancients* (Edinburgh, 1788), 1, facing p. 390; L. Daubeny, *Lectures on Roman Husbandry* (Oxford, 1857), pl. IV, 2. Dickson's short-comings are all the more surprising, since his own work, which is securely based on close attention to the ancient authorities, shows a rare combination of sound scholarship and practical farming knowledge. Unfortunately he was unacquainted with the simple Mediterranan ards.

board, which is so designed as to turn the slice of earth removed by the combined action of the share and coulter, towards the furrow side, and to invert it (see Fig. 98 (b)). The other side of the mouldboard plough, known as the 'landside', consists of a flat smooth piece of wood or steel, which slides slong the furrow-wall as the plough is drawn along (see Fig. 98 (a)). In most temperate regions, where the soils tend to be heavy, and the temperature relatively low, deep tillage and more or less complete inversion of the sod are usually necessary, and the mouldboard plough reigns supreme. The ard, on the other hand, is ideal for shallow tillage, and is very suitable in semi-arid zones, where cereal crops are grown in soil moistened by winter rains, and where the growing season coincides with dry air and high temperatures. Under these conditions a light and frequent stirring of the surface soil is all that is needed. The ard also has a further advantage: 'in sandy soils and under dry conditions it has the advantage of leaving a trash layer on the surface without up-rooting perennials, thus preventing excessive wind erosion and soil drift' (Hopfen, FIATR, 44).

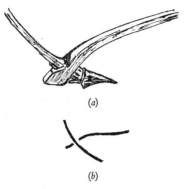

(a)

(b)

Fig. 99. Beam-ard (Iraqi)

There are two main categories of ard, which are usually designated 'beam-ard' and 'body-ard', the respective names being based on the prominence in each type of one or other of the two main members of the implement. The beam-ard consists essentially of a curved plough-beam (Lat. 'bura', 'buris'), pierced by a spear-like body (Lat. 'dentale'), with which is incorporated the stilt (Lat. 'stiva'). In the body-ard, on the other hand, the relationship of plough-beam and body is reversed, the body curving upwards and terminating in the stilt, and being itself pierced by the plough-beam. In some varieties of beam-ard the stilt is almost horizontal, and there are two shares, an arrow-shaped main share and a tanged fore-share which lies above it and is secured in position between a pair of ridges on the upper side of the main share; the type is well known from finds in Scandinavia, and has also been found in Roman Britain; it is usually referred to as the 'bow-ard'. The accompanying diagrams show clearly the different distribution of the parts of the plough in the two main divisions. Both species are still widely distributed in many parts of the world, the beam-ard predominating in central and eastern Spain, south-western France, northern Tunisia, northern Greece, western Turkey, Syria, Lebanon, Israel, Transjordan and Iran, the body-ard in Portugal, western Spain, the Balearic and Canary Isles, Morocco, eastern

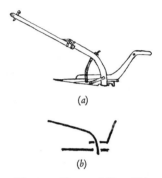

(a)

(b)

Fig. 100. Bow-ard (Spanish)

(a)

(b)

Fig. 101.
Body-ard (Afghan)

127

Algeria, the southern Alpine regions, Italy, Yugoslavia, Albania, Bulgaria, Rumania and Anatolia. Closely related to the body-ard is the sole-ard, a light implement characteristic of dry zones. It has a narrow horizontal body, which in some examples widens out at the rear to make a triangular form. The plough-beam and stilt are separately inserted into the sole, the heel of which usually projects behind the base of the stilt to enable the ploughman to press on it with the foot. It is at present widely used in southern Spain, Morocco, western and southern Algeria, southern Tunisia, Libya, Egypt, southern Italy, Greece, Crete, Cyprus and northern Turkey.

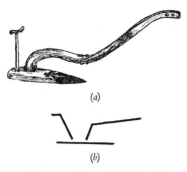

(a)

(b)

Fig. 102. Sole-ard (Pakistani)

2. *To which of these groups did ancient Roman ploughs belong?* Unfortunately we lack both detailed technical descriptions of the Roman plough and its parts, and surviving specimens of the implement (apart from the well-known plough-models). It has been generally assumed that the *aratrum* was a sole-ard, fitted with a socketed plough-share, in which the most important part was the sole or *dentale* (*dentale est aratri pars prima*—Isidore).

This conclusion is based on a variety of considerations, some structural (e.g. the meaning to be attached to Vergil's 'duplex dorsum' at G. 1. 172), others operational (e.g. the stance and actions of the ploughman while guiding the plough through the furrow). These matters are fully discussed under the separate headings for the different parts of the plough (below, pp. 130 ff.). R. Aitken's theory that Vergil's plough was a beam-ard, not a sole-ard, is not accepted here. His paper (*JRS*, XLVI, 1956, 97–106) is examined in detail in Appendix G.

Fig. 103. One-piece plough (Etruscan)

3. *How the Roman plough works*

The simplest form of *aratrum*, like its Greek counterpart (see Appendix G, p. 214), consisted of a sole or share-beam of hard wood set horizontally and drawn through the ground by a pair of oxen yoked to a beam which curved downwards at the opposite end, where it was dowelled into the sole. The movement of the sole through the furrow was controlled both for depth and width of cut by the stilt, which might be either a simple backward extension of the sole, or a separate piece dowelled in at a convenient angle like the yoke-beam. Variations on this basic pattern might include one or two vertical supports joining the yoke-beam to the sole, to

give additional strength. It is obvious that the most primitive form of this plough may well have been made by selecting a convenient branch of a tree, and there is nothing inherently improbable in Vergil's account of an elm being trained *in situ* for the purpose of 'receiving the form of the crooked plough' (G. I. 169–70). Various modifications and extensions of the simple *aratrum* are known from both literary and archaeological evidence; they include a range of devices, designed either to adapt the type for the cultivation of stiffer and heavier soils (e.g. the iron ploughshare to sheathe and protect the wooden sole against the effects of continual friction, or to provide suitable seed-beds under varying conditions of moisture (e.g. the movable ridging-boards, *tabellae*).

4. *The parts of the aratrum* (see the accompanying illustration)

The above description of the essential parts of the *aratrum* by no means disposes of the difficulties encountered in the surviving evidence. Of the six parts mentioned by Varro (*a*), the identification of *vomer*, the share, *stiva*, the stilt, *manicula*, the hand-grip, and *temo*, the yoke-beam or pole, presents no difficulties. The crucial problems are concerned with the other two terms *buris* (Varro's *bura*), and *dentalia* (Vergil), *dentale* (Isidore, = Varro's *dens*). In spite of the clear evidence of the texts, some of the earlier commentators (e.g. Dickson and Daubeny, *opp. citt.*, and several editors of the *Georgics*)

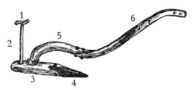

Fig. 104. Sole-ard. 1, Manicula; 2, Stiva; 3, Dentale; 4, Vomer; 5, Buris; 6, Temo

wrongly identified *buris* as the sole or share-beam, and *dentale* as the plough-beam. Yet Varro's identification of *bura* is unequivocal: 'qui quasi temo est inter boves, bura' (referring presumably to the type which had an unjointed pole running from yoke to share-beam); and Isidore's definition of *dentale* is equally clear: 'the sole (*dentale*) is the first part of the plough; the share (*vomer*) is drawn over it as a kind of tooth'. If the editors were unaware of Columella 2. 2. 23–4 or Pliny 18. 171 they need only have consulted Servius at G. I. 172, where he makes it clear beyond doubt that *dentale*, not *buris*, is the share-beam: 'dentale est lignum, in quo vomer inducitur'. This major difficulty being disposed of, we may now proceed to the separate parts of the plough and their functions.

PARTS OF THE 'ARATRVM'

2. DENS, DENTALE   3. BVRIS, BVRA   4. VOMER, VOMIS, VOMERIS
5. TEMO   6. STIVA   7. MANICVLA   8. (i) AVRES, (ii) TABELLAE (Varro),
TABVLA (Pliny)   9. RALLVM   10. ROTVLAE

2. Dentale (-is, n.), Dens (dentis, m.) (Varro, *LL*), Dentalia (Verg.), *the sole* or *share-beam*

In addition to passages ((*a*)–(*k*)) above, the following references are of some importance:

(*a*) Colum. 2. 2. 24 (on the question of light *versus* heavy ploughs). 'Celsus . . . advises the use of small shares and *share-beams* for breaking up land': Celsus . . . censet . . . et exiguis vomeribus et *dentalibus* terram subigere.

(*b*) Pliny 18. 171 (on various types of ploughshare). 'A third type (of share) used in easily worked soil does not present an edge along the full length of the *share-beam* but has only a small spike at the extremity': tertium (genus vomeris) in solo facili non toto porrectum *dentali* sed exigua cuspide in rostro.

(*c*) Verg. G. 1. 172. 'A *share-beam* with double back': duplici *dentalia* dorso.

DISCUSSION

The sole or share-beam (*dentale*) is the essential part of the plough, and indeed can be regarded as a plough in itself. Since it was commonly protected against friction by an iron sheath (the *vomer*) the term *vomer* was often, especially in poetry, used for the whole plough. Friction against the sides of the sole would be considerable, and the sheath of the socketed *vomer* was often long enough to protect a good deal of it (see on 'vomer', below, pp. 132 ff.). The reference from Pliny ((*c*), p. 132) implies that the common type ('vulgare genus' = type 2, p. 133) was so protected.

Vergil's 'share-beam with double back' (*duplici dorso*) has been explained in two ways: according to one theory, *duplex* here means 'grooved', like the 'duplex spina' or 'grooved spine' mentioned among the points of a horse by Vergil, Varro and Columella.[1] Alternatively, it may refer to a share-beam which spreads out at the back to form two sections. Rich, who favours this latter explanation (*Dict. Ant.* s.v. 'dentale', 2), shows an engraving of such a plough 'still in common use amongst the agricultural populations on the bay of Taranto'. The most recent editor of the *Georgics*, H. H. Huxley, gives the ambiguous rendering 'double-ridged share-beam', and offers no comment (Vergil, *Georgics* I and IV, ed. by H. H. Huxley, London, 1963, p. 89). The groove required by the first theory would

[1] Vergil, *G*. 3. 87; Varro, *RR* 2. 7. 5; Colum. *RR* 6. 29. 2.

presumably be a groove made lengthwise along the top of the *dentale* for the purpose of securing the *vomer*, which would be fitted with a longitudinal spline to engage the groove. Unfortunately no specimen of such a *vomer* has been noticed, and existing representations of ploughs show a level, or almost level surface on the *dentale*. The second explanation seems the more natural of the two. It should be noted that the bifurcated form of the share-beam, which is still a common feature of Italian ploughs (see Fig. 97, p. 126), enables the ploughman to clear the furrow, and thus achieve better results than could be obtained by the simple symmetrical plough (the effect is that of trenching with the spade as compared with ordinary digging). The type is well represented by a bronze model from Sussex, now in the British Museum, London (see Plate 11 (*a*)). R. Aitken's theory, that Vergil's plough was a form of beam-ard, involves an entirely different interpretation of G. 1. 172, and cannot be usefully discussed here. For a full discussion see Appendix G (pp. 213 ff.).

3 **Buris,** Bura (Varro, *LL*), *the plough-beam*

The plough-beam, as distinct from the sole or share-beam, is the curved section which joins the share-beam to the yoke-beam or *temo*, through which the motive power is supplied. Some confusion has arisen in relation to this part of the plough, caused partly by inaccurate statements in the authorities, and partly by the historical evolution of the implement. Thus Varro in his account of the parts of the plough (*LL* 5. 134) speaks of the *bura* as a single curved beam running from the share-beam to the oxen. In other references (e.g. Vergil, G. 1. 170–1), the *temo* is quite distinct from the *buris*, though joined to it. The difficulty may be cleared up by considering three types of *aratrum*, all of which are identifiable from surviving types still in use:

(*a*)   (*b*)   (*c*)

Fig. 105. One-piece ploughs (Roman)

(1) A primitive type, in which share-beam, plough-beam and yoke-beam consist of a single piece of naturally branching wood. The type is illustrated by the accompanying drawings (Fig. 105), from Gow (*JHS*, xxxiv, 1914, pl. 17, nos. 15–17).

(2) A second type, in which the curved *buris* is socketed into the horizontal sole, and continues as a straight or curved pole to the yoke: this type is well known from monuments (e.g. the Cherchel mosaic—see Plate 12) and is still in use in the Cherchel area as well as in Cyprus: it is the type referred to by Varro (*loc. cit.*) (see Fig. 106).

(3) The common Roman type, described by Vergil (*loc. cit.*), in which the curved *buris* is socketed into the sole, or share-beam, and attached to the yoke-beam by a pegged joint (see Fig. 104 above); this type is still in

Fig. 106.
Sole-ard (Cypriote)

use in Tunisia, Pakistan and Iraq.[1] Isidore (b) appears to be describing type (2) in which *buris* and *dentale* are quite separate, and the *temo* is continuous with the *buris*.

4. Vomer (-eris, m.), Vomis (-eris, m.), Vomeris (-eris) (Cato), *the plough-share*[2]

(a) Cato, *RR* 135. 2. 'Roman ploughs will be good for strong soil, Campanian for black loam': aratra in terram validam Romanica bona erunt, in terram pullam Campanica.

(b) *Ibid.* 'You will find detachable *ploughshares* the best': vomeris indutilis optimus erit.

(c) Pliny 18. 171–2. 'There are several kinds of ploughshare. The "knife" is the name given to the curved blade used for cutting through very dense soil before it is broken, and for marking out the tracks for the subsequent furrows with incisions which the share, sloping backwards, is to bite out in the course of ploughing. The second type is the ordinary share consisting of a bar sharpened to a point like a beak. A third type for use in light soils does not extend along the whole length of the share-beam, but has only a small spike at the extremity. In the fourth kind this spike is broader and sharper, ending in a point, and using the same blade to break up the ground and with its sharp sides to cut off the roots of the weeds. Recently a contrivance has been invented in the Raetian area of Gaul, consisting of an addition to this type of plough of two small wheels; the local name for this type is *plaumoratum*. The share is spade-shaped': vomerum plura genera: culter vocatur inflexus[3] praedensam priusquam proscindatur terram secans futurisque sulcis vestigia praescribens incisuris quas resupinus in arando mordeat vomer. alterum genus est volgare rostrati[4] vectis. tertium in solo facili non toto porrectum dentali sed exigua cuspide in rostro. latior haec quarto generi et acutior in mucronem fastigata eodemque gladio scindens solum et acie laterum radices herbarum secans. non pridem inventum in Raetia Galliae ut duas adderent tali rotulas, quod genus vocant plaumorati;[5] cuspis effigiem palae habet.

(d) Ovid, *Fast.* 4. 927. 'The beaked *ploughshare*': vomer aduncus.

DISCUSSION

The agronomists have little or nothing to say on the design of shares. Cato's Campanian plough (passage (a)) had a wooden share; the soil was so loose and friable that there would be little wear on the sole. His second reference (b) shows that in his time fixed shares were still in use. Light

[1] J. Bérard, *MEFR*, LII (1935), 133, fig. 3 (type 2, Cherchel, Algeria); H. J. Hopfen, *FIATR*, L, fig. 30d (type 2, Cyprus).
[2] The term 'vomer' is often used, especially in poetry, to denote the whole plough.
[3] inflexus *Silligius* ed. vol. III, 1855; infelix *ll*; inferius *Brot. ex ed. pr. locus nondum sanatus. An* infixus prae dentali? *Mayhoff.*
[4] *Gelenius:* rostratum uti aut rostra uti.
[5] plauromatum sive ploum raeti (?) *Walde–Hofmann.* See further Appendix G.

tanged shares are still in use with body-ards (Hopfen, p. 52, fig. 32, nos. 4 and 5). Surviving examples of detachable shares from the Middle East are dated as early as 1000 B.C. Pliny's discussion of the more important varieties of share and their functions is of considerable interest, since none of the agronomists has provided any information on the subject. At 18. 171–2 (passage (c)) he describes four distinct types of share, adding what he calls a recent invention in the design of the plough itself—the addition of a wheeled forecarriage, known as the *plaumoratum*. Unfortunately, the text at the beginning of the passage is suspect; the descriptions of types two, three and four are orderly and intelligible, and each of them is introduced with the standard formula 'second, third and fourth type'—'alterum genus est ... tertium ... quarto generi'. But the first item, as the MSS have it, appears to describe, not a type of share, but a 'coulter', that is, a curved blade set in front of the share to cut the furrow-slice vertically before it is broken up and turned over by the share. But (a) *culter* with this specific meaning is not attested elsewhere (*Thesaurus* s.v. 'culter' cites only this passage), (b) ploughs fitted with coulters were naturally common enough in the northern provinces, where heavier soils made them necessary, but are not found in the Mediterranean area. Pliny is normally very particular in defining the regional distribution of implements or techniques if they are not found in Italy,[1] and this identification must be rejected. The reading adopted in the text involves only Silligius' *inflexus* for the MS reading *infelix*, which makes no sense. Mayhoff's *infixus* for *infelix* is much more difficult to account for than *inflexus*, and his substitution of *prae dentali* for *praedensam* seems to be based on the widely held notion that *culter* means a 'coulter'. On the reading proposed here Pliny's first type is not, strictly speaking, a share, but a simple form of 'ground-opener', of a type still used in a number of Alpine districts to ease the passage of the share in the subsequent ploughing of heavy soils that have been icebound during the winter.[2] My interpretation of this difficult passage is then as follows:

Fig. 107. Culter? (Austrian)

Type 1. A simple 'ground-opener', for use on very dense or tightly impacted soil, making the first surface cut, and easing the work of the first ploughing.

Type 2. The common kind (*volgare genus*), consisting of a wooden baulk (*vectis*), terminating in a beak, like that on the prow of a ship. Both Pliny's adjective ('rostratus') and that used by Ovid ('aduncus') emphasize the

Fig. 108 (a).
Socketed share

[1] See, for example, 18. 296 (the reaping machine or *vallus*), below, p. 158.
[2] P. Leser, *Die Entstehung und Verbreitung des Pfluges* (Münster in Westphal., 1931), p. 302, Abb. 150 (= Leser, *Entstehung*). See also A. G. Haudricourt and M. J.-B. Delamarre, *L'homme et la charrue à travers les âges* (Paris, 1955), pl. XIV, fig. 48 (= Haudricourt–Delamarre). For similar implements from Portugal seee J. Dias, *Os Arados Portugueses* (Coimbra, 1948), p. 30, fig. 6.

curvature of the beak, which is an essential feature. This shape is very common in surviving ploughshares.[1] For a very different interpretation of this passage, in which 'rostrati vectis' is assumed without argument to be a tanged iron share see below, p. 135, and for a full discussion of the difficulty involved, Appendix G.

Fig. 108(b). Tanged share

Fig. 108(c). Winged share

Type 3. This type, used in easily worked soils, is short, with a small spike (*exigua cuspis*) at the end; sheathing of the entire sole is not necessary, since there is very little friction on it as it passes through this kind of soil. This type is also common in contemporary ards, as the accompanying drawing indicates.

Type 4. In this type we have a double-edged blade, consisting of a vertical edge and two horizontal cutting edges along the sides, designed both to cleave the soil (*scindens solum*) with the vertical cutter, and to cut off the roots of the weeds 'with the sharp edge of its sides (*acie laterum*)'. Heavier soils demand wider and deeper furrows; these in turn demand an increase in the size and weight of the sole and the share, and this means a considerable increase in the resistance of the soil. With Pliny's fourth type the limit of development of this type of plough seems to have been reached. The next step is to assist the traction by mounting the forward end of the sole on a forecarriage. Pliny's fifth type is connected with its immediate predecessor.

Fig. 109. Wheeled plough (medieval)

Type 5. This is an important modification of type 4, introduced in Pliny's time in the Raetian district of Gaul (i.e. the region now known as the Grisons in East Switzerland). The sole is now mounted on a pair of wheels, which would help materially to overcome the resistance of the ground to the wider share. This is the earliest literary reference to the heavy plough which was soon to dominate farming in north-western Europe, and which had apparently already appeared in parts of this region before Pliny's time.[2]

[1] The adjective *aduncus* in the passage cited from Ovid (*d*) refers to an important feature of the share. If the share is absolutely horizontal it tends to slide along the furrow without making a proper 'bite' (cf. Pliny 18. 171 (passage (*c*)). In order to prevent this the ploughshare is turned slightly downwards at the tip. The curved or beaked tip wears down easily: hence the need for periodic resharpening or renewal of the share. Bearing this in mind we can easily understand Cato's preference for sleeved, detachable shares over the tanged variety (passage 3 (*a*) above).

[2] C. F. C. Hawkes, 'The Roman villa and the heavy plough', *Antiquity*, IX (1935), 239–41; F. G. Payne, 'The plough in Roman Britain', *Arch. Journ.* CIV (1947), 82–111; W. H. Manning, 'The plough in Roman Britain', *JRS*, LIV (1964), 54–65.

Pliny's ploughshares and the archaeological evidence

The chief difficulty in comparing the literary with the archaeological evidence is that (a) there are no surviving specimens of Roman ploughs, (b) representations of ploughs on monuments are often difficult to interpret, (c) surviving Roman shares are very rare for Italy (from Pompeii), though common enough on Romano-British sites (Payne, *op. cit.* fig. 1 contains 21 specimens of varying size and weight); many of these, however, belong to the beam-ard, and it is not easy to see how they can be made to fit the literary evidence, as Aitken (*JRS*, XLVI, 1956), and more recently Manning (*JRS*, LIV, 1964) have suggested. The crucial passage is Pliny's description of the 'common variety' of share (p. 132, passage (c)). The ordinary MS reading gives 'alterum genus est volgare rostratum uti (*aut* rostra uti) vectis', emended by Gelenius to 'rostrati vectis'.[1] Aitken (*op. cit.* p. 102) accepts the emendation without comment, and insists that Pliny is referring to a tanged share, although he admits that this type of share is not found in Italy south of Emilia! He further ignores the ambiguity of the term 'vectis', which can be used to denote either an iron bar or one made of timber. Yet this share is the 'common variety'. Thus the weight of the admittedly inconclusive evidence is that Pliny's second variety is a body-ard, with its share-beam of wood shaped to a beak, and fitted with a socketed share. This interpretation is strengthened by the next sentence in Pliny which describes the third variety of share: 'a third type for use in light soils *does not extend along the whole length of the share-beam* [italics mine], but has only a small spike at the extremity'. It is difficult to avoid the conclusion that Pliny's third type is basically the same as his second, but much smaller. My conclusion is that the literary and archaeological evidence at present available cannot be reconciled. Until we have a reasonable quantity of shares of the Roman period from Italian sites we must continue to study the question on the working assumption that Roman ploughs, whether fitted with tanged or socketed shares, were commonly body-ards, not

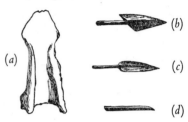

Fig. 110. (a) Vomer; (b) and (c) tanged share; (d) chisel share

---

[1] The common reading = 'beaked like a crowbar' requires explanation. Aitken (*JRS*, XLVI, 1956, 102) accepts the emendation to *rostrati vectis* without comment, and assumes that the reference here is to a tanged share. Manning (*JRS*, LIV, 1964, 60 and n. 48), who generally follows Aitken, here insists that the MS reading is intelligible, and that the reference is to a tanged share, although Aitken admits that tanged shares are not found in Italy south of Emilia. I cannot see why a tanged share should necessarily have the appearance of a beak; surely the method of fitting the share (tanged or socketed) is immaterial to the point; not all tanged shares nor all socketed shares are beak-shaped. In support of the interpretation given in the text it may be added that a crowbar normally has a 'beak' for prising open woodwork or for getting a purchase for lifting a heavy object.

beam-ards of the type suggested by Aitken.[1] For further discussion of the numerous problems raised by Aitken and Manning see Appendix G, pp. 213 ff., 'The Vergilian plough'.

The Roman evidence and the evolution of the plough

It is often asserted, without careful study of the evidence, that Roman agriculture tended to stagnate technically, and that few improvements either in the design of implements or in processes of cultivation are reported by the authorities. This is true only to a limited extent, and there are important exceptions to the general trend. Improvements in the design of manual implements have already been discussed (see above, s.v. 'falx vinitoria', pp. 93 ff.). Pliny's account of *vomeres* is important from the historical point of view: he shows some awareness of the evolution of the ploughshare, and his order of presentation of his material at 18. 171–2 suggests that he was aware of a connection between the technical advance represented by the double-bladed share (type 4) and the invention of the plough with a wheeled forecarriage (type 5). This was a development of great importance, since it enabled farmers in north-western Europe, who had already put into use a type of beam-ard suitable to their soils, to increase arable cultivation; farmers in Britain were able to exploit the heavy clay soils and so expand wheat production in the eastern part of the island. This expansion, it would appear, not only satisfied the heavy demands of the permanent garrison of the Roman province, but eventually made Britain to some extent an exporter of wheat to other areas.[2]

5. Temo (–onis, m.), *the yoke-beam*

Varro, *LL* 5. 134 (see p. 123). 'The *yoke-beam* is so called from "holding" ("*tenendo*") for it holds the yoke': *temo dictus a tenendo; is enim continet iugum.*

Not in Isidore.

The yoke-beam consisted either of a single length of timber, curved at one end and mortised into the sole, or of a shorter length attached to the plough-beam (*buris*) by means of pegs or lashings.[3] Both types are still used. The flexible joint between *temo* and *buris*, which gives greater freedom to the oxen in taking up unevennesses in the work, did not appear before the early Middle Ages. The plough-beam or *buris* was the most vulnerable part

[1] On the paucity of surviving ploughshares and on the confusion caused by doubtful identification see Haudricourt–Delamarre, pp. 97 ff, and esp. pp. 105–6.

[2] E. S. Applebaum, 'Agriculture in Roman Britain', *Agric. Hist. Rev.* VI (1958), part II, 66 ff.

[3] Hopfen, *FIATR*, p. 50, fig. 30 (*e*), from Kurdistan, North Iraq, illustrates the pegged type of fastening between *temo* and *buris*.

of the implement, and was liable to snap off if heavy clods or other obstacles were encountered (see Varro, *RR* 1. 192 (passage (*l*), p. 124)).

Vergil's *temo* was 8 ft long (G. 1. 171). Its great length is well illustrated in the agricultural mosaic from Oudna, now in the Bardo Museum, Tunis. The upper register shows a *temo*, complete with its yoke, propped up against the outer wall of a tall double-storey building (Gauckler, *Inventaire des mosaïques de la Gaule et d'Afrique*, t. II, no. 362; Prêcheur-Canonge, pl. 1).

6. **Stiva** (-ae, f.), *the stilt*

7. **Manicula** (-ae, f.), *the hand-grip*

Manicula is used only by Varro (*LL* 5. 134) to denote the cross-bar of the handle as distinct from the shaft.

(*a*) Varro, *LL* 5. 134 (see above, p. 123). Not in Isidore.

(*b*) Colum. 1. 9. 3 (on the physical type required for a ploughman). 'For, as I have already said, we shall make all the taller ones ploughmen, both for the reasons previously advanced, and also because in the work of the farm there is no task less tiring to a tall man; for in ploughing he stands almost erect, and rests his weight on the *stilt*': nam longissimum quemque aratorem, sicut dixi, faciemus, et propter id, quod paulo ante rettuli, et quod in re rustica nullo minus opere fatigatur prolixior, quia is arando *stivae* paene rectus innititur.

(*c*) Ovid, *Met.* 8. 218. 'The ploughman leaning on his *stilt*': *stivaeque* innixus arator.

(*d*) Ovid, *Fast.* 4. 825. 'Pressing down the *stilt* he marks out the walls with a furrow': premens *stivam* designat moenia sulco.

(*e*) Pliny 18. 179. 'Unless the ploughman bends his back to the work he goes crooked': arator nisi incurvus praevaricatur.

DISCUSSION

1. *Position of the stiva*

There is a discrepancy between the statement of Columella and that of Pliny. Columella recommends that tall men should be selected as ploughmen, on the ground that a tall ploughman will be able to stand more or less erect as he presses on the stilt, while Pliny uses a proverbial expression for good ploughing which implies that the ploughman must bend his back to the work, otherwise he will not plough a straight furrow. The explanation of the discrepancy seems to lie in the varying design, height and 'set' of the stilt. Among ploughs still in use in Italy we find specimens with long stilts set almost vertically to the sole (e.g. Leser, p. 308, Abb. 158 (a

plough from Apulia in south-east Italy with a stilt as long as the sole and set almost vertically), compared with Abb. 156, p. 307, where the stilt is almost horizontal). It may be noted that contemporary Algerian ploughs have almost horizontal stilts, whereas in neighbouring Tunisia they are high and almost vertical. There is no such thing as a 'standard' Italian plough either in ancient or in modern times.

2. *Design of the stiva*

In the body-ard the stilt is in one piece with the sole, either at right-angles to it or at an obtuse angle, and is fitted with a cross-bar inserted through a hole in the handle.[1] In the sole-ard, the type to which the ordinary Roman *aratrum* belongs (see above, p. 128), the *stiva* is socketed at right-angles into the horizontal sole. An interesting variation in the position of the *stiva* appears in two ploughing scenes on a mosaic of the second century A.D. from Cherchel, Algeria.[2] In these examples *temo* and *buris* are in one piece (type 2, p. 131), which is socketed into the back of the *dentale*. Two strong supports are socketed into the front of the *dentale*, passing through the yoke-beam. The front support is the *stiva*, since it is provided with a cross-bar for the ploughman. But is is difficult to see how pressure at this point could be effective in maintaining an even keel, and the arrangement may be no more than an artist's fancy.

3. *The stiva in action*

In certain respects this part of the plough resembles the joystick of an aircraft. While its basic function, like that of a rudder, is to enable the ploughman to drive a straight furrow, and not 'prevaricate' (Pliny, *loc. cit.*), it also has the important task of keeping the implement on an even keel, i.e. maintaining the desired depth of cut. Ploughshares are curved slightly downwards at the point (Ovid's *vomer aduncus*, p. 131). Wheelless ploughs thus have a natural tendency to dig themselves into the ground as they move forward, and this must be counteracted by strong pressure down-

[1] Hopfen, *FIATR*, xlviii, fig. 29 (six examples from different regions).
[2] J. Bérard, 'Mosaïque inédit de Cherchel', *MEFR*, lii (1935), pl. ii, p. 120. Commenting on the Cherchel mosaic, Bérard (*art. cit.* pp. 134 ff.) states that Vergil always represents his ploughmen as bending over their ploughs, and that farmers in the Campagna and in the Abruzzi region of central Italy still use ploughs of a pattern closely resembling the Cherchel type. On the other hand, Haudricourt–Delamarre (p. 103) cast doubt on the effectiveness of such a positioning of the stilt. In reply to Bérard's claim that this type of plough is still found in central Italy, they point out that there is no mention of it in the exhaustive treatment of the subject by P. Scheuermeier (*Bauernwerk in Italien der italienischen und rätoromanschen Schweiz*, Ehrlenbach–Zürich, 1943), adding 'on peut se demander s'il ne s'agit pas d'une déformation expressive de l'artiste qui a voulu montrer le laboureur courbé, s'appuyant à la fois avec le pied sur le dental et avec la main sur le mancheron'.

wards on the stilt.[1] In addition to these control mechanisms, the sole may be turned to either side by means of the stilt, so as to effect partial inversion of the sod, and avoid leaving unploughed balks between the furrows. At 2. 2. 25 Columella explains that in every alternate furrow the ploughman must hold the plough at an angle (*obliquum tenere aratrum*): 'with a straight share laid sloping, the slice of earth (cut by the previous furrow) will turn, because the breadth of the share lifted up on the land side will raise the earth to the opposite side, and this, meeting with the flat of the sole or share-beam, would be turned over by it'.[2] This method of preparing the seed-bed produces an even tilth, with furrows laid close together and no unbroken balks (*scamna*) (Columella 2. 2. 26); it also kills the roots of the weeds (Pliny 18. 176).

These then are the five essential parts of the *aratrum*; the *manicula* (no. 7) is not an essential feature, and is often omitted. Some attachments and improvements remain to be considered.

8. (i) Aures (-ium, f.) (Vergil), 'ears' (cf. aratra aurita, Pallad. *RR* 1. 43. 1)

(ii) Tabellae (-arum, f.) (Varro), Tabula (-ae, f.) (Pliny), *ridging-board(s)*

(*a*) Verg. *G.* 1. 172 (parts of the plough). 'A pair of "*ears*"': binae *aures*.

(*b*) Pallad. *RR* 1. 43. 1 (inventory of implements). 'Ploughs; either simple, or, if the open nature of the terrain permits, *eared*, so that with the latter it may be possible to raise up the plants on a deeper furrow to counteract the high water-table in winter': aratra simplicia vel, si plana regio permittit, *aurita*, quibus possint contra stationes humoris hiberni sata celsiore sulco attolli.

(*c*) Varro, *RR* 1. 29. 2 (on covering the seed after sowing). 'When they plough the third time, after the seed has been broadcast, the oxen are said to "ridge" ("lirare"), that is, with *boards* attached to the ploughshare they both cover the broadcast seed in ridges and at the same time cut ditches to allow the rain-water to drain off': tertio cum arant iacto semine, boves lirare dicuntur, id est cum *tabellis* additis ad vomerem simul et satum frumentum operiunt in porcis et sulcant fossas, quo pluvia aqua delabatur.

(*d*) Pliny 18. 180 (on harrowing). 'This clod-breaking operation is also repeated after the seed has been sown . . . by means of a *board* attached to the plough': sato semine iteratur haec quoque (scil. occatio) . . . *tabula* aratro adnexa.

Design and function of tabellae and aures

Unlike the mouldboard plough the symmetrical ard cannot form ridges (Varro's 'porcae' in passage (*c*), rising up between the furrows like a hog's back). Where these are required for the purpose of covering the seed or

---

[1] See Colum. *RR* 1. 9. 3; Ovid, *Metam.* 8. 218; *Fast.* 4. 825.

[2] F. Harrison, 'The crooked plough', *Class. Journ.* 11 (1916), pp. 323–32. Keeled ploughs, which would facilitate this process, are well attested (e.g. the well-known bronze model from Sussex (Plate 11 (*a*)).

for drainage (Varro (*c*), Palladius (*b*)) detachable wings were used to throw up the soil on either side of the share and make a 'ridge-and-furrow'. Varro's term 'tabellae' is not used elsewhere in this sense; evidently they were straight-sided boards. Pliny's 'tabula aratro adnexa' (*d*) indicates the same type of attachment; a single board, however, would cover the seed, but without clearing the furrow, whereas a pair of boards would, as Varro says, both cover the seed and make a ditch. Modern ridging-ploughs employ wings of steel for the same purpose: Hopfen (*FIATR*, p. 60, fig. 39*e*) shows a ridging device used on an improved version of a traditional Libyan ard. The identity of Vergil's 'aures' is less certain. They may be identical with the 'pin-ears' found today on ploughs used in several parts of Spain, in Tunisia and in Macedonia.[1] But they are not to be confused with mouldboards. The true mouldboard plough with its complicated double curvature designed to effect complete inversion, as well as lateral displacement of the sod, did not appear in Europe before the latter part of the eighteenth century.[2] From the scanty evidence available it would seem that ridging-boards did not appear until after Cato's period. Columella does not specifically mention them, but uses the stock term 'lirare' for a process which had presumably become standard practice (see *RR* 11. 3. 20 on the method of growing garlic). Palladius (*b*) is presumably referring to a type of ridging-plough with fixed 'ears'. Apart from the use of ridging for plants such as garlic or asparagus, ridging and furrowing were essential for the successful raising of autumn-sown cereals, since heavy winter rains could leave the land waterlogged; hence Vergil's injunction to the farmer to pray for clear skies in winter ('hiemes orate serenas') at *G*. 1. 100.

9. **Rallum** (-i, n.), *a scraping tool, ploughstaff*

From the root of *radere*, to scrape. '*radlom* gegenüber *caelum* aus *kaid-slom*' (Walde–Hofmann, s.v. 'rallum'). Not in the lexica or in the lists of equipment.

Pliny 18. 179 (rules for ploughing). 'The share should be cleaned now and then with a goad tipped with a *scraper*': purget vomerem subinde stimulus cuspidatus *rallo*.

Discussion

The above passage is the sole literary reference to this implement, which is familiar from representations on monuments. It consisted of a narrow

[1] For a good discussion of the subject see Aitken, 'Virgil's plough', *JRS*, XLVI (1956), 101 f. On the danger of drawing conclusions from the survival of Latin terms for the plough and its parts see Haudricourt–Delamarre, ch. 3, pp. 45 ff.
[2] Aitken, *art. cit.* p. 101, notes that Schneider's clear distinction between *aures* and mouldboards (edn. of Palladius, 1795) 'appears to have passed unnoticed by Virgilian scholars'. Full account of the whole question of the development of the mouldboard plough in Haudricourt–Delamarre, pp. 329 ff.

iron blade, fitted with a tang for insertion into the end of the ox-goad. It was used for the essential task of keeping the ploughshare free of accumulations of earth which would otherwise check its smooth passage through the ground.

Monuments

Rich (*Dict. Ant.*) does not notice the implement. Daremberg–Saglio (t. IV, 2, s.v. 'rallum') notices three representations: (*a*) the well-known plough-model from Arezzo in Etruria, now in the Museo di Villa Giulia in Rome (fig. 5916); (*b*) another from the necropolis at Vulci in Etruria, now in the Museo Nazionale at Naples (fig. 5917); (*c*) a third (unillustrated) from Acerra in Campania (*Mon. Acad. d. Lincei*, IX, pl. IV, 5).

10. **Rotulae** (-arum, f.), *small wheels*

Used only by Pliny with reference to the wheeled plough of central and northern Europe (see Fig. 109, p. 134).

Pliny 18. 172 (on varieties of ploughshare). 'In the fourth kind this spike is broader and sharper, ending in a point, and using the same blade to break up the ground and with its sharp sides to cut off the roots of the weeds. Recently a contrivance has been invented in the Raetian area of Gaul, consisting of the addition to this type of plough of *two small wheels*; the local name for this type is *plaumoratum*. The share is spade-shaped': latior haec quarto generi et acutior in mucronem fastigata eodemque gladio scindens solum et acie laterum radices herbarum secans. non pridem inventum in Raetia Galliae ut duas adderent tali *rotulas* quod genus vocant *plaumorati*; cuspis effigiem palae habet.

DISCUSSION

The word 'plaumoratum' is found only here. For a detailed discussion of the numerous emendations proposed see Appendix G, p. 213. Many editors have sought to identify one or both of the German words 'Pflug' (plough) and 'Rad' (wheel) in *plaumoratum*. Discussion of this vexed question must begin with Pliny's reference to *rotulae*, and Servius' commentary on the word 'currus' used by Vergil of the plough at G. 1. 174: '. . . and a stilt to turn the base of the *car* from the rear', '. . . stivaque, quae *currus* a tergo torqueat imos'. Serv. *ad loc.*: 'But he calls it the "car" on account of the custom of his own province, in which the ploughs have wheels to assist them', 'currus autem dixit propter morem provinciae suae, in qua aratra habent rotas, quibus iuvantur'. Servius' interpretation of the use of the word *currus* is clearly wrong; the comparison of a plough moving through the furrow with a car is as natural as Catullus' use of the same word to describe the ship *Argo* (Catullus 64. 9), as Huxley points out (Vergil,

Georgics I and IV, ed. by H. H. Huxley, London, 1963, p. 89). But it is clear from Servius that ordinary Roman ploughs of the fourth century A.D., when he wrote this commentary, had no wheels; it is possible that the wheeled plough had come into use in North Italy by the time of Servius. Pliny is not the most careful of writers, but he is usually meticulous in defining the area in which a particular implement or process is to be found, and in such passages it is to be inferred that he is distinguishing between foreign implements and practices and those prevalent in Italy (see p. 133, n. 1). At 18. 172 he is clearly referring to a recent development ('non pridem inventum') in the Raetian area of Gaul, in the shape of a pair of small wheels added to the plough ('ut duas adderent tali rotulas'). Now the addition of a wheeled forecarriage would be a natural development in heavy clay soils, where the simple plough's tendency to dig itself in could not easily be arrested, as in the lighter soils of the south, by the pressure of the ploughman's foot and hand (see the discussion s.v. 'stiva', pp. 137 ff.). Pliny and Servius are thus not in conflict. Leser (*Entstehung*, p. 236) objects that *plaumorati* should refer to a type of ploughshare, not a type of plough; this is surely to demand a more logical treatment than we have a right to expect of Pliny. In any case, if the wheels were not a forecarriage, what were they? The Raetians may have got their wheeled plough from further north, and *plaumoratum* may be a word of Gallic origin, as several editors have suggested. But Pliny's reference must stand as an important piece of evidence on the spread of the wheeled plough; yet it does not conflict, as has often been argued, with the persistence of the simple sole-ard as the ordinary type of plough in use in Italy throughout Roman history.

Monuments

(a) *Extant representations (including models, reliefs, mosaics)*. The famous Arezzo bronze model (Fig. 103, p. 128), now in the Museo di Villa Giulia, Rome, is only one of a number of surviving votive ploughs of different types (Leser, p. 219, Abb. 96, Blümner, *Denkmäler*, I, 13, fig. 15). The model clearly belongs to the 'one-piece' class; the ridges probably represent a method of binding the share to the sole.

The powerful wooden model of a body-ard from Telamon, Etruria (Plate 10 (a)), now in the Museo Archeologico, Florence (inv. no. 70940), is dated to the fourth or third century B.C. (*Not. degli Scavi*, 1877, p. 245). The Telamon model has a single hand-grip, and the straight yoke-beam is at right-angles to the stilt and parallel to the line of the boot-shaped sole. The traction-angle is so acute as to make the implement unworkable if constructed to scale.

Two well-known models in bronze from Roman Germany. The first of these (Plate 10 (*b*)), a small bronze from Cologne, now in the Römisch-Germanisches Zentralmuseum, Mainz, is a typical beam-ard with the heavy tanged share familiar from many sites in north-west Europe. The other is of similar pattern, from a grave at Rodenkirchen, near Cologne, now in the Landesmuseum at Bonn (inv. no. 3492). It is dated to the late fourth century A.D. (see W. Haberey in *Bonner Jahrbücher*, CLIX, 1949, 28, Abb. 2; cf. *ibid.* p. 100, Abb. 4 (another similar model of unknown provenance)). Rather similar to these, but more schematic and therefore less easily classified, is the well-known bronze model from Sussex, now in the British Museum, London (inv. 54. 12. 27. 76; see Plate 11 (*a*)).

Another Romano-British model, with a pair of oxen and a ploughman, found at Piercebridge, Northumberland, looks more like the 'one-piece plough' represented by the Arezzo model (see Plate 11 (*b*)): reproduced in Rostovtzeff, *SEHRE*², pl. XI, 2.

Sculptured ploughs are rare: Espérandieu, *Gaule*, mentions only three specimens, V, 4092, 4243, XIV, 8386 (all from the area round Luxemburg). There is a good example of a sole-ard with a reinforcing member linking the plough-beam (*buris*) to the stilt (*stiva*) on a sculptured tomb-relief found near Maktar in central Tunisia, now in the Bardo Museum, Tunis (Merlin–Poinssot, *Guide du Musée Alaoui*, I, 4th edition, pl. XLVII; G. Picard, *Le Monde de Carthage*, Paris, 1956, pl. 76). I have seen ploughs closely resembling this design at work in the same neighbourhood. They are very common on coins, the ploughing colonist being a stock reverse design on coins issued by veteran colonies (examples in Gow, *art. cit.* pl. XVII, 14–17, p. 131; reproduced in detail, Figs. 105(*a*)–(*c*), p. 131). Fig. 105(*c*) resembles fairly closely the Arezzo model (Fig. 103, p. 128), except that it has a single hand-grip instead of a cross-bar; 105(*a*) and (*b*) seem to have a 'boot-tree' sole like that of the Telamon model (Plate 10 (*a*)). Their yoke-beams are set at normal angles to the sole. Unfortunately this class of evidence is difficult to assess, since the operative parts are always squeezed in between the hindquarters of the oxen and the circumference of the coin, so that the shapes and precise organization of the parts are not easy to discern; Gow (*art. cit.*) seems to have been over-confident in his use of this class of evidence for the historical evolution of Roman ploughs.

Mosaics provide more valuable evidence: the Cherchel mosaic (Bérard, *MEFR*, LII, 1935, pl. II, p. 120; Prêcheur-Canonge, pl. II, 3) contains on the first two registers (Plate 12) two fine representations of the *aratrum simplex* (Fig. 102, p. 128). In both examples the *stiva* is socketed into the centre of the sole, so that the ploughman leans forward in an almost horizontal position (see further pp. 138 ff., on the design of the *stiva*). The design

is very clear in these examples; more commonly the sole is obscured by the furrow, and other parts by the animals, making classification difficult.

The Oudna mosaic (Prêcheur-Canonge, *Inv.* 1. 2; Gauckler, II, 362) depicts a plough propped up against the wall of a shed; the *bura* and *temo* are all in one piece, and the implement is probably an ordinary sole-ard. The Oudna mosaic contains a second plough. In this case the ploughman has just unyoked the oxen; and the back of the sole and the whole of the *stiva* are obscured by the ploughman as he bends forward. The Seasons mosaic from St-Romain-en-Gal (Rhône Valley, S.E. France), now in the Louvre, Paris, contains a ploughing scene (see G. Lafaye in *Rev. Arch.* 3ᵉ sér. t. XIX, 1892, 323–47, no. 25 (Autumn)).

(*b*) *Extant specimens.* None of the whole implement. Iron ploughshares have survived in large numbers, but not all the known types are well represented. Tanged shares, both large and small, are common enough in the collections: they are more usually, though not exclusively, associated with ploughs of the beam-ard type. Among surviving socketed shares by far the most numerous group is the primitive type in which the iron does not fully cover the share-beam, but covers the base only, and is then 'lapped round' to form a socket. The few iron shares so far found on Roman sites in Italy are of this type (e.g. Petrie, *TW*, pl. 67, no. 34, from Pompeii—Naples, Museo Nazionale, inv. no. 110506—see Fig. 110(*a*), p. 135). They are poorly represented in the handbooks (three in Petrie, none in Reinach, very few in the Saalburg Catalogue). Examples from Roman Britain, in which tanged and socketed varieties appear, are well illustrated in Payne (*art. cit.* p. 134, n. 2), fig. 1; a few in Drachmann, *R-E* XIX. 2, 1461, s.v. 'Pflug'. Leser is disappointing: Abb. 30, p. 433, illustrates only the spear-shaped, tanged share which features later in many medieval representations.

Survival

(*a*) *Of the implement.* (i) The simple *aratra*. For the distribution of the various types see the excellent distribution map provided by R. Aitken, 'Virgil's Plough', *JRS*, XLVI (1956), fig. 14, p. 104, where the specific varieties of the beam-ard (*B*) and the sole-ard (*S*) are clearly indicated. There is a convenient selection of common varieties in H. J. Hopfen, *Farm Implements for Arid and Tropical Regions*. See also Haudricourt–Delamarre, *L'Homme et la Charrue*, pp. 224–31, and illustrations, pp. 232–3, 248–9, 264–5. Leser, *Entstehung*, p. 307, Abb. 157, presents an interesting example of the 'ground-wrest' type from Viterbo, Campania, central Italy (for a similar type see Jaberg–Jud, Karte 1455, no. 1). For the simple wooden

plough still widely used in Tunisia see Prêcheur-Canonge, *Inventaire*, p. 44; Bérard, *MEFR*, LII (1935), 133–4.

(ii) Wheeled type. Leser, *Entstehung*, illustrates several interesting examples of the primitive plough with very small wheels (Pliny's 'rotulae') surviving in the Balkans, e.g. p. 272, Abb. 119, p. 277, Abb. 124, 125 (all from Bosnia); id. 280, Taf. 14 (from Rumania).

(*b*) *Of the name*. Fr. 'araire' (f.), the simple wheelless plough, as opposed to 'charrue' (f.), the wheeled plough; for survivals see Haudricourt–Delamarre, *op. cit.* fig. 1 (from Portugal); fig. 31 (from Auvergne, central France). See also D. Faucher, *La vie rurale* (Paris, 1962), pp. 91 ff. It. 'aratro' (m.), the plough. Sp. 'arado' (m.), the plough, etc.

In addition, the names of most parts of the Roman plough survive in the Romance languages, principally in Italian, Spanish and Portuguese. Aitken (*JRS*, XLVI, 1956, 99–100, pl. X, 1–5) cites 'aurillos', 'orejeras' (*aures*), 'dental' (*dentale*), 'estibo' (*stiva*), and 'timourit' (*temo*) from different regions of Spain.

8

HARROWS

1. CRATIS   2. IRPEX

1. Cratis (-is, f.) (in this sense usually pl. Crates, -ium), *harrow*

R-E IV. 2, cols. 1682–5 [Olck].

(*a*) Not in Varro, *LL*.

Fig. 111. Bush-harrow (Austrian)

(*b*) Isid. 19. 10. 17 (on building materials). 'They (*crates*) are in fact frameworks of woven reeds, so called from the Greek verb κρατεῖν, to be strong, that is to say because they hold each other together': sunt enim (crates) conexiones cannarum, dicti ἀπὸ τοῦ κρατεῖν, id est quod se invicem teneant.

(*c*) Varro, *RR* 1. 23. 5 (on planting for profit). '... to provide you with osiers, for making items of basketry, such as wagon-bodies, winnowing-baskets and *bush-harrows*': ... ut habeas vimina, unde viendo quid facias, ut sirpeas, vallus, *crates*.

(*d*) Varro, *RR* 2. 2. 9 (on sheep-rearing). '(The shepherds) bring with them *hurdles* or nets, with which to make sheep-folds in the wilderness': ... portant secum *crates aut retia, quibus cohortes in solitudine faciant. (* for MS *grates*)

(*e*) Colum. 2. 17. 4 (on laying down a meadow). '(after sowing a mixture of hay and vetch) we shall then break down the clods with hoes, and bring on a drag to level off the surface, and we must dissipate the heaps of earth, which are usually made by the drag where it turns round ...': ... tum glaebas sarculis resolvemus et inducta *crate* coaequabimus grumosque, quos ad versuram plerumque tractae faciunt *crates*, disiciamus ...

(*f*) Pliny 18. 186 (on treatment of the corn while growing). 'There are some kinds of soil which are so luxuriant that it becomes necessary to comb the crop while in leaf—the comb is another kind of *harrow* fitted with pointed iron teeth': sunt genera terrae quorum ubertas pectinari segetem in herba cogat—*cratis* et hoc genus dentatae stilis ferreis.

(*g*) Verg. *G*. 1. 94–5 (on preparing soil for wheat). 'He also much improves the fields who breaks the sluggish clods with drag-hoes, and draws *bush-harrows* over them':

> multum adeo, rastris glaebas qui frangit inertis
> vimineasque trahit *cratis*, iuvat arva ...

(*h*) Serv. *ad loc*. 'The *harrow*, which the country folk call the "wolf", obviously used for levelling the fields': ad agrorum scilicet exaequationem *crates*, quam rustici irpicem vocant.

146

DISCUSSION

1. *Design*

The term *crates* was used to denote a variety of articles made of wood, wickerwork or straw, and ranging from hurdles to shields. There is considerable disagreement among modern authorities about the design of this implement: Daremberg–Saglio (t. I, ii, 1556, s.v. 'crates') include this *crates* as one of the eight different meanings of the term, and describe it as a hurdle drawn by oxen for harrowing, which has two functions: (1) to break up the clods after ploughing (i.e. 'occatio'—cf. Pliny 18. 180: 'occatio sequitur ... crate vel rastro', and Part 1, p. 46); (2) to remove surface weeds and roots. In support of this interpretation only Pliny (passage (*f*) above) is cited, and 'densatae' is read for the MS reading 'dentatae' without comment. The word 'densatus' can only mean 'of thicker texture'. Such a hurdle could be used for removing smallish clods, and for reducing the surface to an even tilth; but it would not be capable of breaking heavy clods, still less of eradicating weeds. Careful study of the above passages makes it clear that there were three types of *crates* used for agricultural purposes: (1) the ordinary hurdle, used principally (i) for carting manure (*crates stercorariae*), (ii) for folding sheep (passage (*d*)); (2) the ordinary 'drag', used for levelling (passages (*e*) and (*g*)); (3) the heavy animal-drawn implement mentioned only by Pliny (passage (*f*)). It seems obvious that Daremberg–Saglio are confusing the heavy animal-drawn implement with the 'drag' referred to by Columella (*d*) when describing the best method of establishing a new meadow or restoring an old, run-down one. This is of course the ordinary light drag, which is still used for this purpose in warm climates (in temperate regions the roller is commonly used). The heaps (*grumi*) are formed of small clods which adhere to the under-side of the drag, detaching themselves at the end of the field where the drag is turned round for the next run. Other commentators (e.g. Rich, *Dict. Ant.* s.v. 'crates') give no help towards a solution. Columella (*e*) and Vergil (*g*) are both referring in almost identical terms to a dual operation, the breaking up of the clods left by ploughing, done by means of the *sarculum* (Columella) or the *rastrum* (Vergil), and the reduction of the surface to a fine tilth, done by drawing a brushwood drag over it. Servius' explanatory note (*h*) is intended to inform the reader that it is the light drag that Vergil has in mind. In spite of these clear textual indications, there is confusion among editors. Thus Collart, in his recent edition of Varro, *LL* v, commenting on 'irpex' (q.v.), observes: 'The true harrow mounted on a chassis is called "cratis" (especially in the plural "crates", -ium); the *irpex* appears to have been nothing more than a large frame for harrowing' (i.e.

a bush-harrow) 'drawn by a man or more often by oxen' (*Notes explicatives*, p. 232). In support of this distinction he cites Billiard (*L'Agriculture*, p. 69), without apparently realizing that the latter's explanation of the term 'irpex' (a 'large rake'), is quite different, and indeed erroneous.

2. Functions

We are concerned then with two implements of similar design: (1) the light brushwood drag; (2) the heavy implement mentioned by Pliny (passage (*e*)). On the basis of this passage we must conclude that the *crates dentatae* was a heavy implement fitted with teeth, designed to effect, by means of a single implement, the laborious dual task of breaking up the clods after ploughing and of levelling off the seed-bed. It consisted of a strong wooden frame, capable of being fitted on the under-side with rows of iron teeth. Here again, commentators could have avoided confusion by examining surviving specimens of this type of implement; both are still much used by farmers in southern Europe and the Middle East (see below, under 'Survival', p. 156).

2. Irpex (–icis, m.), *harrow*

(*a*) Varro, *LL* 5. 136. '*Irpices*', *harrows*, consist of a straight piece of wood with numerous teeth, which are drawn by oxen exactly like a wagon, so that they pull up the things that "creep" (*serpunt*) in the ground; they used to be called *sirpices* and later, by some people, *irpices* with the S worn off': *irpices* regula compluribus dentibus, quam item ut plaustrum boves trahunt, ut eruant quae in terra serpunt, sirpices,[1] postea irpices S detrito, a quibusdam dicti.

Fig. 112. Irpex (Italian)

(*b*) Fest. s.v. 'irpices', p. 105. '*Irpices* are a type of iron *rastri*, so called because they have numerous teeth for rooting up weeds in the fields. The word, however, comes from the Greek ἁρπάζω, ἁρπαγή, because it ἁρπάζει, snatches up the weeds. Euripides': irpices genus rastrorum ferreorum, quod plures habent dentes ad extirpandas herbas in agris. est autem a Graeca ἁρπάζω, ἁρπαγή, quia herbas ἁρπάζει rapit. Euripides.

(*c*) Serv. *ad* Verg. G. 1. 94–5. '*crates*, which the country folk call *irpices*': crates, quam rustici *irpicem* vocant.

(*d*) *Corp. Gloss.* s.v. 'erpica'. Erpica egdae (*AS*) v 359. 47; cf. erpicarius egderi (*AS*) v 359. 48 (on the variant forms Bruno, *Apporti*, p. 139, no. 145 *b*).

(*e*) *Gloss. Plac.* v 26. 3. *Hirpices*, tribula.

(*f*) Cato 10. 3 (inventory for an oliveyard). '1 *harrow*': irpicem 1.

[1] Cato calls them 'urpices' or 'hurpices'.

DISCUSSION

1. *Problems of identification*

The confusion that exists concerning these two implements is surprising, since both types are still in use (see below under 'Survival', p. 151). It demonstrates once again the importance of close study of existing implements and techniques for the light which they may throw on those of ancient times.

The fact that the heavier *crates* is not mentioned by any writer before Pliny requires explanation. The régime laid down briefly by Varro (*RR* 1. 29), and in greater detail by Columella (2. 3. 22–5; 4. 1. 5) for repeated ploughing of the fallow, if successfully followed, makes harrowing unnecessary; the furrows should be so numerous and so close together 'that it can scarcely be determined in what direction the ploughshare has been driven' (Columella 2. 4. 1). As for harrowing after the sowing, this was a proverbial example of bad husbandry (*ibid*. 2. 4. 2). There is another passage of Pliny (*g*) which has an important bearing on the matter. Here, after describing the first ploughing (*proscissio*) and the cross-ploughing (*iteratio*) Pliny continues with the text cited above: 'After the cross-ploughing has been done there follows the harrowing (*occatio*) of the clods with a woven framework (*crate*) or a drag-hoe (*rastro*). Where circumstances require it, and where local custom allows, this second ploughing is also repeated after the seed has been sown, by means of a toothed harrow (*crate dentata*) . . .'

Now it is clear from other references in the agronomists that the recommended régime for cereals was to plough the fallow repeatedly (as many as nine times in Tuscany: see Pliny 18. 182). The inference to be drawn from 18. 180 is surely that the use of the heavy animal-drawn harrow enabled the farmer, where local custom allowed, to cut down on the exhausting labour of repeatedly ploughing the fallow. The motive cannot be determined with certainty; but references to shortages of labour are to be found in both Columella and Pliny (e.g. Columella 4. 6. 3; Pliny 18. 181, 261, 300), and it is perhaps significant that one of Pliny's references to a labour-saving device ('compendium operae') follows close on the passage discussed above (18. 180, 181): 'With beans and vetch it is a labour-saving plan involving no loss to dispense with preliminary breaking before sowing', 'at fabam et viciam non proscisso serere sine damno compendium operae est.'

2. *Etymology*

Varro (*a*) is wrong: *irpex* is a dialect form (see Serv. *Georg*. 1. 94–5) related to *(h)irpus*, the Samnite word for wolf (see Ernout–Meillet, 3rd ed. p. 527,

s.v. 'hirpus', and references cited there). The resemblance to the sharp, triangular teeth of the wolf is clear enough; *irpex* is then a 'country' word for *crates*, and may refer to a more primitive type of the implement (see below, under 'Design'), but there is no conclusive evidence on the point. Servius is wrong in equating *vimineae crates* with *irpex*. The bush-harrow does not in the least resemble the teeth of a wolf.

3. *Design*

Billiard (*L'Agriculture*, p. 69) regards the *irpex* as an implement of the same class as the *crates*, but inferior, and used by poor farmers: 'the *marra* and the *irpex* are types of large, heavy rake (*râteau*), fitted with many teeth, and dragged over the ground by an ox, a donkey or by the farmer himself'. There seems to be a confusion here between *rastrum*, *marra* and *irpex*. Billiard offers no evidence in support of this curious assertion, except Vergil, *G*. I. 104–5, a passage which merely describes the process of breaking up the clods on poor soil after sowing, without mentioning the implement used. The identification of *irpex* with *marra* is clearly wrong (see commentary, s.v. 'marra', Part I, pp. 41–2). In the absence of specific evidence it is better to assume that *irpex* is a lighter, and *crates* a heavier version of the same implement.

If Varro's account is to be trusted, we may detect a distinction between the *irpex*, a single beam (Varro's 'regula', passage (*a*)), fitted with one row of teeth, and a likely precursor of the toothed roller of later times, and the *crates dentatae* mentioned by Pliny, which will have consisted of a triangular or rectangular frame fitted with several rows of teeth. Both types are still used (see below, under 'Survival').

4. *Monuments*

(*a*) *Extant representations.* Unfortunately, no identifiable representation of either of these implements has been reported from monumental sources before the medieval period, when they become frequent, especially in illuminated manuscripts. There is an excellent representation of a four-sided *crates*, the rear portion of the frame being wider than the front, in the well-known illuminated MS *Les très riches heures du Duc de Berry*, now in the Musée Condé at Chantilly, Loire, France. The month is October, and the scene represents sowing and harrowing (edition of H. Malo, Paris, 1945). L. Liger, *La nouvelle maison rustique* (8th ed.), vol. I, pl. facing p. 541 (Paris, 1762), reproduced in *HT*, vol. IV, p. 30, fig. 15, shows a farming scene from eighteenth-century France with a harrow almost identical in shape to that of *Les très riches heures* for October. There is a good representation of the common *crates stercorariae* in the Seasons mosaic from

St-Romain-en-Gal, now in the Louvre (G. Lafaye, in *Rév. Arch.* 3ᵉ ser. t. XIV, 1892, Winter, third panel; Billiard, *L'Agriculture*, fig. 6, p. 84).

(*b*) *Extant specimens.* Rare, but there is a good example of the 'single-row' type (see Fest. p. 105—above, passage (*b*), p. 148) in the Saalburg collection (*Saalburgjahrb.* VIII, 1934, Taf. 4, no. 10).

5. *Survival*

(*a*) *Of the implement.* Both types are still common in the Mediterranean area. The writer has seen triangular *crates* in operation in central Sicily and in Palma di Mallorca. Both are featured by Jaberg–Jud, Karte 1431, nos. 3 and 5. Other specimens may be found in Werth, *op. cit.* pp. 157–9, Abb. 50–4, and in Leser, 'Westöstliche Landwirt-schaft', *Festschr.* P. W. Schmidt, 'Anthropos' (Vienna, 1928), pp. 426–8, Abb. 19–27; pp. 465 ff., Abb. 65, 66.

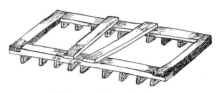

Fig. 113. Irpex (Italian)

(*b*) *Of the names.* (i) Ital. 'graticola' (f.), fire-grate, Eng. 'grate', 'grating'. Span. 'grada' (f.), harrow. Ptg. 'grade' (f.), harrow. (ii) Ital. 'erpice' (m.), harrow; Fr. 'herse' (f.), harrow.

9

DRAGS AND THRESHING
MACHINES

Note. In order to avoid unnecessary repetition of passages in which both 'traha', 'tribulum' and 'plostellum poenicum' appear, the references to all these implements are set down in chronological order of occurrence.

1. Traha (-ae, f.) (Colum.), Trahea (-ae, f.) (Verg.), Tragula (-ae, f.) (Varro, *LL*), Traga (-ae, f.) (Ps. Servius), *drag*
R-E VI A. 2, cols. 2077–8 [Hörle].

Fig. 114. Traha (ancient Egyptian)

2. Tribulum (-i, n.) (Varro, *RR*; Verg.; Pliny (?)), Tribula (-ae, f.) (Colum.; Isid.), Trivolum (-i, n.) (Varro, *LL*; *Corp. Gloss. Lat.*), Trebla (?) (Cato), *threshing-sledge*
R-E VI A. 2, 2426 [Hörle]; *ibid.* V. 2, 1700–6 [Olck] s.v. dreschen.

Fig. 115. Tribulum (Cypriote)

3. Plostellum Poenicum (Varro), *Punic cart*

(*a*) Varro, *LL* 5. 31. 'After this in the harvest comes the threshing (*tritura*), because then the grain is "rubbed out" (*teritur*)': hinc in messi tritura, quod tum frumentum teritur, et trivolum[1] qui teritur.

(*b*) Varro, *LL* 5. 139 (things used for transporting produce, etc.). 'Among the implements drawn by animals the *sledge* ("tragula") takes its name from the fact that the animal "drags" it ("trahere") along the ground': de his quae iumenta ducunt, *tragula*, quod ab eo trahitur per terram.

(*c*) Isid. 20. 14. 10 (repeating Serv. *ad* Verg. G. 1. 164). 'The *sledge* is a type of cart, used for threshing grain, and gets its name from this (i.e. from the verb "terere", "to rub")': *tribula* genus vehiculi unde teruntur frumenta, et ab hoc ita vocatum.

(*d*) *Corp. Glos.* s.v. 'trahea'. *Trahea* τυκάνη τὰς βώλους ἀφανίζουσα II 200. 8. traduco κέστρος, ὄχημα δίχα τροχῶν II 200. 5 (tragula *Salmas.*) etc. *trahae*

[1] trivolum F. *Corp. Gloss. Lat.* II 458. 50 (tribulum = Gk. τυκάνη); cf. II 200. 8; II 201. 37; V 195. 63.

152

sunt vehicula v 624. 32. *trahae* quae rustici tragula vocant v 350. 8. Cf. Varro, *LL* v. 139; Loewe *Prodr.* 418. trahas quidam putant esse quibus in area colligitur pabulum (paululum codd.). Donatus vero dicit vehicla esse trahas sine rotis v 250. 14. Cf. Serv. *Georg.* 1. 164.

(*e*) *Corp. Gloss.* s.v. tribula. *tribula* τυκάνη II 201. 37; III 195. 63 (tyganin). τρυγάνη ἡ τὸν σῖτον ἀλοῶσα II 460. 48. τρικάνη II 459. 12. ρυκάνη II 428. 57. τρικάνη, τρίβολος III 262. 58 (*unde?*). τρίβολος II 458. 50. τριπτηρία II 459. 40. τριβόλιον II 524. 51. machina qua fruges tribulantur v 250. 18. genus vehiculi unde teruntur frumenta et ob hoc ita vocatum v 250. 19. machina ad triturandum II 595. 45. genus vehiculi dictum a terendo, id est quo frumenta teruntur v 527. 8. Cf. Serv. *Georg.* 1. 164; Isid. 20. 14. 10.

(*f*) Cato 135. 1 (on purchasing equipment). 'Carts and *sledges* are obtained at Suessa and in Lucania': Suessae et in Lucania plostra, *treblae*.

(*g*) Varro, *RR* 1. 22. 1 (articles which should be made on the estate). 'Nothing should be bought which can be ... made by the men on the estate; in general articles made of withies and wood, such as hampers, baskets, *threshing-sledges*': quae ... fieri a domesticis poterunt, eorum nequid ematur, ut fere sunt quae ex viminibus et materia rustica fiunt, ut corbes, fiscinae, *tribula* ...

(*h*) Varro, *RR* 1. 52. 2 (on threshing methods). 'The grain should be threshed on the floor. This is done in some districts by means of a yoke of oxen and a *threshing-sledge*. The latter is constructed either of a board roughened with stones or pieces of iron embedded in it, which separates the grain from the ear when it is dragged by a yoke of oxen with the driver or a heavy weight on it; or else of a toothed axle running on low wheels, called a *Punic cart*; the driver sits on it and drives the oxen which pull it; this is the method in use in eastern Spain and elsewhere': e spicis in area excuti grana (oportet). quod fit alibi iumentis iunctis ac *tribulo*. id fit e tabula lapidibus aut ferro asperata, quae cum imposito auriga aut pondere grandi trahitur iumentis iunctis discutit a spicis grana; aut ex axibus dentatis cum orbiculis, quod vocant *plostellum poenicum*; in eo quis sedeat atque agitet quae trahant iumenta, ut in Hispania citeriore et aliis locis faciunt.

(*j*) Colum. 2. 20. 4 (on threshing methods). 'If you have a few teams (of horses), you may hitch them to a *threshing-sledge* and a *drag*, either of which very easily breaks up the straw': si pauca iuga sunt, adicere tribulam et traheam[1] possis, quae res utraque culmos facillime conminuit.

(*k*) Pliny 18. 298 (on threshing). 'After reaping the ear itself is in some places beaten out with threshing-sledges on a threshing-floor': messa spica[2] ipsa alibi *tribulis* in area ... exteritur.

(*l*) Verg. *G* 1. 164 (the farmer's equipment). 'Sledges and drags and drag-hoes of grievous (?) weight': tribulaque traheaeque et iniquo pondere rastri.

(*m*) Servius *ad loc.* 'TRIBVLA, a type of cart, used for threshing grain. TRAHAE. We call those implements *drags* which are used for dragging and piling up the corn. This type of cart gets its name from dragging; they have no wheels':

---

[1] traheam *Lundström*: traham *vulgo*: trahere *SAR*.   [2] Messa spica? *Mayhoff*: messis.

TRIBVLA, genus vehiculi, unde teruntur frumenta. TRAHAE. trahas dicimus, quibus trahuntur frumenta et coacervantur. dictum est autem hoc genus vehiculi a trahendo; nam rotas non habent.

(*n*) Ps.-Servius *ad loc.* '*Drags* are either, as some people say, a board drawn by oxen, which is brought (?) into the threshing-floor to gather up the corn; or a cart without wheels, which they commonly call a "*drag*"': traheaeque vel tabula est, ut quidam dicunt, quae trahentibus bubus areae induci (?) ad pabulum colligendum; vel vehicula sine rotis, quas vulgo *trahas* dicunt.

DISCUSSION

1. *General*

After harvesting, the next process is the separation, first of the ears of grain from the straw, and then of the grains themselves from the chaff. Where the corn had been cut at the top of the stalk, the grain was taken to the granary and either beaten out by hand with flails or trodden out by cattle during the winter, when labourers or oxen were not engaged on other tasks. If the grain had been cut at middle height, and dry weather made it possible to thresh in the open on the threshing-floor, the method recommended by Columella (*j*) was to use an animal-drawn implement, either a *traha* or a *tribulum*, to remove the straw; the grain was then separated from the chaff by tossing the mixture with shovels (*ventilabra*)— (see s.v. 'ventilabrum', pp. 32 ff.). The use of these implements speeded up a process which depended upon a spell of fine weather, and so protected the crop against damage by storms.

2. *The traha (trahea)*

The main difficulty about this implement is the paucity of information in the sources; while the *tribulum* is mentioned by Varro (*a*) and Isidore (*c*) there is no reference in either to the *traha*. In another passage (*LL* 5. 139) Varro mentions an animal-drawn implement which he calls a 'tragula', so called 'because it is "dragged" ("trahitur") through the ground'. The connection with 'trahere' to 'drag' is supported by Ernout–Meillet (*op. cit.* 3rd ed. p. 1234, s.v. 'traho'). The term 'tragula' is used elsewhere to denote a type of javelin used by the Gauls (Caesar, *B.G.* 1. 26. 3, etc.), but it does not occur elsewhere in an agricultural context. That *traha* and *trahea* are alternative forms of the same word seems evident enough; and it is probable that all three forms refer to the same implement. Rich (*Dict. Ant.* s.v. 'traha') defines it as a drag without wheels (see the passage from Servius' commentary on Vergil, *G.* 1. 164 (*k*)), and concludes from the phrasing in Columella 2. 20. 4, 'adicere tribulam et traheam possis', that the *trahea* 'was sometimes drawn behind the *tribula*, to complete what had

been left imperfectly threshed'. This inference is not justifiable, for Columella (*j*) goes on to say that 'either of these implements will very easily break up the straw'. Vergil's reference (*j*) gives no help towards a solution of the problem. Servius defines the *trahea* as a cart for removing the threshed grain from the threshing-floor and piling it up. This must be discarded, since it is in direct conflict with the express statement of Columella (*loc. cit.*). On the evidence available it is not possible to say more than that the *traha* or *trahea* was another, perhaps a simpler form of threshing implement than the *tribula* or *tribulum*; *tragula* (Varro) and perhaps *traga* (Ps.-Servius) were alternative names for implements of the same basic type.

3. *Tribulum, tribula*

Varro (*h*) gives an accurate description of the *tribulum*, which corresponds to surviving specimens of an implement that is still widely used. It consists of a heavy wooden board with flints or iron teeth embedded in the underside; the roughened under-surface releases the grain from the straw, leaving only the chaff to be removed in a further process. It was an obvious improvement on the ancient method of treading out the grain with animals. Another variety was the 'Punic cart' ('plostellum poenicum'), which was constructed on a somewhat different principle: the straw was broken up, not by the rubbing action (hence 'tribulum', 'rubber') of a sledge passing over it, but by a toothed roller which crushed as it revolved. Rich (*Dict. Ant.* s.v. 'plostellum' (2)) and Daremberg–Saglio (t. IV, 2, 924 *b*) refer to the modern counterpart of this implement which is still used in Egypt under the name of 'noreg'; the former includes a drawing of the Egyptian machine.[1] But Varro's *plostellum* differs in one important respect from the *noreg* as depicted by Rich: the *plostellum* was not a sledge with rollers, but a small wagon with wheels, and a driver mounted upon it; the small wheels (*orbiculi*) would be necessary to the operation, since the spiked axles must have been elevated somewhat above the ground; otherwise they would merely have pushed the straw along instead of riding over it and crushing it.

4. *Plostellum poenicum*

See also the discussion of *tribulum* (above, Section 3). If Varro's description (*h*) is correct, the *plostellum poenicum* may be regarded as an improved

[1] 'The *noreg* is a machine consisting of a wooden frame, with three cross-bars or axles, on which are fixed circular iron plates, for the purpose of bruising the ears of corn and extracting the grain, at the same time that the straw is broken into small pieces; the first and last axles having each four plates, and the central one three; at the upper part is a seat on which the driver sits, his weight tending to give additional effort to the machine' (Sir J. G. Wilkinson, *The Manners and Customs of the Ancient Egyptians*, revised ed. ed. by J. Birch, London, 1878, II, 423).

version of the *tribulum*, imported probably from the Carthaginian farmers of Spain. Although its rotary action will have made it more efficient than the *tribulum*, the absence of any reference in Columella's lengthy treatment of threshing methods (2. 20. 3–5) would imply that it had not found favour in Italy.

5. *Monuments*

No representations of these implements are known to me from monumental sources, but numerous examples of threshing-floors of considerable antiquity are known; they are prevalent in Palestine, Syria, Greece and Spain. Many of them bear on their surfaces clear marks of the grinding action of flints or iron teeth.

6. *Survival*

(a) *Of the implement.* The *tribulum* survives unchanged in many parts of the Mediterranean region and the Middle East. R. J. Forbes (*HT*, II, 106, fig. 70) illustrates the design of the implement from a specimen still in use in Cyprus, which is studded with flints (from a photograph taken by O. G. S. Crawford). 'The *plostellum punicum* is still in use in the Lebanon and Syria' (Daremberg–Saglio, *loc. cit.*). E. Hamy, *Comptes rend. de l'Acad. des Inscr.* (1900), p. 22, reported that the Berbers of North Africa were still using an implement of similar design, known locally as the 'kerita'. A good specimen from Transcaucasia, consisting of a pair of spiked rollers and a toboggan-type body, surmounted by a table, is featured by E. Werth, *Grabstock, Hacke und Pflug* (Ludwigsburg, 1954), p. 211, Abb. 131. This closely resembles the Egyptian *noreg*, reproduced as Fig. 117.

Fig. 116. Tribulum (Cypriote)

(a)

(b)

Fig. 117. Plostellum poenicum (Egyptian)

(b) *Of the name.* (i) *Traha, trahea:* Ital. 'treggia' (f.), a sledge. Span. 'treilla' (f.), a leveller (for soil). (ii) *Tribulum:* Ital. 'trebbia' (f.), a flail; 'trebbiare' (v.t.), to thresh; 'trebbiatore (m.), threshing-machine. Span. 'trilla' (f.), a harrow. Ptg. 'trilhar' (v.t.), to thresh.

Note. On the regional distribution in Italy of various methods of threshing, see now Parain, *Verbreitung*, 362.

10

REAPING MACHINES

Vallus (-i, m.), *a frame*, *a reaping machine*

R-E VIII A. 1, cols. 291–2 [W. Schleiermacher].

Note. Vallus is only used in the latter sense by Pliny (18. 296). Palladius calls the machine which he describes at 7. 2. 2 a *vehiculum* (four times); for the container of his machine, which he mentions specifically only once, he uses the word *carpentum*. The lexical and etymological references, which are of special importance in connection with the machine, are set out below:

(*a*) VALLVS

Schleiermacher, *R-E*, *loc. cit.*, derives the term from 'vannus', the winnowing-fan, *vallus* being a diminutive form; the container of the

reaping machine gets its name from a resemblance to the winnowing basket. The etymological authorities are divided: Walde–Hofmann deny any connection with the masculine word *vallus*, a stake, while Ernout–Meillet derive it from *vallus*, a stake, without discussion.

Fig. 118. Vallus (reconstructed)

(*b*) CARPENTVM

R-E III. 2, 1606–7: *carpentum* a two-wheeled carriage indicating more than one type of vehicle, viz. (1) a town carriage for ladies, (2) a war chariot used by Gauls and Britons, (3) a cart for carrying dung, citing Palla-

Fig. 119. Carpentum (reconstructed)

dius 10. 1. 2; Palladius 7. 2. 2. is not cited! Ernout–Meillet give only the first meaning, and describe *carpentum* as an ancient loan-word from Gallic, citing Livy 41. 21. 17 'carpentis Gallicis'. Walde–Hofmann suggest a possible connection with 'corbis' a basket.

DESCRIPTION

THE LITERARY EVIDENCE

Pliny 18. 296 (on reaping methods). 'On the vast estates in the provinces of Gaul very large frames (*valli*) fitted with teeth at the edge and carried on two wheels are driven through the corn by a pack-animal[1] pushing from behind; the ears thus torn off fall into the frame': Galliarum latifundiis *valli* praegrandes dentibus in margine insertis duabus rotis per segetem impelluntur iumento in contrarium iuncto; ita dereptae in vallum cadunt spicae.

Pallad. 7. 2. 2–4 (on harvesting grain). 'In the more level plains of the Gallic provinces they employ the following short cut or labour-saving device (*compendium*) for harvesting. With the aid of a single ox the machine outstrips the efforts of labourers and cuts down the time of the entire harvesting operation. They construct a cart carried on two small wheels. The square surface of the cart is made up of planks, which slope outwards from the bottom, and so provide a larger space at the top. The height of the planks is lower at the front of this container (*carpentum*); at this point a large number of teeth with spaces between are set up in line to match the height of the ears; they are bent back at the tips. At the back of the vehicle are fastened two very small yoke-beams, like the poles of a litter; at this point an ox is attached by means of a yoke and chains, with his head pointing towards the cart; he must be docile, so that he will not exceed the pace set by the driver. When the latter begins to drive the vehicle through the standing corn, all the ears are seized by the teeth and piled up in the cart, leaving the straw cut off in the field, the varying height of the cut being controlled from time to time by the cowherd who walks behind. In this way, after a few journeys up and down the field the entire harvesting process is completed in the space of a few hours. This machine is useful on open plains or where the ground is level, and in areas where the straw has no economic value': pars Galliarum planior hoc compendio utitur ad metendum, et praeter hominum labores, unius bovis opera spatium totius messis absumit. fit itaque vehiculum, quod duabus rotis brevibus fertur; huius quadrata superficies tabulis munitur, quae forinsecus reclines in summo reddant spatia largiora; ab eius fronte carpenti brevior est altitudo tabularum; ibi denticuli plurimi ac rari ad spicarum mensuram constituuntur in ordinem, ad superiorem partem recurvi; a tergo vero eiusdem vehiculi duo brevissimi temones figuntur, velut amites basternarum. ibi bos capite in vehiculum verso iugo aptatur et vinculis, mansuetus sane, qui non modum compulsoris excedat. hic ubi vehiculum per messes coepit impellere, omnis spica in carpentum denticulis comprehensa cumulatur, abruptis ac relictis paleis, altitudinem vel humilitatem plerumque bubulco moderante, qui sequitur; et ita per paucos itus ac reditus brevi horarum spatio tota messis impletur. hoc campestribus locis vel aequalibus utile est, et iis quibus necessaria palea non habetur.

THE MONUMENTAL EVIDENCE

The above passages constitute the whole of the surviving literary evidence for a mechanical reaper. But Palladius' detailed description is strikingly confirmed by four pieces of monumental evidence, the most recent of

[1] I.e. horse, donkey or mule (see p. 160).

which came to light as recently as 1958. They are set out below, with descriptions as full as the state of the monuments permits.

1. *The Tableau of the Seasons* from the Porte de Mars at Reims in north-east France. The panel depicting the *vallus* is one of a series of panels in low relief surrounding a large medallion on the soffit of the central arch of a three-arched gate. The monument is still standing, but the reliefs were already much damaged when the drawings, on which all modern discussion of the reliefs is based, were made in the eighteenth century. The plaque for the month of August depicts a reaping machine. Prior to the 1958 discovery (see section 3 below) no scholar had identified it as such, but there is now no doubt about its identity. The monument is usually dated to about the end of the second or the beginning of the third century A.D.   Pl. 13

2. *The Arlon Relief.* This is a fragment of a funerary monument dis-covered at Arlon (*Orolaunum Vicus*), a Roman site near Luxemburg, in 1854. It depicts the machine being pushed from the rear by an animal, and guided, also from the rear, by a man. The poor condition of the fragment (the surface is considerably damaged, and only part of the hindquarters and the tail of the animal are visible) made identification difficult; it was not until 1926 that Rostovtzeff made a correct guess when he wrote: 'the operation represented is probably reaping by means of a machine drawn by a team of oxen' (*SEHRE*, I, pl. XXIX, fig. 4, Oxford, 1926), though he postulated several animals instead of one, and placed them in front instead of behind the machine.   Pl. 14

3. *The Relief from Montauban-Buzenol* (often referred to as the Buzenol relief). The third monument, and the most important as well as the best preserved of the three, found at Montauban-Buzenol in southern Belgium, not far from Arlon, in 1958, consists of a panel in low relief which formed part of a large funerary monument. The Buzenol find, first published by J. Mertens, 'Sculptures romaines de Buzenol', *Le Pays Gaumais*, XIX (1958), 17–124, has provoked much discussion: the most important contributions are mentioned in the discussion below.   Pl. 15

4. *The Trier fragment.* Part of a mutilated relief panel unearthed in 1890 during gardening operations behind the Landesmuseum in Trier, West Germany. The surviving fragment, which must have been originally more than twice its present size, contains only the nearside wheel, part of the nearside shaft, the lower part of one of the forelegs of an animal and a sizeable portion of its muzzle, the profile of its chest, and the back portion of the frame. H. Cüppers (*Trierer Zeitschr.* XXVII, 1964, 151 ff.), has correctly identified the fragment as depicting part of a *vallus* in operation. Unfortunately the slab has broken off slantwise across the right-hand face, leaving only the right-hand rear portion of the container, and the boss of   Pl. 16

the offside wheel visible, but it is evident that the machine, while closely resembling the Buzenol *vallus*, had a different type of container, and a different arrangement of the container on the machine. The teeth have suffered complete destruction, together with the greater part of the animal. The wheels are of similar pattern to those of no. 3, but have only eight spokes compared with the latter's ten.

DISCUSSION

1. *The literary evidence*

According to Pliny's brief description the *vallus* consisted of a very large frame fitted with teeth and mounted on a pair of wheels. The frame was driven through the corn by an animal, which was probably but not certainly a mule, pushing from behind. The ears were torn off by the teeth and fell into a receptacle. Pliny's machine is thus no more than a mechanized 'pecten' (see above, s.v. 'pecten', pp. 113 ff.) and had nothing in common with modern reaping-machines, which cut the stalks at the base of the plant by the operation of a set of knives moving across a cutter-bar. The successful operation of a machine designed to tear off the heads involves the solution of three problems:

(1) The teeth must be so shaped and arranged that they will be able to catch and tear off the heads without serious clogging of the blades, and without undue loss of grain by falling.

(2) Since the stalks are not of uniform height throughout a field of corn, there must be some device for raising and lowering the rows of teeth at will.

(3) The animal must be so harnessed to the vehicle that he can propel it easily and at an even pace.

Pliny's account offers no information on these problems; we therefore turn now to the detailed account given by Palladius. The author begins by referring to the terrain in which such machines were used, viz. the flat plains of the Gallic provinces. The machine can only be used on level ground. His next point is that the machine is a labour-saving device (*compendium*). The implications of this are fully discussed below (pp. 169 f.). The design of the machine is then discussed in detail: it is a *vehiculum* or carriage mounted on two small wheels, on the platform of which is built a square container, the *carpentum*, made of planks (*tabulae*). The sides of the container slope outwards from the bottom to the top (*forinsecus reclines*) so that the space at the top is wider. In other words the container is of the familiar 'tumbril' type.

The ordinary Roman wagon, the *plaustrum*, was a simple platform set on two or four wheels, on which various containers might be mounted.

160

Palladius' 'vehiculum' is the wheeled platform, and 'carpentum' is the container mounted on it; thus far the *vallus* conforms to a common type of vehicle. Next we come to the main working part, the teeth. Pliny merely says that the frames (*valli*) are fitted with teeth 'at the edge' (*in margine*); Palladius begins this part of his account by stating that the planks on the front of the container do not reach the same height as those at the sides and back; here teeth are set up in a row 'to fit the height of the ears' ('ad mensuram spicarum'). They are 'numerous' ('plurimi') and 'spaced out' ('rari'). The adjective 'rarus' seems out of place here, that is, in its usual sense of 'widely spaced'; Renard suggests (*art. cit.* pp. 99–100) that the basic meaning of 'rarus' is something that provides interstices: hence 'open' soil (*rarum solum*) as opposed to 'dense' (*spissum*), and that this is the meaning here. The line of teeth is set up above the top layer of planking at the front, and they are 'curved back' ('recurvi')—that is, the points are higher than the blades. This is an important, indeed an essential feature: the curvature would induce a scooping action, restricting the 'intake' of ears and preventing the machine from clogging. Thus the first of our three technical problems, that of enabling the teeth to catch and tear off the heads without clogging or undue loss of grain appears to have been satisfactorily solved by the arrangement as described by Palladius. Palladius' next point is the harnessing and control of the ox; the animal is harnessed to a pair of short shafts which are attached to the back of the cart 'like the poles of a litter' ('velut amites basternarum'). The last phrase clearly implies that the arrangement was unfamiliar to the reader; harnessing between shafts for pulling is certainly attested for Roman imperial times: E. M. Jope (*HT*, II, 544, fig. 489) shows a boy's chariot with shafts from a bas-relief on a third-century sarcophagus from Trier; the Gallic provenance of the monument may well be significant. Unfortunately Palladius gives no details of the harnessing system, but merely refers to a yoke (*iugum*) and chains (*vincula*).

The animal, says Palladius, must be 'docile' ('mansuetus') so that he will keep up a steady pace under the control of the driver. Thus the third condition for successful operation is satisfied. The final paragraph of Palladius' account describes the actual operation of the machine. The ears are all grasped by the teeth and piled into the container, leaving the straw behind. The ox-driver (*bubulcus*) controls the height of the teeth from behind. Precisely how this is effected is not explained in the text. Here, as at several other points, the problem is illuminated by the evidence of the surviving monuments. Palladius then rounds off his account by referring to the time saved by the machine, adding that it is for use on open plains or where the ground is level, and that its use is limited to areas where the straw has no

economic value. This last point reminds us of an important passage in Pliny (*d*), p. 98, where reference is made to a saving of labour by 'cutting the stalks at middle height and missing out the shorter ones'; see the discussion on the economics of the reaping machine (below, p. 170).

2. *The monumental evidence*

1. *The Porte de Mars tableau.* In spite of the fact that the monument is still *in situ*, and has not apparently been damaged since attention was first drawn to it in 1816 (A. de Laborde, *Les monuments de la France*, Paris, 1816, pl. CXIII), we are still dependent on a drawing made by Bence in the eighteenth century. H. Stern,[1] who examined the original some years ago, vouches for the accuracy of Bence's drawings, but includes no photographs. Reinach[2] thought that Bence's drawings were 'rather contrived'. From the drawing, as reproduced by Renard (*art. cit.* pl. XVII, 1) it appears that the sculptor was attempting no more than a purely decorative scheme. The only parts depicted are the left side of the toothed frame, seen from the side, but sloping downwards so as to display the teeth in front view, and the left wheel. A man is shown walking in front of the vehicle, and turning half round in the act of unclogging the teeth with a short scraper, exactly as if he were cleaning the teeth of a very large comb. No other part of the machine is visible. All that we learn from the tableau is that the machine required a labourer to keep the blades clean. Bence's drawing suggests that he took the stick to be the handle of a rake, and the *vallus* its teeth; he identified the scene as that of a man harrowing.

2. *The Arlon Relief.* Although the relief is fragmentary and mutilated it is clear that the object depicted is part of a *vallus* seen from the rear. It shows clearly the driver walking behind, and part of the animal, which is evidently an equine. The long shafts which enclose both the animal and his driver are joined together at the rear by a cross-bar, clearly visible in the relief. The angle of the shafts, and the position of the driver's arms and body, suggest that he is tilting the *vallus* downwards into the corn.

3. *The Buzenol Relief.* The Buzenol relief is by far the most important of the four surviving monuments. It is more naturalistic than the Porte de Mars panel, and in a far better state of preservation than either the Arlon or the Trier fragment. Also it provides the only detailed evidence we have concerning the shape and design of the teeth and their frame. J. Mertens's publication (*La Suisse Primitive*, XXII, 4, Dec. 1958, figs. 46, 47) shows on the left a labourer, wearing the same type of short tunic as the Arlon driver, facing the vehicle from in front. Both his legs are severely damaged, and

[1] H. Stern, *Le calendrier de 354*, Étude sur son texte et ses illustrations (Paris, 1953), p. 208 and pl. XXXVIII, fig. 4.
[2] S. Reinach, *Répertoire de reliefs gr. et rom.* (Paris 1909), t. I, 231, fig. 2.

it is not absolutely certain whether he is standing or walking; this question can only be resolved by detailed discussion of the operation on which he is engaged. He is evidently engaged in freeing the teeth of chaff and other clogging matter, which seems, from close examination of the slab, to have been cut off from the right-hand side of the frame as far as the seventh and eighth blades, which are in process of being cleaned. At this point the material is shown at an angle to that on the already cleaned blades, and the blade of the cleaning implement is obscured by it (Plate 15). The edges of the blades appear to be almost parallel to each other, and with this arrangement very frequent, or indeed continuous clearing of the blades will have been necessary; otherwise, as more and more heads were caught between the blades, those nearest to the tips would be forced against those which had not yet been severed, and might be torn up by the roots. This operation could be carried on in one of two ways—either by stopping the machine at frequent intervals, or by a continuous process of cutting off the clogged areas by a side-to-side movement over the surface of the frame. This latter arrangement would have required the labourer to work from one side, and it involves the assumption that the Buzenol sculptor was representing the less efficient version of the operation, or alternatively that he sacrificed accuracy of presentation to the artistic requirements of the subject, and to the size of his slab. He has indeed chosen a good angle of sight in order to expose to view the various parts of the machine. In the extreme foreground, to the right is shown the left or nearside wheel, and immediately behind it the toothed frame terminating in a raised board of the same length as that of the blades, with a downward-sloping concave profile at its forward end. This feature, not shown or mentioned elsewhere, served as a guide-board to draw the corn into the frame and prevent its fouling the wheel. At the extreme left-hand side the standing corn is clearly shown as it passes through the comb, the thick heads of grain being clearly visible between the right leg of the labourer and the projecting blades (Mertens, *art. cit.* p. 51, fig. 47). The top right-hand corner of the slab shows the axle and the right or offside wheel, both in very low relief, but perfectly distinct, and a wooden beam which appears to meet the base of the comb-frame at right-angles, but to be separate from the axle. Thus the entire frame will have been mounted on the axle, but running free, so that the machine could be raised or lowered at will, exactly as described by Palladius in connection with the larger machine. At the extreme right-hand edge appears the head of a donkey or mule, and part of a throat-harness; a halter (?) hangs loosely between the animal and the back of the frame. There is no sign of the body of the container for the reaped ears. This is not surprising, since the angle of sight chosen by the sculptor would exclude it from view, except

for the opening or 'throat' behind the row of teeth which is clearly visible; the left side of the container would also be obscured by the stalks passing under the machine. The structure of the frame would require the container to be a long, coffin-shaped box, running the full length of the frame, its depth being determined by the diameter of the wheels, estimated by E. P. Fouss[1] as between 70 and 75 cm (between 2 ft 3 in. and 2 ft 6 in.). If the front of the container was hinged along the bottom edge, and secured with a catch at the top, the contents could have been easily discharged when the container was full. This particular problem does not seem to have engaged the attention of any of the numerous commentators on the Buzenol *vallus*, with the exception of J. Kolendo ('La moissonneuse antique', *Annales* (*ESC*), 15° année, no. 6, Nov.–Dec. 1960, pp. 1112–13). Kolendo supposes that the container was removable, and made of light wickerwork, which does not seem at all satisfactory. In Fouss's model in the Arlon museum the container is an integral part of the frame (see Renard, pl. III, 2).

4. *The Buzenol and Arlon reliefs compared.* It is clear that the damaged reliefs from Arlon (2) (see Plate 14) and Trier (1) (see Plate 6), in spite of their mutilated condition, depict a *vallus* in motion, while the Reims panel (1) (see Plate 13) and the Buzenol relief show it at rest; this important distinction is made clear by J. Mertens in his discussion of the monument (*art. cit.* pp. 52–3), but the accompanying drawing (*loc. cit.* fig. 48), in which the two fragments are tentatively joined together, is slightly misleading, since it prompts the suggestion that two men were employed on the machine. Mertens refers to 'the driver or his assistant', thus leaving open the question whether one or two men were required. But the driver could easily stop the machine single-handed both to empty the container and to clean the blades; there is nothing in the surviving monuments which presupposes a second workman, nor does Palladius mention more than one.

5. *The Trier vallus.* The Trier *vallus*, in spite of its mutilated condition, evidently belongs to the same class as the Buzenol machine, having a rather shallow frame. It differs from the latter, however, in two important respects: (1) The ends of the frame are roughly triangular in section, and the surviving portion of the frame suggests a resemblance to the grass-box of a lawn-mower; its shape *may* imply a greater capacity than that of the Buzenol machine. (2) The positioning of the teeth cannot be precisely determined, but they must have been set well below the level of the top of the container, giving a much deeper throat, whereas those of the Buzenol

[1] E. P. Fouss, 'Le "vallus" ou moissonneuse des Trévires', *Le pays gaumais*, XIX (1958), 130 ff., and figs. 6 and 7.

machine were set somewhat higher up, leaving a rather narrow throat opening into a container which appears to have been slung below the level of the frame (see p. 164 above). Dr Cüppers's reconstruction (see Plate 16) is not altogether satisfactory; the set of the blades is incorrectly arranged in relation to the floor level of the container (at the angle shown the heads of grain would tend to fall forwards), and the harnessing is unworkable. It is dangerous to infer too much of the probable operational technique from such a mutilated fragment, but it does indicate that more than one design of the lighter *vallus* was tried out. Such experiments would be quite in keeping with Gallo-Roman skill in the construction of wheeled vehicles of many kinds, and with their ingenuity in the harnessing of animals.[1] The Trier *vallus* may represent an attempt to improve on the Buzenol type, with the object of redesigning the container so as to increase its size and thus reduce the number of stoppages during the reaping operation.

3. *The evidence considered as a whole*

In the first excitement following the Buzenol discovery, it was perhaps natural to assume, as several commentators have done, that we now have before us an accurate representation in stone of the machine described in detail by Palladius. J. Kolendo, for example, not only regards the Buzenol discovery as confirmation of Palladius' description, but goes on to suggest that his account was not derived from earlier literary sources, but is based on personal observation, adding with caution that the author's supposed Gallic origin is not otherwise sufficiently established. But it is evident that none of the surviving monuments depicts the Palladian machine, and it is virtually certain that all three of them represent examples of a lighter version, with a container slung partially or wholly below the toothed frame. This is properly a *vallus*, and this is the term used by Pliny. Palladius' machine, on the contrary, while operating by means of a similar row of teeth for tearing off the heads of grain, was of different construction, being built up of rows of planking into the shape of a tumbril (*carpentum* is his word), and fitted with a pair of short shafts, as contrasted with the long-shafted *vallus* depicted on the Arlon fragment.

4. *The two types of reaping machine*

Heitland, writing in 1920, and probably unaware of the limited monumental evidence then available, said he believed that there was 'no record of any attempts to improve the original design' (*Agricola*, Cambridge, 1921, p. 398). At that time none of the three known monuments had been correctly identified, and the Buzenol relief was still undiscovered. The

[1] See p. 13, n. 3, and references cited there.

evidence now available makes it clear that two main types of harvester were in use on the Gallic *latifundia*: (1) the *vallus* or shallow-frame type with underslung container, steered by a man walking behind the animal, which was either a mule or a donkey; (2) the *carpentum* or tumbril type of machine, with a large container mounted above the wheels, pushed by an ox, not by a mule or donkey, and controlled by a man walking beside, not behind, the machine.

5. *The two varieties of the vallus*

Close examination of the Buzenol and Trier reliefs shows that two varieties of *vallus* were in use. Although the container of the Buzenol machine is not visible, except for the narrow 'throat' behind the row of teeth, the general structure would require the container to be a long, shallow, coffin-shaped box running the full width of the frame, its depth being determined by the diameter of the wheels (*c*. 70–75 cm—see p. 168). With a frame about 1 m 20 in width, the container may have measured about 4 ft × 1 ft × 1 ft 3 in., giving a capacity of 5 ft³. The container of the Trier *vallus* was, as we have seen (above, p. 164), of a different shape, and set higher above the ground, providing a greater capacity and thus reducing the number of stoppages of work for emptying the container.

6. *The design of the carpentum*

Kolendo (*art. cit.* pp. 1112–13), in suggesting that the body of the smaller machine was probably a light basketry container, links this view with the name 'vallus', which he defines as the diminutive of 'vannus' (f.), a winnowing basket. Palladius' machine, which was evidently a large heavy affair, with a container made of solid planking, is never referred to by him as a *vallus*, but as a 'vehiculum' (a general term for a wheeled vehicle), or a 'carpentum' (the etymology of which is uncertain).[1] As the numerous reconstructions of the *carpentum* indicate,[2] the design and positioning of the container must have given this machine a very different appearance from

---

[1] Mau (*R-E* III. 2, cols. 1606–7, s.v. 'carpentum') shows that *carpentum* was basically a two-wheeled vehicle, the meanings including a town-carriage for ladies (numerous references), a Gallic or Britannic war-chariot, and a dung-cart. The etymologists are divided: Ernout–Meillet cite Livy 41. 21. 17 in support of the view that it is a loan-word from Gallic, but Meyer–Lübke stresses the difficulties of this view. Walde–Hofmann suggest a possible derivation from the root of 'corbis' a basket. Mau does not cite Pallad. *RR* 7. 2!

[2] Conveniently reproduced by M. Renard, 'Technique et agriculture en pays trévire et rémois', *Latomus*, XVIII (1959), part 1, figs. 1–7 and pl. XV. While it is true that the Buzenol discovery has greatly stimulated interest in the history of the *vallus* (for full references see bibliography), it is astonishing that W. Schleiermacher, writing on this topic in 1955 (*R-E* VIII A. 1, cols. 291–2), had not encountered a single reconstruction of Palladius' machine.

that of the Buzenol *vallus*. The container will have projected equally on either side of the axle, and consequently the shafts, unlike those of the *vallus*, were, as Palladius says, very short ('brevissimi') (see the reconstruction, Fig. 119).

The wheels are described as small ('rotae breves'); those of the *vallus*, by contrast, with a diameter of between 70 and 75 cm, could scarcely be referred to as 'small'. There is no reason, however, for assuming that the wheels of the *carpentum* were solid, as all the reconstructions represent them. Spoked wheels are standard on all the numerous types of carts and wagons depicted on the monuments of Gaul,[1] and the Saalburg museum contains two well-preserved specimens.[2] Apart from these differences the two machines were clearly related. The teeth of the Buzenol relief correspond closely in shape and setting to Palladius' description. The harnessing arrangements will have been somewhat different; the most convenient fastening for an ox pushing a load by means of a yoke and chains would be a frontal or forehead yoke of the type still used in parts of the Middle East;[3] most of the reconstructions favour this system. To either end of the yoke were fitted iron chains (*vinculi*), which in turn were attached to the ends of the short shafts (*brevissimi temones*). It should be remarked that the shafts required for the larger machine would be much stouter than those of the smaller *vallus*; if they were too long, the balance of the cart would be affected, and control by the driver of the varying height would be difficult. Jope (*HT*, I, 96, fig. 64), reproducing the earlier drawing made by Quilling, correctly shows the driver walking beside the *carpentum*, controlling its direction, and raising or lowering the teeth by means of the shaft beside him, in contrast to the driver on the Arlon relief (above, p. 162), who controls the height from behind by applying or releasing his weight on the shafts.

7. *Size and weight of the machines*

We have no means of determining the size of the larger machine. E. P. Fouss (*Le pays gaumais*, XIX, 1958, 150 ff.) has attempted to estimate the dimensions of the Buzenol *vallus* by comparing the proportions of the driver, the animal, and certain parts of the machine. His calculations give

[1] Espérandieu, *Gaule*, t. IV, no. 3522 (Dijon), t. V, nos. 4031, 4092 (Arlon), t. VI, no. 5759 (Neumagen).

[2] *Saalburgjahrb.* III (1912), 68 ff., Abb. 27, 28. The first of these wheels has a diameter of 88 cm, the second is slightly smaller; each of them is fitted with ten spokes.

[3] See Hopfen, *FIATR*, s.v. 'Yoke and harness systems', p. 22, fig. 11. There are no difficulties about the harnessing required for Palladius' machine, but the lighter *vallus* presents harnessing problems which, owing chiefly to the fragmentary state of the evidence, still await solution. For a full treatment of these problems see my article, 'Gallo-Roman harvesting machines' (*Latomus* (forthcoming)).

the width of the toothed frame as between 1 m. 20 and 1 m. 30 (*c.* 4 ft and 4 ft 3 in.), and the width including the wheels as between 1 m. 44 and 1 m. 54 (*c.* 4 ft 8 in. and 5 ft). This latter width corresponds very closely with the known widths of wheel-ruts in the streets of a number of Gallic cities. A similar calculation gives the wheel-diameter as approximately 70–75 cm or 2 ft 3 in.–2 ft 6 in. This, as M. Renard points out (*art. cit.* p. 97), makes them smaller than many surviving carriage-wheels, which is precisely what we should expect. The wheels would need to be high enough to allow sufficient ground-clearance between the earth and the bottom of the container. On the other hand, wheels of too large a diameter would involve too severe a 'dip' in adjusting the teeth to the height of the crop. The wheels of the Buzenol *vallus* have ten spokes, which is the most common arrangement on Gallo-Roman monuments depicting animal-drawn vehicles. There is a remarkable contrast between the well-balanced design of the Buzenol *vallus* and the clumsy appearance of even the most satisfactory reconstructions of Palladius' machine; this impression is accentuated by the solid, heavy wheels which appear on all the reconstructions, and for which there is no warrant in the sources.

It is impossible to believe that Gallic wagon-builders, whose technical skill is very evident from our abundant monumental sources, were incapable of building a better-designed machine, and it is not surprising to find E. A. Thompson setting Nachtweh's reconstruction of the *vallus* alongside the quaint war-machines of the Anonymus' *De Rebus Bellicis* with the comment: 'If the machine of Pliny and Palladius were not known to have been successfully used, we may be sure that scholars would have dismissed it as far-fetched, wrong-headed and impracticable' (*A Roman Reformer and Inventor*, Oxford, 1952, p. 81). These observations were made long before the Buzenol discovery, of which E. P. Fouss wrote that its perfect adaptation of form to function made it not only 'un chef-d'œuvre de technique élémentaire, mais aussi d'élégance rustique' (*art. cit.*).

8. *The reconstructed vallus at Buzenol*

The small-scale model of the Buzenol *vallus* in wood, made by E. P. Fouss, and now in the Musée Gaumais at Virton, South Belgium, is light in weight, and on the whole carefully constructed. The blades, however, are flat, instead of curved upwards at the points, and the outer edges of the frame are not splayed out so as to draw the stalks in, and prevent the wheels from being clogged by corn left standing as the machine moves forward. Close observation of the scultured slab shows that both these features are present, and an experiment, made subsequently to the discovery of the slab, has proved that both are essential to the successful operation of the imple-

ment. A full-size replica of the *vallus* was constructed and put into operation on a field of wheat, using two labourers and a donkey.

The replica is now on the site behind the museum at Buzenol. It was constructed of heavy timber, the wheels were too large and too heavy, the teeth were perfectly flat, and the edges of the frame were not splayed out. Consequently the machine was not successful; it was too heavy for the animal, the wheels became entangled, the absence of curvature in the blades impeded the essential scooping action, and the wooden edges proved unable to make an effective cut.

It is to be hoped that a fresh attempt will be made to construct a working model from which the above-mentioned faults have been eliminated, since it is only by such exact experiments that the working of such machines can be fully understood and their economic potential assessed.

9. *Merits and defects of the reaping machines*

Pliny offers no comment, but Palladius fully appreciates the economic advantage of the machine, and refers to the saving effected both in man-power and in time. He gives no precise information about the savings effected, beyond stating that the whole process is completed in a few hours. Since man-days per *iugerum* is the regular base for calculations of time expended on various operations,[1] it is tempting to assume that Palladius' reference to 'a few journeys up and down' (7. 2. 4) means on a field of one *iugerum*; even this would not help us very much, since the time reference to the space of a few hours (*loc. cit.*) is almost as vague. Columella (2. 12. 1) gives an average of $1\frac{1}{2}$ man-days per *iugerum* for reaping wheat. On the basis of Fouss's calculation of the width of the Buzenol *vallus* (*art. cit.* fig. 6), a field of one *iugerum* would occupy the machine for two hours. Even if we assume two workmen per machine, this is equivalent to four man-hours per *iugerum* against twelve for manual reaping. A better result could be expected from the larger machine. Against these savings must be set a number of defects as compared with manual reaping. These include tearing of the heads, clogging of the teeth, and considerable losses of grain, apart from damage to the straw through trampling. In assessing the importance of these factors we should first remember that the use of the machines was restricted to large estates, given up presumably to wheat production, where losses under the first two heads would be compensated by savings in time and man-power. The man-power aspect is fully discussed below (see the section on the economics of the *vallus*, pp. 170 f.). As for the losses in grain and straw, Kolendo (*art. cit.* pp. 1107 ff.) draws attention to the importance of sheep- and swine-raising in north-east Gaul (Varro, *RR*

---

[1] See my article, 'The productivity of labour in Roman agriculture', *Antiquity*, xxxix (1965), 102 ff.

1. 53, etc.), and the fallen grains and the straw would provide useful fodder after the harvest (see *CIL* VI, 2305–6—a rustic calendar for the month of August—also Pliny 18. 300).

Where the operating units are large enough and the soil fertile, these losses are not economically important. Furthermore, there was the special hazard over most of north-west Europe of a breakdown in the weather at harvest-time. August is notoriously a wet month in these areas, whereas the earlier harvesting season in Italy often exposed the farmer to a quite different hazard. There it was not a disastrous break in the dry weather that was feared, but rather a persistent succession of windless days that forced him to adopt the tedious process of winnowing with the winnowing-fan (see Part I, s.v. 'ventilabrum', pp. 32 ff.).

10. *The economics of the reaping machine*

In Italy, where intensive methods on relatively small farming units generally prevailed, the introduction of a harvesting machine could not be justified. Neither Varro, whose *De Re Rustica* no doubt preceded the invention, nor Columella, who may have known of it but rightly judged it to be irrelevant to the needs of Italian farmers, mentions it. That the saving of manpower was important in Gaul in the time of Pliny is clear from 18. 261 where, although the text is far from sound, it is evident that labour was saved in haymaking by the use of a larger and more efficient two-handed scythe (see under 'falx faenaria', pp. 100 ff.). The shortage will have been most acute at harvest-time when hired labour was most frequently employed. Doubts have been expressed about the validity of the labour-saving argument, on the grounds that there is unlikely to have been any shortage of man-power in Gaul during the Early and Middle Empire; M. Renard (*art. cit.* p. 321) cites archaeological evidence for a high density of population. But this may still be consistent with a shortage of agricultural labour. There are several references in the agricultural literature of the period to high labour costs making it unprofitable to harvest a crop (e.g. Pliny 18. 38), and the growing prosperity of Gaul during the first two centuries of our era would easily account for such shortages of casual labour.

In a recent paper M. I Finley[1] has discussed the failure of the Romans to raise productivity to any significant extent so as to meet the challenge presented by the ever-increasing burden of taxation on the land. In the course of the discussion the *vallus* is described as a 'rude, ox-powered mechanical reaper . . . used on the latifundia in the northern districts of Gaul'. Finley regards the *vallus* as an isolated invention which neither spread

[1] M. I Finley, 'Technical innovation and economic progress in the ancient world', *Econ. Hist. Rev.* 2nd ser. XVIII, I (1965), 29–45.

to other areas nor stimulated the development of labour-saving machinery in other branches of agriculture (*art. cit.* p. 30). Finley's first contention lies outside the scope of this study, but his second point demands consideration here. The first thing to be considered is that of the possible areas into which the *vallus* might have been introduced with advantage. We should need to look for wheat-producing areas in which both the nature of the terrain itself made for large, flat, open fields, and where the existing pattern of land use would not have obstructed the employment of new methods of harvesting. The spread of a new agricultural invention is also affected by the availability of suitable areas for its use in reasonably close proximity to the original source.[1] In the absence of contrary evidence we must assume that the *vallus* was invented in some part of north-east Gaul, that its use extended eastwards to the Moselle, and so to within close proximity to the Rhine frontier; westwards it has been found at Reims, and may have extended into the Paris basin. Beyond these rough limits a long distance separates the Gallic *latifundia* from major producing areas with similar conditions. Of these Egypt, the most important wheat-producer, is ruled out, since it never appears to have suffered from any shortage of agricultural labour. Elsewhere in the Mediterranean area the major factor working against the use of the *vallus* would seem to be the growth habit of autumn-sown wheat. The sowing rate is normally half that required in more temperate areas, and the tillering habit of the plant, plus the generally thinner crop, will probably have ruled out the adoption of a mechanical reaper, quite apart from the loss of the straw to which Palladius refers (*RR* 7. 2 *fin.*).[2]

Reference should also be made here to another important invention, the wheeled plough. In his very brief reference to the wheeled plough Pliny says that the people of the Raetian area of Gaul have recently invented an addition to an existing type of plough in the form of a pair of small wheels (for text and technical discussion see pp. 141 ff.). It is possible that the inhabitants of this area obtained their new plough from Gaul (on the linguistic evidence see Appendix G, p. 213). Other evidence of its use in Gaul is discussed by J. Kolendo (*art. cit.* pp. 1108–9), who makes the significant comment that the wheeled plough both reduces the labour of hoeing, and produces an even tilth with no ridges, thus making the ground very suitable for reaping with the *vallus*.

---

[1] It is worth remarking that the spread of the heavy plough of the early Middle Ages, which depended on the interaction of a number of interlocking elements, including animal husbandry and land tenure, was remarkably slow, covering a period of several centuries (see Lynn White, jr., *Medieval Technology and Social Change*, Oxford, 1962, pp. 41 ff., esp. 53 ff.).

[2] See my article, 'Wheat farming in Roman times', *Antiquity*, XXXVII (1963), 209.

Conclusions

Thus the reaping machine, and possibly the wheeled plough, were employed in areas where the special conditions prevailing both in regard to the size of agricultural units and to supplies of man-power tended to favour the use of labour- and time-saving methods of production. This pattern is quite consistent with the incomplete information presented in our sources. It is clear that these developments were exceptional, and for that reason they deserve special attention.[1] Much detailed research needs to be carried out on the sites of the Gallic *latifundia*, and particularly on the pattern of land-use, before the full significance of these technical inventions can be apprehended.

Monuments

(*a*) *Extant representations.* (i) The Tableau of the Seasons from the central arch of the Porte de Mars at Reims (see Plate 13). Still *in situ*. From recent photographs it is evident that there has been considerable deterioration since Bence's drawings were made.[2]

(ii) The Arlon relief, now in the museum at Arlon, South Belgium. There is an excellent replica in the Musée Gaumais at Virton (*Le pays gaumais*, 1963–4, p. 31, fig. 8). The original panel is at present (1964) in an outside courtyard, in a position where it is impossible to study the details of the design. The relief is also reproduced by Rostovtzeff (*SEHRE*, 2nd ed. Oxford, 1958, pl. 37, 4), and by E. Espérandieu, *Gaule*, t. v, no. 4037.

(iii) The Buzenol relief, now in the museum recently erected on the site at Montauban-Buzenol, South Belgium. A replica has been placed in the original position of the find, and there is another in the Musée Gaumais at Virton.

(iv) The Trier fragment, discovered in 1890, now in the Rheinisches Landesmuseum, Trier, West Germany. The monument has been photographed, reconstructed and discussed briefly by H. Cüppers in *Trierer Zeitschr.* (1964).

(*b*) *Extant specimens.* None. The small model and the full-scale reconstruction are discussed on p. 207.

---

[1] On the historic division between the extensive *latifundia* of north-east Gaul and the intensive pattern of land-use in the remainder of the country, a division which has persisted into modern times, see for example R. Dion, *Essai sur la formation du paysage rural français* (Tours, 1934). On problems of productivity in wheat cultivation, 'Wheat farming in Roman times', *Antiquity*, xxxvii (1963), 207–12.

[2] The reliefs, which are in a difficult position for successful photography, were recently (1961) photographed by P. Jahan. Their present condition, as revealed by these photographs, is reported by H. Stern ('Le cycle des mois dans les reliefs de la Porte de Mars', in *Hommages à Albert Grenier*, *Coll. Latomus*, 1962, pp. 1441–6).

Survival

None known. It is worth remarking, however, that the general design of the earliest modern reaping machine which actually worked, that of Patrick Bell (manufactured in the 1850's and marketed as the Beverley reaper), is very similar in general appearance to the *vallus*. The main difference is that in Bell's machine the crop was swept on to the knives by means of rotating sails. The motive power was supplied, as in the *vallus*, from the rear, but in this case by a pair of horses. A similar type of machine, known as Ridley's stripper, was extensively used in Australia during the nineteenth century, and a few machines of the same type were manufactured in England in the late 1940's, but were soon eclipsed by combine harvesters designed to meet English conditions.

CATALOGUE RAISONNÉ
OF ALL IMPLEMENTS
ILLUSTRATED IN THE TEXT

MANUAL IMPLEMENTS

1 Pala (Roman)   p. 17

Pointed iron spade, with tapering sides, made of two plates with an inset socket for the handle.

Handle normally long and straight, with no hand-grip. For trenching and turning over the soil. The annexed example is unusually long in the blade, for deep digging in vineyard or orchard.

From Pompeii.

Petrie, *TW*, pl. 67, no. 22; now in the National Museum, Naples (inv. no. 71764).

Dimensions: length of blade: 30 cm; width at top: 18·8 cm.

2 Pala (Italian)   p. 20

Spade with iron blade, triangular in shape, curving only slightly from the line of the handle; long, straight handle with no hand-grip.

From Mandanice, near Messina, N.E. Sicily.

Jaberg–Jud, *Atlas*, Karte 1429, no. 23, P 819.

Italian name: 'pala'.

Dimensions: blade: 29 cm deep, 33 cm wide; handle: 144 cm.

3 Bipalium (Roman)   p. 20

Spade with iron blade, fitted with a cross-bar for greater penetration than the ordinary *pala*, which it otherwise closely resembles.

From a sepulchral bas-relief.

R. Fabretti, *Inscriptionum antiquarum* . . . , Romae 1679, c. VIII, no. LX, p. 574.

Rich, *Dict. Ant.* s.v. 'bipalium', p. 86.

Daremberg–Saglio, t. I, pl. 7, p. 711, fig. 859.

4 Bipalium (Italian)   p. 23

Spade with iron blade, triangular in shape, with a point for penetrating the ground, fitted with a single, adjustable foot-rest for deeper penetration. Straight handle, with no hand-grip.

From Pescarolo, near Cremona, N. Italy.

Jaberg–Jud, *Atlas*, Karte 1429, no. 27, P 285.

Italian name: 'la vanga Cremonezza'.

Dimensions: blade: 18 cm deep, 25 cm wide; handle: 90 cm long.

5 Bipalium (Italian)   p. 23

Spade with iron blade, shaped like an isosceles triangle with a rounded point, fitted with an adjustable foot-rest for deeper penetration; edges of blade somewhat dished; blade set at a shallow angle with the line of the handle; long straight handle, with no hand-grip.

From Pescarolo, near Cremona, N. Italy.

Jaberg–Jud, *Atlas*, Karte 1429, no. 28, P 285.

Italian name: 'la vanga bersana'.

Dimensions: blade: 32 cm deep, 30 cm wide; handle: 153 cm long.

6 Scudicia (Italian)   p. 25

Short-handled spade with iron blade, very concave, with straight sides meeting in a sharp point; no hand-grip. For trenching and removing soil around vines and orchard-trees.

From Campania, Central Italy.

L. Savastano, *Arboricoltura*, p. 743, fig. 259, v.

Italian name: 'vanga accartocciata da cavatore'.

Dimensions: blade: 24 cm deep; 12 cm wide; handle: 66 cm long.

7 Pala cum ferro (Gallo-Roman)   p. 27

Wooden spade of rectangular pattern, fitted with iron sheath around blade, providing a sharp cutting edge.

From Compiègne, N.E. France.

Now in the Museum of National Antiquities, Saint-Germain-en-Laye, Paris.

S. Reinach, *Cat. Ill.* fig. 279, no. 15914 a.

See also P. Corder, 'Roman spade-irons from Verulamium', *Arch. Journ.* C (1945), 224–31; L. Schmidt, 'Spatenforschungen...', Wien, 1953, 76 ff.

8 Rutrum (Roman)   p. 28

Long-handled shovel-shaped spade, capable both of turning over the soil and of shifting soil from place to place. Blade wide, rounded at the end, and dished, set at an angle of *c.* 20° to the handle. Handle slightly recurved.

From Saalburg, near Frankfurt, W. Germany.

Now in the Saalburg Museum.

Blümlein, *Bilder*, p. 86, Abb. 267, no. 5.

Dimensions: blade: 24 cm wide, 24 cm deep; handle: 84 cm long.

9 Rutrum (Roman) p. 29
Medium-handled, shovel-shaped spade, capable both of turning over the soil and of shifting soil from place to place. Blade wide, rounded at the end and dished. Set at an angle of *c.* 20° to the handle. Handle straight, with hand-grip in form of cross-bar.

From Saalburg, near Frankfurt, W. Germany.

Now in the Saalburg Museum.

Blümlein, *Bilder*, p. 86, Abb. 267.

Dimensions: blade: 17 cm wide at top, 12·6 cm deep; handle: 70 cm long.

10 Ventilabrum (Cretan) p. 32
Of similar type to the Roman *ventilabrum*. Short-handled winnowing implement, of wood, handle straight, slightly backward-curving, blade rectangular in profile, but strongly dished, and terminating in a series of widely spaced teeth.

From Crete: formerly in the Fitzwilliam Museum, Cambridge.

Now in the Museum of Archaeology and Ethnology, Cambridge. (cat. no. 1901. 285).

J. E. Harrison, *JHS*, XXIII (1903), 303, fig. 9.

Dimensions: tines: 10 cm long; maximum width of blade: 25 cm; length of handle: 100 cm; total length: 128 cm.

11 Ventilabrum (Greek—modern) p. 34
Simple winnowing-shovel, commonly used in combination with a fork, the fork being used to separate the broken straw from the chaff and grain, the shovel then being employed to toss the mixture into the wind to separate the grain.

From Tripolis, Arcadia, Greece; purchased there by R. C. Bosanquet.

Harrison, *JHS*, XXIV (1904), 246, fig. 3; cf. *ibid.* 248, fig. 6 (from Palestine).

Dimensions: shovel: 44 cm long, 27 cm wide; handle: 158 cm long.

12 Ventilabrum (Italian) p. 35
Four-pronged wooden winnowing-fork; straight handle; wide wooden tines set fairly close together at an angle of *c.* 30° to the line of the handle, the tines slightly curved to assist in holding the material to be winnowed.

From Pescarolo, near Cremona, N. Italy.

Jaberg–Jud, *Atlas*, Karte 1485, no. 1, P 285.

Italian name: 'la forca da ventolare'.

Dimensions: tines: 25 cm. long, 34 cm wide; total length: 140 cm.

13 Ventilabrum (Italian) p. 35
Narrow shovel with high sides and a straight handle, used for winnowing. Plain shovels of this type are found as early as vth–dynasty Egypt.

From Pescarolo, near Cremona, N. Italy.

Jaberg–Jud, *Atlas*, Karte 1485, no. 10, P 285.

Italian name: 'la pala da ventolare'.

Dimensions: length of shovel: 40 cm; total length: 120 cm.

14 Sarculum (Roman) p. 33
Small digging-hoe with shield-shaped blade set at right-angles to the straight handle.

From a bas-relief depicting a scene in the Circus. This *sarculum* was used for digging a trench to mark off an area for athletic contests.

Provenance not stated.

Rich, *Dict. Ant.* s.v. 'sarculum', p. 574.

15 Dolabra (Roman) p. 36
Long-handled iron axe; the blade is double-headed, one side being furnished with a sharp cutting blade, the edge of which lies parallel to the haft, the other side with a crooked pick.

From Aquileia, N.E. Italy. Taken from a sepulchral monument, which also contains the inscription DOLABRAR(IVS) COL(LEGII) FAB(RVM), the deceased being an axe-maker.

CIL v, 908; *Diz. Epigr.* fasc. 61, p. 1929, s.v. 'dolabrarius'.

Rich, *Dict. Ant.* s.v. 'dolabra', p. 246 (*a*).

16 Ligo (Roman) p. 37
Heavy mattock with split blade (*fractus ligo*) curving inwards, to enable the operator to clear the broken clods. Used in both Roman and modern times for breaking ground on slopes too difficult for ploughing, and in garden cultivation.

Provenance not stated. From an engraved gem depicting Saturn as an agricultural labourer.

Rich, *Dict. Ant.* s.v. 'ligo', p. 383.

17 Ligo (Italian)   p. 39
Heavy, long-handled mattock with short blade, for breaking ground in hilly country.

From Mirano, in the estuary of the Po, near Venice, N. Italy.

Jaberg–Jud, *Atlas*, Karte 1429, no. 1, P 375.

Italian name: 'la sapa'.

Dimensions: blade: 22 cm deep, 8 cm wide; handle: 170 cm long.

18 Ligo (Italian)   p. 39
Long-handled heavy digging mattock, with wedge-profiled blade, tapering from cutting edge to junction with haft.

From S. Elpidio a Mare, S. of Ancona, E. Italy.

Jaberg–Jud, *Atlas*, Karte 1429, no. 4, P 559.

Italian name: 'la sapa'.

Dimensions: blade: 17 cm deep, 14 cm wide (edge), 8 cm wide (haft); handle: 150 cm long.

19 Ligo (Italian)   p. 39
Short-handled heavy mattock with split blade for easier penetration into hard ground.

From Camaiore, in the hills N.W. of Lucca, N.W. Italy.

Jaberg–Jud, *Atlas*, Karte 1429, no. 7, P 520.

Italian name: 'il marone'.

Dimensions: blade: 15 cm deep, 10 cm wide; handle: 110 cm long.

20 Ligo (Italian)   p. 40
Short-handled heavy mattock with split blade, for digging in hard ground. Sides of blade shaped out towards cutting edges, which are square.

From Omignano in the foothills of the Alps, N. of Milan, N. Italy.

Jaberg–Jud, *Atlas*, Karte 1429, no. 8, P 740.

Italian name: 'la tsappa'.

Dimensions: blade: 30 cm deep, 25 cm wide (across blades), 12 cm wide (at haft).

21 Marra (Italian)   p. 40
Long-handled mattock fitted with a long narrow blade, which by its design as well as by its name ('marrucola') suggests a descendant of the Roman *marra*.

From Carmignano, near Acerra, Campania, Central Italy.

Jaberg–Jud, *Atlas*, Karte 1429, no. 3, P 522.

Italian name: 'la marrucola'.

Dimensions: blade: 38 cm deep, 8 cm wide; handle: 140 cm long.

22 Sarculum (Gallo-Roman)   p. 43
Swan-neck hoe with spear-shaped blade, for light tillage. Fitted with a long iron socket for additional strength. The handles of this type are usually backward-curving. Angle of hoe with shaft, *c*. 70°. The type is still commonly used by gardeners.

From Compiègne, N.E. France. Now in the Museum of National Antiquities, Saint-Germain-en-Laye, Paris.

Reinach, *Cat. Ill.* fig. 279, no. 15880 A. Cf. *ibid.* nos. 15880, 15881.

French name: 'sarcloir à lâme triangulaire'.

Dimensions: blade: 15 cm long, 6 cm wide (max).; socket: 40 cm long.

23 Sarculum (Gallo-Roman)   p. 46
Large swan-neck hoe with spear-shaped blade and short thick handle. The surface of the blade is scooped.

From Compiègne, N.E. France.

Reinach, *Cat. Ill.* fig. 279, no. 15881.

Dimensions: blade: 18 cm long, 6 cm wide (max.); socket: 20 cm long (measured straight).

24 Sarculum (French)   p. 46
This shallow-bladed French weeding-hoe or 'sarcloir' has the swan-neck structure typical of some surviving *sarcula*, but the blade is of a different shape from any known from Roman times.

From the Paris basin.

Larousse du XX° siecle, t. vi, s.v. 'sarcloir'.

Dimensions: not given.

25 Sarculum (Italian)   p. 47
This common Italian implement, known as the 'zappetta da cavatore', is a small digging and cultivating hoe used for the same range of operations as those performed with the *sarculum*. The implement illustrated here is one of a series[1] used in vine and orchard cultivation; its chief use is for turning over the soil so as to keep down weeds and aerate the surface soil. The square blade bends inwards from the socket to form an angle of *c*. 70° to the handle.

[1] See nos. 6 and 26.

From Campania, Central Italy.

Savastano, *Arboricoltura*, p. 743, fig. 259, II.

Dimensions: blade: 20 cm long, 11 cm wide; handle: 60 cm long.

26 Sarculum (Italian)   p. 47
Light, pear-shaped digging-hoe with pointed iron dibble at end of handle. One of a group of five specialized implements used for trenching and root-cleaning of vines and orchard trees (see nos. 6 and 25). The blade is pear-shaped to avoid wounding the plant while the soil is being removed in the process of 'ablaqueatio', and the dibble is used for clearing the earth from the roots.

From Central Italy.

Savastano, *Arboricoltura*, p. 743, fig. 259, III.

Italian name: 'la zappetta da cavatore appuntita con piolo ferrato'.

Dimensions: blade: 22 cm long, 10 cm wide; dibble: 15 cm long; handle: 57 cm long.

27 Bidens (Roman?)   p. 47
Heavy two-tined *rastrum*, the long tines widely set, and pointed, with slight inward curvature. For breaking heavy ground, and destroying clods left after ploughing. Fitted with handle to show the complete implement.

For shape of tines see no. 29.

From Greece (Roman period?).

Now in the Polytechnic Museum, Athens.

Petrie, *TW*, pl. 67, no. 52.

Dimensions: length of tines: 24 cm; gap between tines: 8·4 cm; thickness of tines: 1·5 cm.

28 Bidens (Gallo-Roman)   p. 49
A double-bladed implement of the same type as no. 27, consisting of a pair of parallel heart-shaped blades, used for removing the earth from the base of the plant in the process known as 'ablaqueatio'. The shape is designed to prevent wounding of the plant.

From a Gallo-Roman find near Autun (Augustodunum) in Central France.

Now in the Museum at Autun.

Billiard, *La Vigne*, p. 323.

Dimensions: not given. The blades are set slightly inwards from the cross-bar.

29 Bidens (Greek—Roman period)   p. 50
Heavy two-tined *rastrum*, the long tines widely set, and pointed, with slight inward curvature. For breaking heavy ground, and destroying clods left after ploughing. For reconstruction of the implement with handle, see no. 27.

From Greece (Roman period).

Now in the Polytechnic Museum, Athens (see no. 27).

30 Bidens (Roman)   p. 50
Short-handled double-bladed hoe. The flat blades are curved to form a horse-shoe, socketed at the top of the curve to receive the handle, which is straight and set at an acute angle to the blades. For surface tilling and weeding in orchard and garden.

From the Terence MS in the Vatican Library (Vat. lat. 3226), at *Heaut.* I, i, 36.

R. Billiard, *L'Agriculture*, p. 58, fig. 2.

31 Bidens (Italian)   p. 52
A heavy two-pronged *rastrum* of the same type as no. 27, but contemporary. The thick prongs are set at an angle of *c.* 80° to the handle. The prongs are wider at the extremities than at the junction.

From S. Elpidio a Mare, S. of Ancona, E. Italy.

Italian name: 'l'abbidente'.

Jaberg-Jud, *Atlas*, Karte 1429, no. 18, P 559.

Dimensions: blade: 27 cm deep, 13 cm wide (at ends); handle: 127 cm long.

32 Rastrum quadridens (Roman)   p. 52
Heavy drag-hoe, with four teeth, the outer tines curving towards the centre, the middle pair straight and shorter. For breaking heavy soils and for harrowing and clod-smashing after ploughing.

From the Naples area.

Now in the National Museum, Naples (uncatalogued).

Petrie, *TW*, pl. 67, no. 56. Scale 1:6.

Dimensions: width across top: 27 cm; length of outer tines: 6 cm; length of inner tines: 7 cm.

33 Capreolus (Portuguese)   p. 58
No implement identifiable as a *capreolus* has been found, or located on a monument. The name requires a diminutive two-pronged hoe, with blades shaped like the horns of the wild goat, and set close together. The implement illustrated here is a Portuguese two-tined digging-hook (dimensions not given).

Hopfen, *FIATR*, p. 42, fig. 27 *b*.

34 Securis (Roman)   p. 60

Simple single-bladed socketed axe, used by carpenters and coopers. The shapes vary enormously in this group; see, for example, Reinach, *Cat. Ill.* fig. 272; Petrie, *TW*, pl. 9.

From Alise, Côte-d'Or, France. Now in the Museum of National Antiquities, Saint-Germain-en-Laye.

Reinach, *Cat. Ill.* fig. 272, no. 20217.

Dimensions: total length of axe-head: 22 cm; width of cutting edge: 5 cm.

35 Ascia/securis (Italian)   p. 60

Adze-axe (modern) but of similar shape to surviving implements of the type.

From S. Elpidio a Mare, S. of Ancona, E. Italy.

Jaberg–Jud, *Atlas*, Karte 1429, no. 19, P 559.

Dimensions: length of blades (total): 41 cm; width of adze-blade: 6 cm; length of handle: 100 cm.

36 Dolabra (Roman)   p. 61

Heavy adze-axe, resembling the modern English mattock, except that the adze section is subsidiary to the heavy axe. For working in woodland areas, where the axe-head was used for felling and chopping out stumps, and the adze for cutting roots.

From Pompeii, Central Italy.

Now in the National Museum, Naples (inv. no. 72012 F).

Petrie, *TW*, pl. 14, no. 54. Cf. Cichorius, *Traianssäule*, Taf. LXXXVIII, 117, Bild 316 (a felling and clearing scene).

Dimensions: total length: 34 cm; width of axe-blade: 6 cm; length of axe: 12 cm; length of adze: 16 cm.

37 = Fig. 15.   p. 62

38 Dolabra (Roman)   p. 63

Small adze-axe, of the same straight type as Fig. 36, but with wide axe-blade. For chopping out stumps and cutting roots in wooded land (especially in clearing old vineyards).

From Boscoreale, Vesuvius area, Central Italy.

Petrie, *TW*, pl. 14, no. 53.

Dimensions: total length: 19 cm; width of axe-blade: 4·8 cm; length of axe: 6 cm; width of adze: 1·6 cm; length of adze: 8 cm.

39 Dolabra (Roman)   p. 64

Small short-handled hatchet, with wide cutting edge, and twisted, upturned pick. From a log-splitting scene on Trajan's Column. The upturned pick was probably used for log-rolling.

Cichorius, *Traianssäule*, Taf. LIII, 73, Bild 189.

40 Dolabella (Roman)   p. 65

Small *dolabra*, with a short handle, and an axe-head balanced on the opposite side by a down-turned pick. Used, especially in the vineyard, for removing dead wood and loosening the earth around the roots of vines (*ablaqueatio*). Similar to Fig. 39, but with down-turned pick.

From a sepulchral marble (provenance not given).

Rich, *Dict Ant.* s.v. 'dolabella', p. 246.

41 Ascia (Roman)   p. 66

Adze-hammer, the adze-blade being attached by means of bands to a straight handle; the opposite end is reduced to a rod ending in a ball-hammer. An essential tool in carpentry for shaping and smoothing wood.

From Pompeii, Central Italy.

Now in the National Museum, Naples (inv. no. 71959).

Petrie, *TW*, pl. 18, no. 140.

Dimensions: total length: 26 cm; width of adze-blade: 2 cm; width of strap: 5·6 cm; length of adze section: 12 cm; length of hammer: 12 cm; length of iron brace: 12·5 cm.

42 Ascia/rastrum (Gallo-Roman)   p. 67

Double-headed implement, consisting of an adze on one side, the blade being set at right-angles to the line of the haft, balanced by a two-tined *rastrum* (i.e. a *bidens*) on the other. The type still survives (Fr. 'serfouette'). Used for breaking up ground, clearing and hoeing.

From Compiègne, N.E. France.

Reinach, *Cat. Ill.* fig. 277, no. 15869.

Dimensions: total length: 17 cm; length of *ascia*: 6 cm; length of *rastrum*: 6 cm; gap between tines: 2 cm.

43 Ascia/rastrum (Romano-British)   p. 67

Heavy dual-purpose implement with a very wide blade, curved cutting edge, and strong, short tines.

From Lydney, Gloucester, S.W. England.

181

Petrie, *TW*, pl. 67, no. 18.

Dimensions: total length: 39 cm; approx. width of ascia-blade: 19 cm; length of tines: 11 cm; gap between tines: 6 cm; maximum thickness of tines: 1·8 cm.

44 Ascia/rastrum (Roman)   p. 67
Heavy, dual-purpose implement, with wide adze-blade and long, inward-curving tines.

From Roman Germany.

Saalburgjahrb. III (1912), Taf. 8, no. 17.

Dimensions: overall length: 34 cm; length of axe: 8 cm; width at edge: 6 cm; length of tines: 11 cm; thickness of tines: 8 mm; gap at points: 1·2 cm.

45 Ascia/rastrum (Roman)   p. 68
Small dual-purpose implement, consisting of a broad, short adze-blade on one side, balanced on the other by a pair of short tines, widely spaced. For breaking up and digging heavy soils; the adze-blade also used for chopping out stumps in wooded land.

From Velleia, Po Valley, N. Italy.

Now in the Parma Museum.

Petrie, *TW*, pl. 67, no. 19. Scale: 1:6.

Dimensions: total length: 15 cm; width of blade: 6·6 cm; length of tines: 4·8 cm.

46 Ascia   p. 68
Short-handled mattock with a wedge-shaped blade, used mainly for trenching and clearing land; very similar in design to the Italian farm-worker's 'zappa'.

From Trajan's Column (Cichorius, *Traianssäule*, Taf. XL, 56, Bild 139); Rich, *Dict. Ant.* s.v. 'ascia', 4, p. 62, correctly describes the figure, but the reference is incorrect.

47 Ascia/rastrum (Italian)   p. 68
Dual-purpose implement of heavy design, comprising a wide mattock blade balanced on the other side by a *bidens* with heavy, widely spaced tines. For breaking up and digging heavy ground.

From Palmoli in the mountainous Molise/Abruzzi region of Central Italy.

Jaberg–Jud, *Atlas*, Karte 1429, no. 14, P 658.

Dimensions: total length: 33 cm; blade: 9 cm wide; *bidens*: 12 cm wide; handle: 100 cm long.

48 Ascia/rastrum (Italian)   p. 68
Heavy dual-purpose implement, similar in design to no. 46, but with longer tines and blade for deeper penetration; mattock-blade tapered to cutting edge.

From Galliate on the River Ticino, W. of Milan, N. Italy.

Italian name: 'i sapi'.

Jaberg–Jud, *Atlas*, Karte 1429, no. 15, P 139.

Dimensions: total length: 45 cm; blade (at edge) 8 cm wide; *bidens*: 12 cm wide; handle: 120 cm long.

49 Cultellus (Nigerian)   p. 70
Surviving examples of the straight-bladed tree-pruning knife are comparatively rare. The annexed figure is a common matchet, as used in the forest areas of West Africa and elsewhere. The blade is usually slightly convex, with no hook, the head either straight (as here), or slightly rounded, and wider than the haft end.

From Western Nigeria (European manufacture).

Dimensions: blade: 45 cm long; haft: 16 cm long, width at end of blade: 8·4 cm.

50 Cultellus (Roman)   p. 7
Small pruning-knife with strongly recurved blade, almost semicircular in shape, with slightly curved handle. For pruning vines and orchard trees. See also Fig. 75.

Found at Nattenheim, Rhineland, W. Germany, in 1907.

Now in the Landesmuseum, Trier (inv. no. 0799).

Dimensions: length: *c.* 11·5 cm.

51 Falx messoria (Roman)   p. 7
Small semicircular sickle, for reaping millet or other small cereals.

From an inscribed brick found at Agen (*Aginnum*) on the river Garonne, S.W. France. The sickle is flanked by the inscription D(IS) M(ANIBVS), showing that it is a funerary monument. The blade is toothed, a common feature in sickles of this type.

Del Pelo Pardi, *Attrezzi*, p. 5, fig. 3.

52 Falx messoria (Roman)   p. 8
Large open-bladed sickle, plain-edged, of the balanced Roman type, for reaping wheat or barley. The blade has a large gathering curve, and half the blade lies almost in a circle around the hand, so as to give a sawing cut from the wrist.

From Pompeii.

Now in the National Museum, Naples (N. 71703, 11235–6).

Petrie, *TW*, pl. 54, no. 31.

Dimensions: span: 48 cm; width of blade (uniform): 4 cm.

53 Falx messoria (Roman) p. 80

Plain-edged balanced sickle with typical open blade, sharply bent towards the handle; back of blade reinforced.

From Pompeii, Central Italy.

Del Pelo Pardi, *Attrezzi*, p. 5, fig. 2. Cf. Petrie, *TW*, pl. 54, 33.

No dimensions given.

54 Falx messoria (Italian) p. 80

Serrated sickle, of elliptical, almost circular curvature, with a blunt tang.

From G. A. de Herrera, *Libro de Agricoltura* (Madrid, 1520), trans. into Italian by M. R. di Fabriano (Venezia, 1557).

Del Pelo Pardi, *Attrezzi*, p. 6, fig. 6 N.

No dimensions given.

55 Serrula ferrea (Roman) p. 82

Curved saw-blade attached at an acute angle to a backward-curving handle. This illustration, taken from an Egyptian painting, suggests the design of the implement mentioned by Varro (1. 50. 2) as used for reaping wheat in the Picenum district of N.E. Italy.

Rich, *Dict. Ant.* s.v. 'falx', no. 3, p. 273.

56 Falx veruculata rostrata (?) (Welsh) p. 83

This implement, mentioned only by Columella (2. 20. 3), was evidently a specialized form of reaping sickle, fitted with a spit (*veruculum*), which in this variety must have presented a beak-like appearance. No sickles answering to the requirements appear to have survived, and various interpretations, from cradle-scythes to toothed frames fitted over the blade, have been suggested (see Appendix E(2)). The figure is taken from the catalogue of an English farm implement manufacturer, of Stourbridge, Worcestershire, dated 1899. The notched tip to the blade presumably served to engage the bundle of stalks as the sickle was put in.

Dimensions: not given.

57 Falx veruculata denticulata (?) (La Tène) p. 83

Reaping sickle of open shape, mainly serrated, with a tooth-like extension forged on; a possible precursor of Columella's implement. (See Appendix E(2).)

Pre-Roman, La Tène period. Found at La Tène, Switzerland. Now in the British Museum, London (inv. no. 80. 12–14. 7).

Unlike the rest of the blade, the extension is square in section.

Dimensions: span: 32·8 cm; total length of blade: 41·7 cm; serrated section: 25·8 cm long; plain section: 7·6 cm long; 'veruculum' (square in section): 8·8 cm long; tang: 10·8 cm long.

58 Falx arboraria (Roman) p. 85

Heavy, short-handled billhook, for cutting saplings and lopping branches. Blade wide and straight, head heavily convex. Hook angled at *c.* 85°. Short, thick handle with knob to assist the grip.

From Pompeii, Central Italy.

Now in the National Museum, Naples (inv. no. 71711–17, 110514–15).

Petrie, *TW*, pl. 57, no. 44.

Dimensions: total length: 38 cm; length of blade: 22 cm; length to bend: 16 cm; maximum width of blade: 9 cm; length of bill: 9 cm; width from beak to shoulder of blade: 19 cm.

59 Falx arboraria (Roman) p. 86

Tree-pruning billhook, with crescent-shaped blade and tapered hook. The backward curve and narrow bill are typical of the implement as used in the vineyard and orchard. Handles are either socketed, as here, or tanged (see no. 60) for greater strength.

From Pompeii, Central Italy.

Now in the National Museum, Naples (inv. no. 71710).

Petrie, *TW*, pl. 57, no. 49.

Dimensions: total length: 36 cm; span: 17·2 cm; width of blade from butt to bend: 4 cm; approx. length of bill: 12 cm.

60 Falx arboraria (Roman) p. 87

Tree-pruning billhook, with crescent-shaped blade and tapering hook. The long curve of the blade, and the gathering-in shape, are typical of the implement as used in vine-growing areas (see nos. 59 and 62). Note the powerful tang.

From the Mainz district, Rhineland, W. Germany.

Now in the Römisch-Germanisches Zentralmuseum, Mainz.

Petrie, *TW*, pl. 57, no. 47.

Dimensions: total length: 38·4 cm; span: 22 cm; maximum width of blade at bend: 6·4 cm; width at butt: 5 cm; width at edge: 2·4 cm.

61 Falx arboraria (Roman)   p. 87
Short pruning-hook, for vines. The semicircular blade enables the pruner to enclose the branch to be cut. Fitted with a short tang and a metal band for the end of the handle. A beautifully designed implement.

From Rheinhessen, Rhineland, W. Germany.

Now in the Römisch-Germanisches Zentralmuseum, Mainz (inv. M. 3. 3. 4).

Petrie, *TW*, pl. 57, no. 62.

Dimensions: total length: 25 cm; span: 12 cm; maximum width of blade: 6 cm; approx. length of bill: 9 cm; length of tang: 8 cm; diameter of ring: 4 cm.

62 Falx arboraria (Roman)   p. 87
Light tree-pruning hook, of slender design, with the typical recurved blade, and a shortish bill. Socketed handle. For the vineyard and orchard.

From Boscoreale, Vesuvius district, Central Italy.

Petrie, *TW*, pl. 57, no. 48.

Dimensions: total length: 36·5 cm; span: 21·6 cm; approx. length of bill: 9 cm; maximum width of blade: 4·8 cm; length of socket: 12·8 cm.

63 Falx arboraria (Roman)   p. 87
Hedge-bill, with straight blade, short heavy hook, and projection at the back for withdrawing the branch after lopping. Long socket and handle for reaching high branches.

From Compiègne, N.E. France.

Now in the Museum of National Antiquities at Saint-Germain-en-Laye, Paris.

Reinach, *Cat. Ill.* fig. 273, no. 15894 A.

Dimensions: length of blade: 9 cm; length of socket: 32 cm; approx. length of bill: 3 cm; length of back projection: 4 cm.

64 Falx ruscaria (?) (Romano-British)   p. 89
No identifiable examples of this specialized implement appear to be known. The annexed example from Roman Britain has the short bill and straight blade required. (Contrast the vine-pruning types, Figs. 58–61.)

From Wookey, Somerset, England.

Now in the Wells Museum, Wells, Somerset.

Petrie, *TW*, p. 57, no. 42.

Dimensions: total length: 25 cm; span: 16 cm; length of bill: 4 cm; width of blade at butt: 6 cm; width of blade at bend: 4·8 cm.

65 Falx sirpicula (?) (Roman)   p. 89
Heavy tanged billhook of shallow curvature, without angle or bill. Designed for cutting reeds.

From Bretzenheim, above Mainz, W. Germany.

Now in the Römisch-Germanisches Zentralmuseum, Mainz.

Petrie, *TW*, pl. 56, no. 25.

Dimensions: total length: 34 cm; span: 18 cm; length of tang: 8 cm; maximum width of blade: 6 cm; width at butt: 4·4 cm.

66 Falcicula brevissima tribulata (?) (Gallo-Roman)   p. 90
There is complete uncertainty about this implement, mentioned only by Palladius among the agronomists, as used for cutting bracken. The implement illustrated here is taken from a sepulchral monument in the form of a brick, inscribed D(IS) M(ANIBVS), found at Agen (Aginnum) on the Garonne, S.W. France (see no. 47). A small circular serrated blade would correspond with the requirements (see also no. 51).

Del Pelo Pardi, *Attrezzi*, p. 4, fig. 3.

67 Falcastrum (Roman)   p. 91
Long-handled scythe-like implement for cutting down brambles. The blade resembles that of an open-curved sickle (as Fig. 53), but has a long tang. Described by Blümlein (*loc. cit.*) as a scythe, it is in fact a long-handled billhook.

From Cologne district, W. Germany.

Blümlein, *Bilder*, p. 88, Abb. 275 (*a*).

Dimensions: not given.

68 Falcastrum (French)   p. 93
Long-handled billhook with crescent-shaped blade, as used by French gardeners and foresters.

Larousse du XXᵉ siècle, s.v. 'croissant'.

Le Gall, p. 59.

69 Falx vinitoria (Roman)   p. 93
Vine-dresser's knife in its fully developed form, as described in detail by Columella (*RR* 4. 25.

1–3), where he also discusses the specific uses of the six parts of this multi-purpose pruning implement (see Fig. 70).

From an ancient MS of Columella.

70 Falx vinitoria (Roman)   p. 94
As Fig. 69 but enlarged, with the parts numbered for identification.

71 Falx vinitoria (Gallo-Roman)   p. 96
Vine-dresser's knife, of heavier type than Fig. 69, and lacking the *mucro* or spike; the hatchet heavier and straight-edged, the bill much heavier and thicker, the haft set back at a wider angle from the blade.

From a funeral stele in the Museum at Nîmes, S. France. (inv. no. 879. 2. 2).

Le Gall, pl. VI, 2; Espérandieu, *Gaule*, I, 472.

Dimensions: total length: 20 cm; chord: 6 cm; width at butt: 5 cm; axe projects: 3·5 cm; length of handle: 7·5 cm.

72 Falx vinitoria (Italian)   p. 96
The continuity of type in this implement is well illustrated in this example, which approximates closely in design to Fig. 69, except that it lacks a *mucro* or spike.

From a miniature painting in the Codex Virgilianus which once belonged to the poet Petrarch.

Del Pelo Pardi, *Attrezzi*, p. 14, fig. 19.

73 Falx vinitoria (Roman)   p. 96
Vine-dresser's knife of typical shape, with heavy, slightly convex *securis*, and straight, rather heavy bill (contrast the lunate *securis* and tapered bill of Fig. 69). The shape is identical to that used by Italian vine-dressers today.

Found by G. del Pelo Pardi near Benevento, Apulia.

Del Pelo Pardi, *Attrezzi*, p. 15, fig. 20.

Dimensions: not given.

74 Falcula vineatica (Roman)   p. 96
The miniature sickle, used for cutting off the bunches of ripe grapes from the vine. Sickle of open curvature, tanged.

The example illustrated has its tang bent at the end (presumably damaged).

From the Moselle valley, near Trier, W. Germany.

Blümlein, *Bilder*, p. 94, Abb. 306.

Dimensions: total length: 16 cm; span: 7 cm; point of blade to point of handle: 12 cm; maximum width of blade: 2·4 cm.

75 Falcula vineatica (Roman)   p. 97
Small grape-cutting knife with blade of billhook shape and iron haft. Corresponds well to Columella's term 'ungues ferrei' (iron hooks) at 12. 18. 2. See also Fig. 50.

From Heddernheim, W. Germany.

Now in the Historisches Museum, Frankfurt am Main (cat. no. 2299).

Loeschke, *Denkmäler vom Weinbau*, p. 13, Abb. 11, no. 7.

Dimensions: length: 13 cm; span: 4 cm; maximum width of blade: 1·4 cm; length of haft: 8 cm.

76 Falx faenaria (Roman)   p. 98
Blade of mowing-scythe, with the typical elliptical curvature. The handle end is short (unlike that of the sickle) and flattened to receive the snath or handle, which is straight, and attached by means of two rivets.

From W. Germany.

Now in the Römisch-Germanisches Zentralmuseum, Mainz (inv. no. 46. 825).

Blümlein, *Bilder*, p. 88, Abb. 275 a.

See also Petrie, *TW*, pl. 54, no. 22.

Dimensions: not given.

77 Falx faenaria (medieval French)   p. 99
Two types of mowing-scythe are reported by Pliny (18. 261): (1) the two-handed, long-handled type used on the large estates in Gaul; (2) a short, one-handed type, as here. The illustration is taken from a fourteenth-century MS in the British Museum (see Plate 1). The blade is long and deep, and terminates in an upward-curving bill, the short, stout handle is provided with a hand-grip. The medieval operator has in his left hand a long stick, the end of which is not visible, but which may be a hook for enclosing the amount to be cut, as in the English hook and sickle method of reaping corn. See also the discussion of Fig. 78 (scythette).

Dimensions (approx.): length of handle: 46 cm; length of hand-grip: 15 cm; length of blade: 30·5 cm; length of bill: 15 cm.

78 Falx faenaria (modern) p. 99

This later version of the single-handed implement (no. 74) was once widespread in north-eastern Europe. The slightly arched blade is about 46 cm long with the tang bent steeply upward, and the handle, which is somewhat shorter than the blade, is bent at the top to end in a hoof-shaped hand-grip. In his left hand the scythette-operator holds a long hook with which he separates the standing crop and clears a way for the cutting blade.

Hopfen, *FIATR*, pp. 100 f., fig. 72.

Dimensions (approx.): length of handle: 26 cm; length of hand-grip: 14 cm; length of blade: 46 cm.

79 Falx faenaria (Gallo-Roman) p. 101

Long scythe-blade with upper edge reinforced with metal. The handle-end tapers sharply to a point, and the single metal peg suggests a method of attaching the blade which resembles the modern ring-fastening. Contrast Fig. 76.

From Compiègne, N.E. France.

Now in the Museum of National Antiquities, Saint-Germain-en-Laye.

Reinach, *Cat. Ill.* fig. 278, no. 15888.

Dimensions: length from tip to tang (estimated): 55 cm; length of tang: 15 cm; maximum width of blade: 5 cm.

80 Falx faenaria (Gallo-Roman) p. 101

Short-bladed mowing-scythe, resembling in shape the British Museum example (Fig. 77), but lacking the pronounced bill. The angle at the back is square, not rounded, and there appears to be a tang-fastening.

From the Côte d'Or district, around Dijon, Central France.

Now in the Museum of National Antiquities, Saint-Germain-en-Laye.

Reinach, *Cat. Ill.* fig. 278, no. 1481, who says it might also be a sickle, which is most unlikely.

Dimensions: length from tip to tang: 25 cm; length of tang: 15 cm; maximum width of blade: 6 cm.

81 Furca (ancient Egyptian) p. 104

Pitchfork, from an Egyptian tomb, showing the most rudimentary of the types of this implement, which consisted of a suitably shaped branch of a tree.

Lepsius, *Denkmäler*, II, 80; cf. Petrie, *TW*, pl. 67, no. 41.

82 Furcilla (Italian) p. 105

Three-pronged wooden hay-fork with recurved tines, which are square in section, splayed out so as to form wide gaps at the points. For lifting and stacking hay in field or stockyard. The design is traditional and occurs all over Europe.

From Montanaro, in the foothills of the Alps, N.E. of Turin, N. Italy.

Italian name: 'la forca da paglia'.

Jaberg–Jud, *Atlas*, Karte 1485, no. 2.

Dimensions: total length: 150 cm; length of prongs: 30 cm; gap between prongs (at point): 9 cm.

83 Furcilla (Roman type) p. 106

Conjectural representation of a forked vine-prop, designed to bear the weight of the ripe clusters. Drawn to the scale of the implement recommended by Varro (1. 8. 6), viz. about 2 ft long (60 cm).

84 Furca ferrea (Roman) p. 108

Two-pronged pitchfork, of iron with a long socket for extra strength, for lifting and stacking hay or straw. The traditional set of the prongs, bowed slightly outwards from the bifurcation, and closing slightly at the points, has remained unchanged over the centuries.

From Compiègne, N.E. France.

Now in the Museum of National Antiquities, Saint-Germain-en-Laye.

Reinach, *Cat. Ill.* fig. 278, no. 29023.

Dimensions: total length (prongs + dowel): 40 cm; length of prong: 20 cm.

85 Furca ferrea (Gallo-Roman) p. 108

A three-pronged fork of strong construction with a long socket, similar in design to the northern digging-fork. The digging-fork is unknown to the Mediterranean area, and this example, from N.E. France, may be an early example of the digging-fork.

From Compiègne, N.E. France.

Now in the Museum of National Antiquities, Saint-Germain-en-Laye.

Reinach, *Cat. Ill.* fig. 278, no. 29020 (A).

Dimensions: total length (prongs + dowel): 50 cm; length of prongs: 20 cm; gap between prongs: 7 cm.

86 Furca ferrea (?Romano-British)   p. 109
Two-pronged iron pitchfork, of typical spur-shape design, for lifting and stacking hay or straw.

Found in a bog forming the bank of the old river at the junction of the Nene at Horsey, near Peterborough, England.

Rich, *Dict. Ant.* s.v. 'furca' (1), p. 308.

Dimensions: None given; probably similar to no. 78.

87 Pastinum (Roman)   p. 109
Short two-pronged fork for light surface cultivation, especially in the kitchen-garden and nursery. About the same size as the modern implement, which is three-pronged.

From Pompeii.

Now in the National Museum, Naples (inv. no. 71739).

Petrie, *TW*, pl. 67, no. 45.

Dimensions: total length: 20 cm; length of tines: 7·5 cm; distance between tines: 6 cm.

88 Pastinum (Roman)   p. 110
Small two-pronged fork, similar in shape to no. 89, but with very short, widely spaced prongs. Probably a double dibble for planting.

From Pompeii. Now in the National Museum, Naples (inv. no. 71741).

Petrie, *TW*, pl. 67, no. 44.

Dimensions: total length: 14 cm; length of tines: 3·6 cm; distance between tines: 7·2 cm.

89 Pastinum (modern)   p. 110
Long-handled planting stick for planting out seedlings. The hollowed metal head makes a hole and then serves to press the soil around the roots. Isidore's implement consists of two close-set prongs, and is still employed for this purpose under the names 'trivella' and 'cruccia'. No examples were available for illustration. The implement shown here is of traditional shape.

Hopfen, *FIATR*, p. 85, fig. 60.

Dimensions: not given.

90 Mergae (ancient Egyptian)   p. 110
Flat pieces of wood fitted with hand-grips for tossing the mixture of grain and chaff in winnowing are well known from Egyptian times onwards. *Mergae* were used for stripping the ears from the stalks, but no representations are known from Roman times. The annexed illustration is of a pair of winnowing boards in the Petrie collection of Egyptian implements now in University College London. They are shown here as representing the kind of implement required for the process. Since most of the literary references identify *mergae* as forks, it is probable that the edges were serrated. They may well have been joined together by a cord, as in the Georgian examples cited by Steensberg (p. 112).

Petrie, *TW*, pl. 78, nos. 64 and 65.

From a photograph.

Dimensions: total length: 22 cm; width: 7 cm.

91 Pecten (ancient Egyptian)   p. 113
Comb-shaped wooden implement for removing the heads of grain, leaving the straw. No specimen seems to have survived, and the illustration is conjectural, based on an Egyptian type.

From the tomb of Paheri, El Kab (Egypt).

Harrison, *JHS* XXIV (1904), fig. 2, p. 245; Egypt Exploration Fund, Eleventh Memoir, Tylor and Griffith, 1894: *The Tomb of Paheri at El Kab*, pl. iii, pp. 12–14.

92 Serrula (Roman)   p. 116
Part of a two-way saw-blade. The concave shape suggests that it is a pruning-saw rather than a carpenter's tool.

From Pompeii.

Now in the National Museum, Naples.

Petrie, *TW*, pl. 50, no. 34.

Dimensions: total length (in present incomplete state): 21 cm; width at butt: 6 cm.

93 Serrula manubriata (Roman)   p. 117
Small two-way pruning-saw. 'Scie a guichet'.

From Presles-St-Audebert, Dept. of Aisne, N.E. France.

Reinach, *Cat. Ill.* fig. 275, no. 38146.

Dimensions: total length: 32·5 cm; length of blade: 28 cm.

94 Serrula (Roman)   p. 117
Small saw with offset horn handle and straight two-way blade.

From the Roman fort at Newstead, Scotland.

J. Curle, *A Roman Frontier Post and its People* (Glasgow, 1911), pl. LXVIII, no. 6, and p. 290.

Petrie, *TW*, pl. 50, no. 33.

Dimensions: total length: 15 cm; length of blade: 8 cm.

95 Forpex (Roman)   p. 119

Pair of shears, with intersecting blades joined by spring steel for single-handed operation. For sheep-shearing.

From Pompeii, Italy. Now in the National Museum, Naples.

Petrie, *TW*, pl. 58, no. 11.

Dimensions: length (total): 17·2 cm; length of blade: 10 cm; width of blade at base: 2 cm.

96 Forpex (Roman?)   p. 119

Pair of shears, with long intersecting blades, resembling those of a scissors, joined by a spring steel rod bent outwards and flattened at the head. For sheep-shearing.

From W. Germany.

Now in the Römisch-Germanisches Zentralmuseum, Mainz (inv. no. 3. 3. 5).

Blümlein, *Bilder*, p. 96, Abb. 314 (*a*) 2.

Petrie, *TW*, pl. 58, no. 19.

Dimensions: total length: 24 cm; length of blades: 14 cm; width of blades at base: 2·8 cm.

MACHINES

97 Sole-ard: symmetrical type (Italian) p. 126
The broad flat sole (*dentale*) is triangular in shape, wider at the back where it bifurcates to receive the plough-beam (*buris*). The broad, triangular share (*vomer*) is socketed. Behind the share, a wooden upright passes through the yoke-beam and is wedged in position to support it. The ploughtail (*stiva*), which is dowelled into the end of the yoke-beam, consists of a short vertical pole with a handle (*manica*) at right-angles to it.

From Serrone, near Lagonegro, Valle di Diano, S. Italy.

Jaberg–Jud, *Atlas*, Karte 1455, no. 1, P 654; cf. Lesser, *Entstehung*, p. 307, Abb. 157 (from Viterbo, S. Tuscany).

98 Mouldboard plough (modern English) p. 126
(*a*) Modern horse-drawn general-purpose mouldboard plough (left side). Both pole and stilt are mounted on a solid steel base which in turn is welded to the sole. The coulter is mounted on this pole so as to bring its vertical cutting edge in close proximity to the horizontal cutting edge of the share. The forward end of the pole is supported on a pair of wheels, that on the land-side being much smaller in diameter than the wheel on the mouldboard side, which remains in the furrow. The stilt has two handles.

C. Davies, *Field Machinery* (London, 1949), p. 38, fig. 36.

(*b*) The same, right-hand view, showing the mouldboard. English manufacture.

C. Davies, *op. cit.* p. 48, fig. 45.

99 Beam-ard (Iraqi): (*a*) drawing; (*b*) diagram
p. 127
In this type of plough the curved yoke-beam (*temo*) is pierced by a spear-shaped body-handle unit, which is curved and inserted at a suitable angle to enable the plough to run horizontally. Note the heavy socketed share, which is turned down slightly at the point; this helps to keep the plough on an even keel. The design suggests that the beam-ard has developed from the hoe.

From C. Iraq.

Hopfen, *FIATR*, p. 46, fig. 28 (*c*).

100 Bow-ard (Spanish): (*a*) drawing; (*b*) diagram
p. 127
In this type of plough the plough-beam, which is either continuous with the yoke-beam or jointed to it, as here, is the most prominent part of the implement, being pierced by the stilt and the share-beam (see diagram). The stilt extends well forward of its junction with the plough-beam, and the tanged or bar-share (see Fig. 110 *b–d*) is gripped between the extension of the stilt and the share-beam.

From Catalonia, N.E. Spain.

Leser, *Entstehung*, p. 328, Abb. 177; cf. Abb. 176; for further discussion of these Spanish ploughs see R. Aitken, 'Virgil's plough', *JRS*, XLVI (1956), 97 ff. Aitken's theory is fully discussed in Appendix G.

101 Body-ard (Afghan): (*a*) drawing; (*b*) diagram
p. 127
This type of plough has an upward-inclined body which tapers off to form the stilt, which in turn is pierced by the yoke-beam. Used for comparatively deep tillage in soils with sufficient moisture. The ancient Etruscan body-ard from Telamon in Tuscany (Plate 10 (*a*)) is very similar in design.

From Afghanistan.

Hopfen, *FIATR*, p. 48, fig. 29 (*a*).

102 Sole-ard (Pakistani): (*a*) drawing; (*b*) diagram
p. 128
This type of plough normally has a long shallow horizontal body, which in some regions is widened out to make a triangular form, as in the Italian plough shown above (Fig. 97). This clears the bottom of the furrow (see also the plough-model from Cologne (Plate 10 (*b*))). Plough-beam (*buris*) and stilt (*stiva*) are separately inserted into the sole (*dentale*), the heel of which usually remains clear to provide a step for foot-pressure by the ploughman when required, as shown in the Cherchel mosaic (Plate 12). Plough-beam and yoke-beam are connected by a pegged joint. For surface cultivation.

Hopfen, *FIATR*, p. 50, fig. 30 (*a*).

103 Primitive one-piece plough (Etruscan)
p. 128

Etruscan bronze group from Arezzo, now in the Villa Giulia Museum, Rome. Note the heavy bands which fasten the share to the share-beam. Note also the upright stilt, which would require to be lifted to prevent the oblique share from digging in. For deep cultivation.

104 Aratrum (Roman type)　　　　p. 129
As Fig. 102, but with the parts numbered for reference.

105 One-piece ploughs　　　　　p. 131
These ploughs bear some similarity to the one-piece Etruscan model from Arezzo (Fig. 103). In types (a) and (b) the plough-beam has the solid shape of a boot-tree. Compare the Telamon model (Plate 10 (a)). Type (c) seems the closest in design to the Arezzo plough.

From three silver *denarii* of C. Marius (*c.* 82 B.C.).

Grueber, *Coins of the Roman Republic*, I, 354, nos. 2850, 2853, 2855; Gow, *art. cit.* pl. XVII, nos. 15–17.

106 Sole-ard (Cypriote)　　　　p. 131
Similar to the common Roman sole-ard (Fig. 102), but having a short pole mortised into the sole in front of the plough-beam, and piercing the latter to give support and regulate the depth. In this example plough-beam and yoke-beam are continuous, with double curvature.

Hopfen, *FIATR*, p. 50, fig. 30(d). Cf. Haudricourt–Delamarre, *L'Homme et la charrue*, p. 145, figs. 39 (from Malaga, Spain), 40 (from León, Spain).

107 Culter (Austrian)　　　　p. 133
A simple 'ground-opener', consisting of a strong steel 'tooth', curving forward slightly to the point, and with a sharp leading edge, attached to a horizontal beam which is drawn through the soil to make a preliminary cut before ploughing: 'in some parts of Europe with moist soils, the body-ard (Fig. 101) was preceded by a separate ristle (Fr. "coutrier"), a coulter-like implement, to achieve a greater depth' (Hopfen, *FIATR*, p. 47). Later this ristle was combined with the share to make the vertical and horizontal cut in the same operation. Still used in parts of Spain and Portugal, and in some Alpine districts, as a separate 'ground-opener'.

From Unterkärnten, S. Carinthia.

Leser, *Entstehung*, p. 302, Abb. 150 (after K. Rhamm).

108 (a) Socketed share (modern)　　p. 133
Socketed ploughshare of the common 'beaked' (*rostratum*) type, with chisel-shaped extension to give additional strength, and counteract wear on the sole.

Pliny's second type (18. 171).

Hopfen, *FIATR*, LII, fig. 32(3).

108 (b) Mortised share (modern)　　p. 134
Small, cusp-like share mortised into the head of the plough-beam (Pliny's third type—p. 169).

Hopfen, *FIATR*, p. 52, fig. 32(4).

108 (c) Winged share (modern)　　p. 134
Socketed ploughshare with cutting-edges at the sides to slice off roots of weeds. This type is commonly found in association with medieval wheeled ploughs (see, for example, Fig. 109 below).

Hopfen, *FIATR*, p. 52, fig. 32(2).

109 Wheeled plough (medieval French)　p. 134
Wheeled plough with coulter from a twelfth-century manuscript in the Bibliothèque Nationale, Paris (probably from northern France).

Pliny's fifth type.

Cod. Paris, Lat. 15675.

Gow, *art. cit.* p. 261, fig. 14.

For a similar primitive wheeled plough with large coulter see J. B. Passmore, *The English Plough* (Oxford, 1930), pl. II (a Saxon plough of the tenth century, from Caedmon's MS (British Museum)).

110 (a) Lapped share (Roman)　　p. 135
Very rare specimen of a Roman share from Pompeii, now in the National Museum, Naples. Much worn, especially on the right side of the lapping. The broad arrow-head tip has been broken off at its extremity.

Petrie, *TW*, pl. 67, no. 34.

Dimensions: length: 32·4 cm; maximum width: 12·6 cm, tapering to 9 cm; length of arrow head: 13·8 cm; maximum width of arrow head: 12 cm.

110 (b)–(d) Ploughshares of various types p. 135
(b) tanged, with triangular spear-head.
(c) tanged, with narrow spear-head.
(d) chisel share.

All from Hopfen, *FIATR*, p. 53.

111 Bush-harrow (cf. Vergil's 'vimineae crates')
p. 146

Sledge-type frame, the twigs being held under tension by three cross-members, two above, and one below.

From Enns, Upper Austria.

Jaberg–Jud, *Atlas*, Karte 1431, no. 3, P 5.

112 Irpex (Italian) p. 148

Italian 'erpice', consisting of a simple triangular wooden frame, strengthened by cross-members. On the undersides rows of wooden pegs (28 in all) for reducing clods and making an even tilth after ploughing.

From Campori, N. of Pisa, N.W. Italy.

Jaberg–Jud, *Atlas*, Karte 1431, no. 5, P 511.

Dimensions: not given.

113 Irpex (Italian) p. 151

Italian 'erpice', consisting of a simple rectangular wooden frame, with two battens nailed across the middle to keep the angle joints tight; underneath the longer sides two rows of wooden tines (18 in all). For clod-breaking and harrowing in heavier soils than Fig. 112.

From Camaiore, N. of Pisa, N.W. Italy.

Jaberg–Jud, *Atlas*, Karte 1431, no. 6, P 520.

Dimensions: frame: 2·3 m × 1 m; depth of tines: 7·5 cm.

114 Traha (ancient Egyptian) p. 152

Light animal-drawn drag (Lat. 'traha'). The sides of the sled are joined by five wooden rods.

From an Egyptian tomb.

Rich, *Dict. Ant.* s.v. 'traha', p. 681.

No dimensions given.

115 Tribulum p. 152

Heavy animal-drawn threshing-sledge, fitted on the underside with rows of flints or metal teeth.

Rich, *Dict. Ant.* s.v. 'tribulum', p. 685.

No provenance given.

116 Tribulum (Cypriote) p. 156

Fig. 115 viewed from the underside to show the arrangement of the teeth.

From Cyprus.

R. J. Forbes, *A History of Technology*, II, 106, fig. 70 (from a photograph taken by O. G. S. Crawford).

Dimensions: length: 1 m; width at front, 20 cm, tapering to 17 cm at rear.

117 (a) Plostellum poenicum (Egyptian threshing-sledge) p. 156

Heavy threshing-sledge of similar design to the *traha* (Fig. 114), but equipped with two sets of four small wheels, and one set of three, on its three axles. The three central wheels are positioned so as to cover the intervals between the wheels of the front and rear axles (see Fig. 117 (b)). The driver is mounted on a seat athwart the machine so that advantage may be taken of his weight while he drives the sledge round the threshing-floor. The drawing is of an Egyptian machine, the 'noreg', of similar design to the machine mentioned by Varro (*RR* I. 52. 1) and known as the 'Punic wagonette' (*plostellum poenicum*).

Wilkinson, *Manners and Customs of the Ancient Egyptians*, 2nd ed. revised by J. Birch (London, 1878), II, 423.

117 (b) Plostellum poenicum p. 156

The noreg viewed diagrammatically from underneath, so as to show the arrangement of the wheels and axles on the chassis.

118 Vallus (reconstructed) p. 157

Lighter type of reaping machine or 'header'. The machine, which was propelled from the rear by a mule or donkey, removed the ears of grain as they passed between the rows of teeth, and deposited them in a hopper.

Drawn by H. Cüppers, from a reconstruction of the machine based on the Buzenol, Arlon and Trier reliefs (see Plates 14–16).

Dimensions, as estimated by E. P. Fouss: width of toothed frame: 1 m 20–1 m 30; width including wheels: 1 m 44–1 m 54; diameter of wheels (approx.): 70–75 cm.

119 Carpentum (reconstructed) p. 157

Heavier type of reaping machine or 'header', as described by Palladius (7. 1). The machine, which was of the tumbril type, with a large container, and smaller wheels than the machine illustrated in Fig. 118, was propelled from behind by an ox.

Drawn by L. A. Thompson on the basis of Palladius' description.

Dimensions: no estimate possible in the absence of any surviving representation.

I Miniature from a French manuscript of the fourteenth century, depicting farming operations.

2 (a) Large square digging-spade. (b)–(d) Iron single-bladed digging-hoes.

3 Digging with the *bidens*. Part of a large mosaic pavement from the Palace of the Emperors, Constantinople.

4 Winter operations in the vineyard. Above, *ablaqueatio* (échausselage); below, *sarritio* (sarclage). Parts of a large mosaic from Cherchel, Algeria.

5 (*a*) Heavy iron drag-hoe with five tines.

5 (*b*) Six-pronged iron drag-hoe.

6 (*a*) Heavy plain woodman's axe used for tree-felling.

6 (*b*) Plain woodman's axe, lighter than (*a*).

6 (*c*) Iron hatchet with plain hammer back.

6 (*d*) Iron adze-axe.

7 (*a*) Bronze tanged sickle.

7 (*b*) Iron tanged sickle.

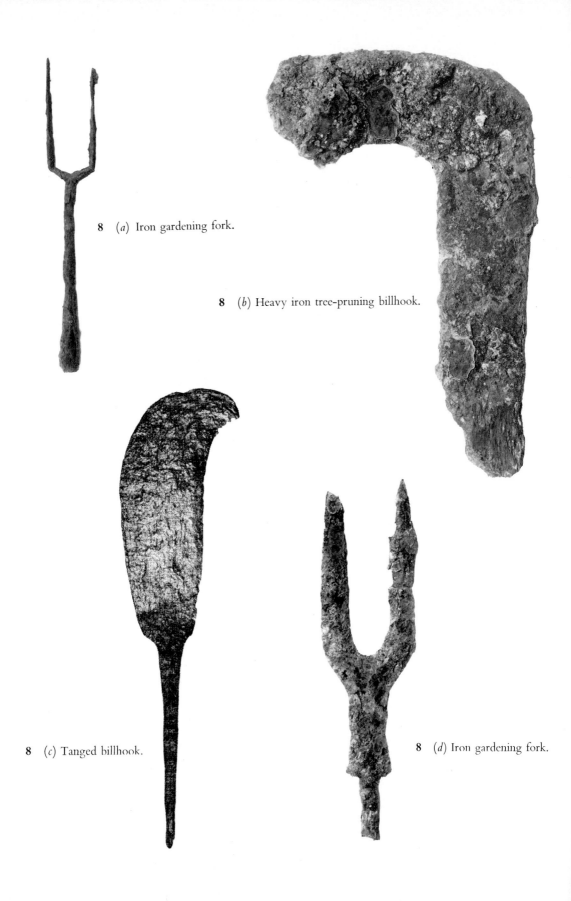

8   (*a*) Iron gardening fork.

8   (*b*) Heavy iron tree-pruning billhook.

8   (*c*) Tanged billhook.

8   (*d*) Iron gardening fork.

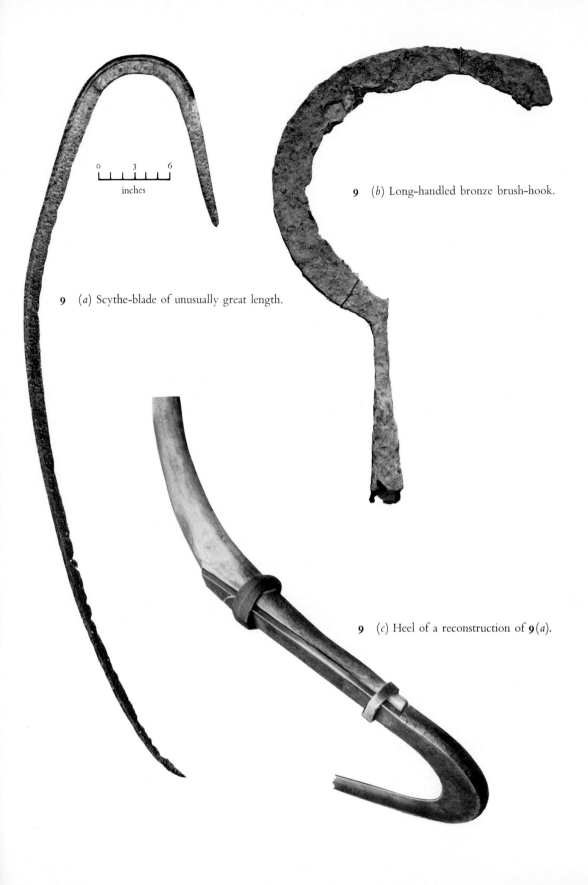

9   (*b*) Long-handled bronze brush-hook.

9   (*a*) Scythe-blade of unusually great length.

9   (*c*) Heel of a reconstruction of **9**(*a*).

0   3   6

inches

10 (*a*) Wooden votive model of a body-ard.

10 (*b*) Bronze votive model of a beam-ard.

11 (*a*) Bronze votive model of a keeled beam-ard.

11 (*b*) Bronze model of a ploughing team and ploughman.

12 Ploughing operations. Above, ploughing and clod-breaking; below, sowing and ploughing in the seed. Parts of the Cherchel mosaic.

13 Seasonal operations. Two panels from the Porte de Mars at Reims. Lower panel, left, haymaking (July); upper panel, right, reaping with the *vallus* (August).

14 Rear portion of a sculptured relief panel depicting a *vallus*.

15 Front portion of a sculptured relief panel depicting a *vallus*.

16   Central portion of a sculptured relief panel depicting a *vallus*.

APPENDICES

APPENDIX A

LIST OF IMPLEMENTS DISCUSSED, WITH NAMES OF AUTHORS IN WHOSE WORKS THEY OCCUR

	Cato	Varro (*LL*)	Varro (*RR*)	Colum.	Pliny	Pallad.	Isid.	Vergil
Acus	—	—	—	—	—	*L	—	—
Aratrum	V★O	★	★	★	★	(1) simplex (2) auritum	★	★
Ascia	—	—	—	—	—	★	★	—
Bidens	—	—	—	★	★	*L	—	—
Bipalium	★	—	★	★	★	—	—	—
Capreolus★	—	—	—	★	—	—	—	—
Crates	—	—	★	★	★	—	—	★
Cultellus	—	—	—	—	—	*L	—	—
Culter	—	—	—	★	★	—	—	—
Dolabella	—	—	—	★	—	—	—	—
Dolabra	—	—	—	★	—	★	—	—
Falcastrum★	—	—	—	—	—	—	★	—
Falcicula★ b.t.	—	—	—	—	—	—	*L	—
Falcula ★ *ruscaria*	V★	(rustaria) ★	—	—	—	—	—	—
Falcula vineatica	V★	—	★ (Cato)	★	—	—	—	—
Falx	—	★	★	★	★	*L	(falcis) ★	★
F. a tergo	—	—	—	—	—	*L	—	—
F. arboraria	V★O	★	—	—	—	—	—	—
F. faenaria	★O	★	—	—	★	★	—	—
F. lumaria	—	★	—	—	—	—	—	—
F. messoria	—	—	—	—	—	*L	—	—
F. putatoria	—	—	—	—	—	*L	—	—
F. silvatica	V★	—	—	—	—	—	—	—
F. sirpicula	V★	★	—	—	—	—	—	—
F. stramentaria	★O	—	—	—	—	—	—	—
F. veruculata★	—	—	—	★	—	—	—	—
F. vinitoria★	—	—	—	★	—	—	—	—
Ferrea(*furca*)★	V★O	—	★ (Cato)	—	—	—	—	—
Forfex	—	—	—	★	★	—	—	—
Fossorium	—	—	—	—	—	—	★	—
Furca	—	—	—	—	★ (= prop)	—	—	★

	Cato	Varro (LL)	Varro (RR)	Colum.	Pliny	Pallad.	Isid.	Vergil
Furcilla	—	—	★	—	—	—	★	—
Irpex	★O	★	—	—	—	—	—	—
Ligo	—	★	—	★	★	★L	★	—
Lupus★	—	—	—	—	—	★L	—	—
Marra	—	—	—	★	★	—	—	—
Mergae	—	—	—	★	—	—	—	—
Merges	—	—	—	—	★	—	—	(= sheaf) ★
Pala	V★O	★	—	★	★	—	—	—
Pala lignea	V★	—	—	—	—	—	★	—
Pastinum	—	—	—	★	—	★ (pastinatum)		—
Pecten	—	—	—	★	★	—	—	—
Plaumoratum★	—	—	—	—	★	—	—	—
Plostellum★ poenicum	—	—	★	—	—	—	—	—
Rallum	—	—	—	—	★	—	—	—
Rastelli	—	★	★	★	—	★	—	—
Rastella	V★	—	—	—	—	★	—	—
Rastrum	★O	—	—	★	★	★	★	★
Runco	—	—	—	—	—	★	★	—
Rutrum	V★O	★	—	—	—	★	—	—
Sarculum bicorne	—	—	—	—	—	★L	—	—
Sarculum simplex	★O	★	(Cato)	★	★	★	—	—
Scudicia★	—	—	—	—	—	—	★	—
Securis s.	★	—	—	—	—	★	—	—
Serrula	—	—	★	★	—	minores L	★	—
Traha	—	—	—	★	—	★	—	(trahea) ★
Tribulum	—	—	—	★	—	—	—	(tribula) ★
Vallus	—	—	—	—	★	★	—	—
Vanga	—	—	—	—	—	★L	—	—
Ventilabrum	—	★	★	★	—	—	★	—

Double implements

	Cato	Varro (LL)	Varro (RR)	Colum.	Pliny	Pallad.	Isid.	Vergil
Securis dolabrata	—	—	—	—	—	—	★	—
Ascia/rastrum	—	—	—	—	—	—	★	—

Parts of aratrum

	Cato	Varro (LL)	Varro (RR)	Colum.	Pliny	Pallad.	Isid.	Vergil
Aures	—	—	—	—	—	★(auritum)	—	★
Tabellae	—	—	★	—	★(tabula)	—	—	★
Buris	—	(bura) ★	—	—	—	—	★	★

	Cato	Varro (LL)	Varro (RR)	Colum.	Pliny	Pallad.	Isid.	Vergil
Parts of aratrum (cont.)								
Dentale	—	(dens) ★	—	—	—	—	★	★ (dentalia)
Manicula	—	★	—	—	—	—	—	—
Rallum	—	—	—	—	★	—	—	—
Rotulae	—	—	—	—	★	—	—	—
Stiva	—	★	—	★	—	—	—	★
Temo	—	★	—	★	—	—	—	★
Vomer	?★V	★	—	★	★	—	★	★?
form vomis	★	—	—	—	—	—	—	★

Note.

★ under an author indicates one or more occurrences in that author.

★ against the implement indicates that it is found only once.

L indicates that the word occurs in Palladius' list of equipment (RR 1. 43).

O indicates that the word occurs in Cato's list of equipment for olive cultivation.

V indicates that the word occurs in Cato's list of vineyard equipment.

(falcis) a word in parentheses indicates a spelling or meaning peculiar to that author.

(Cato) an author's name in parentheses indicates that the word occurs in a quotation from that author.

APPENDIX B

LIST OF MUSEUMS CONTAINING IMPORTANT COLLECTIONS OR INDIVIDUAL ITEMS DISCUSSED IN THE TEXT

Note. Since the publication in 1917 of Petrie's invaluable *Tools and Weapons*, no comprehensive collection of available specimens has been made. The list which follows is therefore far from complete, since it is based entirely on the author's personal knowledge of particular collections, or references in journals and catalogues available to him, and on references kindly supplied by many colleagues. A comprehensive catalogue is an obvious desideratum.

Arles, Provence, France. Museon Arelaten. The vast collection of material illustrating the history and customs of Provence, includes several wooden ards, both beam-ard and sole-ard types being represented.

Arlon, Luxemburg Province, Belgium. Musée Provincial Luxembourgeois. Rich in sculptured reliefs illustrating Gallo-Roman life. Contains the Arlon *vallus* (Plate 27).

Basel, Switzerland. Museum für Völkerkunde. Contains an important collection of wooden ploughs from many parts of the world.

Beaune, Côte d'Or, France. Musée du vin de Bourgogne. Contains a good collection of vine-dresser's knives of all periods, including some Gallo-Roman specimens, and much other material relating to the history of viticulture. The exhibits are arranged so as to illustrate the history of the implements and operations employed in viticulture (Lagrange, A. 'Catalogue du Musée du Vin', *Arts et traditions populaires*, XIII, 2, 1965, 107 ff.).

Bonn, West Germany. Landesmuseum. Contains an interesting collection of bronze models of implements, including yokes, forks, axes, billhooks, *bidentes*, shears and spades, as well as the important plough-model mentioned in the text (p. 143). (W. Haberey, in *Bonner Jahrb.* CXLIX, 1949, 98, Abb. 2.)

Cambridge, England. University Museum of Archaeology and Ethnology. Contains a good collection of Romano-British implements, including the Great Chesterford hoard (very long scythe-blades (Plate 9 (*a*)), mowers' anvils, reaping-hooks). (R. C. Neville in *Arch. Journ.* XIII, 1 (1856), 1 ff.)

Carpentras, Vaucluse, France. Musée Bernus. Contains a good collection of agricultural implements.

Chicago, U.S.A. Museum of Natural History (formerly Field Museum of Natural History). Contains a small but valuable collection of Roman implements from the villa of Julius Florus at Boscoreale, near Pompeii. The collection includes a number of vineyard *sarcula*, as well as the items illustrated on Plates 2, 5, 6, 7, 8.

Cirencester, Gloucestershire, England. Corinium Museum. Good collection of iron implements.

Colchester, Essex. Colchester and Essex Museum. Good collection of implements from the Roman colony of Camulodunum.

APPENDIX B

Cologne, West Germany. Römisch-Germanisches Museum. Contains some implements.

Edinburgh, Scotland. National Antiquities of Scotland. Contains a fine collection of implements from Trimontium (Newstead), including *dolabrae*, small *f. messoriae*, and a unique 7-tined *rastrum*. (J. Curle, *A Roman Frontier Fort and its People*, Melrose, 1911.)

Florence, Italy. Museo Archeologico. As well as a representative collection of manual implements (Plates, 2 (*c*), 5 (*a*)), the museum also contains the wooden plough-model from Telamon, in Etruria (Plate 10 (*a*)).

London, England. British Museum. The Sub-department of Prehistory and Roman Britain contains a good collection of implements from numerous Romano-British sites, including billhooks, sickles and socketed ploughshares, as well as a number of bar-shares. Contains two important plough-models from Piercebridge (Plate 11 (*b*)), and Sussex (Plate 11*a*)). The fine collection of La Tène implements includes a possible precursor of the *falx veruculata* (Appendix E (2)). Recent accessions include two scythe-blades closely resembling the Great Chesterford specimens (Appendix E (3)).

Mainz, West Germany. Römisch-Germanisches Zentralmuseum. Contains a large collection of implements drawn from many parts of the Rhineland and adjacent areas, and includes the plough-model from Cologne (Plate 10 (*b*)).

Montauban-Buzenol, Ardennes Province, Belgium. Musée. Contains the Gallo-Roman sculptures discovered in 1958, which include the well-known *vallus* (Plate 15).

Naples, Italy. Museo Nazionale. Contains the largest existing collection of Roman agricultural implements, drawn from the whole of Campania. Many items are still uncatalogued, but the entire collection is in process of being inventoried. There are large numbers of most of the common implements, except for the *bidens*, and the collection is particularly rich in *dolabrae* and *secures* in a great variety of weights and sizes (see Plates 2 (*a*), 6 (*a*), 6 (*c*), 7(*a*), 9 (*b*)).

Paris, France. Museé des antiquités nationales, Saint-Germain-en-Laye. The collection, which is housed in a former château, contains very large numbers of implements used in agriculture, forestry and woodworking, most of them well preserved. Most of the specimens come from a large hoard found at Compiègne. Billhooks form the largest single category, but there are numerous hoes and spades, as well as scythe-blades. (S. Reinach, *Catalogue illustré du musée des antiquités nationales*, Paris, t. I, 1917, t. II, 1921.)

Reading, England. City Museum. Contains a fine collection of implements from Calleva Atrebatum (Silchester), all catalogued. These include a fine series of *dolabrae, asciae/dolabrae*, and *secures*.

Rome, Italy. Museo di Villa Giulia. The splendid collection of Etruscan and early Italian antiquities includes the famous bronze plough-model from Arezzo (Fig. 103).

Rouen, France. Musée de ferronnerie. Le Socq-de-Tournelles. Specialized collection illustrating the history of iron-working, including implements.

Saalburg, near Frankfurt am Main, West Germany. Saalburgmuseum. This museum, which forms part of the reconstructed Roman fort at Saalburg on the German *limes*, contains a fine collection, in which all the usual agricultural implements are well represented. (L. Jacobi, *Das Römerkastell Saalburg*, Homburg vor der Höhe, 1897; *Saalburg jahrbuch*, Frankfurt am Main, 1910–. Considerable space is devoted in the journal to agricultural implements, with excellent drawings to scale, and full documentation.)

St Albans, Herts, England. Verulamium Museum. Important collection of iron implements, including several varieties of spade-irons (see text s.v. 'pala cum ferro').

Speyer, W. Germany. Landesmuseum. Contains a large collection of implements, viticulture and forestry being strongly represented.

Strasburg, France. Musée archéologique. Good collection of iron implements, including some agricultural specimens.

Trier, West Germany. Rheinisches Landesmuseum. Contains one of the best collections of implements used in viticulture, incorporating the contents of the former Weinmuseum of Trier. (S. Loeschke, 'Denkmäler vom Weinbau aus der Zeit der Römerherrschaft am Mosel, Saar und Ruwer', *Trierer Zeitschr.* VII, 1932.)

Valencia, Spain. Museo Provincial de Bellas Artes. Contains some agricultural implements, including a plough-model and several good *asciae/dolabrae*. For the plough, R. Volant y Simorra, 'Un arado ibérico', *Zephyrus*, IV (1953), 119 ff.

Virton, Luxemburg Province, Belgium. Musée gaumais. This museum, which is the folk museum for the area known as 'le pays gaumais', includes much Gallo-Roman material, particularly a model of the Buzenol *vallus*, by E. P. Fouss, and replicas of the Buzenol and Arlon sculptures. (*Le pays gaumais*, special edition, 1964.)

APPENDIX C

AGRICULTURAL IMPLEMENTS AND OPERATIONS DEPICTED IN MOSAICS CHIEFLY FROM ROMAN AFRICA

Note. In the following table the first entry is the inventory number in Thérèse Prêcheur-Canonge, *Inventaire des mosaïques romaines d'Afrique du nord*, in *La vie rurale en Afrique romaine*, Publ. de l'Univ. de Tunis, Paris, n.d. (1962), pp. 5 ff.

I. 1. ZLITEN. 1st cent. A.D. Tripoli, Museum.

   (*a*) Labour: hoeing.
   (*b*) Threshing corn with animals.
   (Cf. S. Aurigemma, *I mosaici di Zliten*, *Africa Italiana*, ii (1926), ch. III.)

I. 2. OUDNA. 2nd cent. A.D. Tunis, Musée du Bardo.

   (*a*) Ploughing.
   (*b*) Plough propped against a wall.
   (*c*) Olive-picking.
   (Cf. P. Gauckler, *Inventaire. . .* t. II, no. 362.)

I. 5. CHERCHEL. Early or middle 3rd cent. A.D. Cherchel, Museum.

   (i) Ploughing in a field planted with olives.
   (ii) Sowing and ploughing in the seed.
   (iii) *Ablaqueatio*.
   (iv) Hoeing.
   (Cf. J. Bérard, 'Une mosaïque inédite de Cherchel', *MEFR*, LII, 1935, 1 ff.)

I. 6. TABARKA. Early 4th cent. A.D. Tunis, Musée du Bardo.

   Central tableau. Vines.
   Third tableau. Vines.
   (Cf. P. Gauckler, *Inventaire*, t. II, no. 940.)

I. 9. UTICA. End of 4th cent. A.D. Tunis, Musée du Bardo.

   Bottom right of scene. Olive-picking.
   (Cf. P. Gauckler, *Inventaire*, suppl. to t. II, no. 929).

II. 11. LA CHEBBA.

   Summer with sickle.
   (Cf. P. Gauckler, *Inventaire*, t. II, no. 97.)

II. 16. CARTHAGE. Tunis, Musée du Bardo.

   Winter with *bidens*.
   (Cf. P. Gauckler, *Inventaire*, t. II, no. 627.)

II. 21. CARTHAGE. Tunis (Carthage), Musée St Louis.

   Winter armed with *sarculum*.
   (Cf. P. Gauckler, *Inventaire*, t. II, no. 825.)

II. 27. DOUGGA (Thugga). Tunis, Musée du Bardo.
Summer with sickle.
(Cf. P. Gauckler and A. Merlin, *Inventaire*, suppl. to t. II, no. 560*b*.)

II. 28. TIMGAD. Timgad, Musée.
Summer with billhook (?).
(Cf. de Pachtère, Inventaire, t. III, no. 166.)

II. 33. AUMALE. Alger, Musée.
Winter armed with *sarculum*.
(Cf. de Pachtère, *Inventaire*, t. III, no. 350.)

APPENDIX D

LIST OF ARTICLES REFERRING TO IMPLEMENTS, MACHINES OR OPERATIONS IN PAULY–WISSOWA–KROLL 'REALENCYCLOPÄDIE DER CLASSISCHEN ALTERTUMSWISSENSCHAFT'

Since many of the entries contain little or no reference to the agricultural meaning of the word in question, and since the articles vary greatly in value, brief critical notes have been provided.

Note 1. An asterisk prefixed to a word indicates that there is no entry.

Note 2. In Daremberg–Saglio, *Dictionnaire des Antiquités Grecques et Romaines*, the coverage is more nearly complete, and there is a classified index of agricultural terms.

I. IMPLEMENTS AND MACHINES

Aratrum	See s.v. 'Pflug', XIX, 2, 1461–72 (Drachmann)
Ascia	II, 2, 1522–3 (Mau)—of little value for agriculture
Bidens	III, 1, 428–9 (Olck)—little apart from main references
Bipalium	III, 1, 487–8 (Olck)—good discussion
Capreolus	III, 2, 1548–50 (Olck)—good discussion
Crates	IV, 2, 1682–5 (Olck)
Culter, cultellus	IV, 2, 1752–3 (Mau)—no references to agriculture
Dolabra, dolabella	V, 1, 1274–5 (Mau)—no references to agriculture
Falcastrum	See s.v. 'Sichel'
Falx	See s.v. 'Sichel'
Ferrea (*?furca, ?pala*)	See s.v. 'pala'
Forpex, forfex	VI, 2, 2853–6 (Mau)—good discussion
Furca, furcilla	VII, 1, 305–17 (Hitzig)—no references to agriculture
Irpex	—
Ligo	XIII, 1, 525 (Hug)
Lupus	XIII, 2 (no. 12, 3), 1852 (Grosse)—no discussion
Marra	—
Mergae	—
Pala	XVIII, 2, 2441–3 (E. Schuppe)
Pastinum	—
Pecten	XIX, 1, 7–11 (Herzog-Hauser)—only defines *pecten* as = *rastrum* or *irpex*!
Pflug	XIX, 2, 1461–72 (Drachmann)—full discussion; some *vomera* illustrated in the text
Plostellum poenicum	See s.v. 'tribula' (Hörle) (full references)
Rastelli	—

203

Rastrum	I A, I, 257–8 (Orth)—good discussion
Runco	I A, I, 1228 (Orth)
⋆Rutrum	—
Sarculum	I A, 2, 2436 (Orth)—inadequate treatment
⋆Scudicia	—
Securis	II A, 2, 1000 (Kleinfeller)—no reference to agriculture
Serra, serrula	II A, 2, 1738–42, no. I (Hug)—very good treatment
Sichel	II A, 2, 190–3 (Hug)—cursory treatment, but see s.v. 'Ernte'
Traha, trahea	VI A, 2, 2077–8 (Hörle)—full treatment with all essential references
Tribula, *tribulum, trebla*	VI A, 2, 2426 (Hörle)—full treatment with all essential references. See also s.v. 'dreschen', 'Getreide'
Vallus (1) = *vannus* (2) = *Mähmaschine*	VII A, I, 291–2 (Schleiermacher)—good treatment, but knows of no attempted reconstruction of a *vallus*!
⋆Vanga	—
⋆Ventilabrum	See s.vv. 'pala'; 'Ernte'

2. OPERATIONS

Drainage	V, 2, 1645 (Olck)—cursory; nothing on the implements used in drainage
dreschen	V, 2, 1700–6 (Olck)—comprehensive, including full discussion of *tribulum*
Ernte	VI, I, 472–82 (Olck)—inaccurate on technique of haymaking; good discussion of corn-harvesting
Pastinatio	XVII, 4, 2106–7 (Schuppe)—no reference to *pastinum*
Getreide	IX, 2, 1348 (Orth)—confusion between scythes and sickles! There is no entry s.v. 'Sense'

APPENDIX E

SOME SPECIAL PROBLEMS RELATING TO 'FALCES'

I. ON THE VARIOUS MEANINGS OF 'FALX'

(a) *Genera*

See Varro, *RR* 1. 22. 5 (reference to types of *f.*).
Pliny 18. 261 (short and long mowing scythes)

(b) *falx = falx messoria* (★ = *f. faenaria*)

Varro, *RR* 1. 49. 1; 1. 50. 1
★Varro, *RR* 1. 49. 2
Verg. *G.* 1. 348
Prop. 4. 2. 25
Ov. *Am.* 1. 15. 12 (cf. *Anth. Lat.* 477. 6)
Avien. *Arat.* 615
Ov. *Am.* 3. 10. 12; ★ *Pont.* 1. 53; *Fast.* 4. 914
Sen. *Phoen.* 371
Colum. 2. 17. 2; 2. 20. 30
Plin. 18. 169, 261, 296
Juv. 14. 149
Gell. 2. 29. 14
★Apul. *Met.* 6. 1
★Ulp. *Dig.* 50. 16. 31 (pratum est, in quo ad percipiendum fructum falce . . . opus est)
Firm. *Err.* 3. 2
Carm. epigr. 1238. 1 (saec. III)
Vulgate (several times)
Claud. 2. 6. 463; 28. 389
Carm. min. 31. 41
★Sidon. *Epist.* 1. 6. 3
Drac. *Mens.* 6
Ennod. *Epist.* 1. 3 p. 6, 14; *Carm.* 1. 3. 17

(c) *falx = falx vinitoria*

Verg. *Ecl.* 3. 11; 4. 40; *G.* 3. 365; *A.* 7. 179
Hor. *Carm.* 1. 31. 9
Tib. 1. 7. 34
and very freq. (36 entries all told, 17 from Columella)

(d) *falx = falx putatoria*

Cic. *Tusc.* 5. 65 (locum dumosum)
Catull. 64. 40
Lucr. 5. 936
Varr. *RR* 1. 40. 6
Colum. 5. 11. 4
Colum. *Arb.* 3. 4; 5. 2; 26. 4
Plin. 17. 109
Verg. *G.* 1. 157; 2. 416, 421
Hor. *Epod.* 2. 13
Ov. *Met.* 9. 383
Colum. 5. 6. 9; *Arb.* 29. 1 (cf. Plin. 17. 251)
Ov. *Met.* 14. 628 (cf. Colum. 10. 328); *Fast.* 4. 743
Colum. 5. 6. 11; 5. 6. 13, 14; 5. 9. 3
Calp. *Ecl.* 1. 21; 5. 98
Plin. 15. 4; 16. 251; 17. 69, 101, 200; 24. 57
Stat. *Silv.* 5. 2. 69
Quint. *Inst.* 2. 4. 11
Isid. 20. 14. 4
and very freq. in metaph. sense

(e) *falx = securis* (very rare)

Tib. 2. 5. 28
Prop. 4. 2. 59
Culex 86
Martial 6. 73. 1 (cf. Ov. *Epist.* 5. 22)

2. THE IDENTIFICATION OF THE 'FALX VERVCVLATA'

Our sole evidence for the implement is Columella *RR* 2. 20. 3:

Sunt autem metendi genera complura. multi falcibus veruculatis[1] atque iis[2] vel rostratis[3] vel denticulatis medium culmum secant, multi mergis, alii pectinibus spicam ipsam legunt.

The text has been much discussed; the following are the most important commentaries:

J. M. Gesner, *Scriptores Rei Rusticae Veteres Latini* (Leipzig, 1735).
  (*a*) Note *ad loc.*
    Vericulatas falces esse vericulo illo vel hastili munitos, quibus utuntur non foeniseces modo, sed avenae etiam, et brevioris cuiuscumque culmi messores.
  (*b*) Index s.v. *rostratus*
    rostratae (falces): quae continuam habent aciem.

J. G. Schneider, *Scriptores Rei Rusticae Veteres Latini* (Leipzig, 1794).
  (*a*) Note *ad loc.* s.v. *rostratis*.
    Gesneri Index interpretabatur, quae continuam habent aciem. Male! Ipse enim noster IV. 25 rostrum partem aduncam (falcis) interpretatur. Sunt igitur aduncae, denticulatae rectae. Ita nunc video interpretari *denticulatas* etiam n. Dickson II., p. 357, sed is tamen denticulas aciei addi volebat. In verutulatis plane errabat vir doctus quod a retis verriculi similitudine dictas putabat vericulatas.
  (*b*) Note *ad loc.* s.v. *veruculatis*.
    Gesnerus veruculatis edidit et recte de falce veru infixa seu hastili interpretatus est. Graeci δορυδρέπανα dicunt. A veru quod et ligneum et ferreum esse potest fit veruculum, quo usus est Plinius. Alii verutum dixerunt. Ex lectione Polit. et Sang. verutulatis effeci, quod magis probo veruculatis.

A. Steensberg, *Ancient Harvesting Implements* (Copenhagen, 1942), p. 212.
    According to Columella the straw was cut in the middle either with a toothed blade or with a beak-shaped blade . . . Sickles with a serrated edge are usually longer and more open than the smooth-edged balanced sickle. In all probability the implements illustrated in Daremberg and Saglio from Pompeii are such toothed sickles, though they are described as pruning-knives (Daremberg–Saglio, II. 2, p. 970, figs. 2869–70). It is possible that the beak-shaped blade in Columella is merely a smooth-edged balanced sickle.

Discussion

The implement is clearly not, as many have supposed,[4] a scythe. The scythe (*f. fenaria*) operates at ground level, and could not be used to cut a crop at middle height.

---

[1] verutulatis *SA*: vericulatis *R*.   [2] iis *S*: his *A*: his *vel* hiis *R*.
[3] rostratis *acd ed. Ald.*: nostratib; *SAR vett. codd.*
[4] E.g. Orth, *RE*, s.v. 'Getreide', col. 1348, refers to Columella's implement as 'die Sense (*falx foenaria, veruculata* (!)) zum Grasmähen gebraucht'. The same author later describes *f. enticulata* as the serrated sickle!

The word *veruculum* is the diminutive form of *veru*, a spit, or small spear (Gesner's *hastile*), so that the adjectival form should have the meaning 'fitted with a spit'. Steensberg's view, that Columella is referring merely to ordinary plain and serrated sickles must, I think, be rejected on the evidence of the text. Columella is not a writer who spends much time relating the obvious; hence we should not expect reference at 2. 20. 3 to the commonest method of all. Further, even if the use of *complura* can be restricted to three terms in a series, the following references to *mergae* and *pectines* suggest that the author is dealing with methods that were common, but not necessarily familiar to his readers.

Sickles vary in overall size, length of span, and curvature, according to the type and density of the crop to be reaped, the relative toughness of the straw, and personal, regional or traditional preference. The range of types and shapes is very great, but certain broad divisions may be noticed:

(*a*) *Smooth and serrated types.* Serrated sickles tend to be preferred in particularly dry climates, where the straw lacks moisture. Smooth sickles, like mowing scythes, work most efficiently where there is sufficient moisture to assist the action, which somewhat resembles that of shaving with an open razor. Steensberg is therefore wrong in stating that serrated sickles are usually longer and more open than smooth-edged balanced sickles; in the semi-desert areas of northern Ghana and northern Nigeria millet is reaped with a small, almost semi-circular sickle with a serrated edge. The language used by Columella indicates a narrower classification than this; his implements are evidently sub-species of a basic type called *f. veruculata*, and must therefore be similar in their basic design. Schneider (s.v. *rostratis*) is clearly right in stating that the difference between them is that between a curved (*rostratus*) and a straight (*denticulatus*) appearance. But this does not carry us far. We now come to Gesner's note on the passage.

(*b*) *Attachment or modification?* Gesner's note is somewhat confused; his opening sentence seems to suggest a simple form of attachment to a *scythe*, in the form of a spike, which was commonly used up to the late eighteenth century, when it was superseded by the cradle-scythe. The purpose of this form of attachment was to make the cumbersome task of gathering and stacking the sheaves easier by inserting a device which caused the cut sheaves to be laid in an orderly manner (Gesner's 'ordinate'). But he then goes on to say that the implement is also used in his day in cereal harvesting as well as in haymaking, and complicates the question still further by referring to yet another modified *falx*, which in this case is clearly a sickle, not a scythe, fitted with some kind of rake or comb (*rastellum quoddam sive pectinem adiunctum . . . falci*). An attachment of this kind would involve a complete change in the cutting operation; the reaper would have to employ a chopping instead of a sawing action. Although Gesner claimed to have seen such a modified form of the implement, it does not appear to have been recorded elsewhere, and we must conclude that he has confused the un-identified implement with one of the known modifications of the scythe. An alternative is to suppose that *veruculatus* implies a modification of the blade itself, and this is a much more feasible hypothesis. Reaping with the sickle is a multiple operation; the reaper first passes the point of the sickle into the standing crop ('putting in' the sickle); he next grasps a handful of heads (*manipulus*), and then cuts through the stalks at the determined height with a backward sawing move-ment. The wider the arc of the blade, the larger the individual bundle. On the supposition that 'veruculatus' means 'fitted with', or 'drawn out to form', a spit, such an extension of the blade would be useful in a heavy crop, for it would

facilitate the 'putting in' phase of the operation, and would increase the speed of the process. If we return to Gesner's note, we may notice that his phrase 'vericulo munitos' is not inconsistent with a spit-like extension of the blade. Schneider, on the other hand, is very misleading (note s.v. 'veruculatis'); he misinterprets Gesner with 'veru infixa', and then identifies the implement with δορυδρέπανον, which means a halberd, not an agricultural implement!

(c) *Modification. A surviving specimen of 'f. veruculata'?* The text of Columella, in spite of its lack of precision, seems to imply a modification or extension of the blade of the sickle rather than any form of attachment to it. The next step is to examine the surviving specimens of the implement in the hope of finding some feature pointing in this direction. Detailed investigations of specific implements, apart from the plough and the *falx vinitoria*, are rare. I have so far been unable to identify any such extension on any specimens of the Roman period, but there is an important and well-preserved specimen from the great La Tène hoard, now in the British Museum (inv. no. 80, 12–14, 7), which seems to provide a clue to the identification of our implement. This sickle, which is of the open type, with a rather shallow curvature of the blade, and a pronounced S bend to the tang, measures 32 cm across the span, with a blade of 48 cm. The blade is serrated for two-thirds of its length. At this point the serration ends, and the blade continues for 7·5 cm, and is then united to an extension, square in section, and tapering for the remaining 8·5 cm to end in a spike. The welding is clearly visible. This extension could without any distortion of language be described as a *veruculum*. It also resembles a fang (? *denticulatum*). The implement, though pre-Roman in date, meets very well the basic demands set by the phrase *falx veruculata denticulata*. Systematic examination of the immense number of surviving Roman sickles may produce a specimen to match the La Tène implement.

(d) *f. veruculata rostrata.* Assuming that the two varieties are varieties of an extended sickle, the adjective *rostrata* calls for a beak-shaped, as contrasted with the tooth-shaped *f. veruculata denticulata*. Notching at the tip of the blade occurs in later practice, e.g. in the 'Pembroke sickle' used up to a century ago in south Wales, but its purpose is now unknown. One may conjecture that a beaked extension on a shallow sickle would serve to hold the furthermost stalks of a bundle while the stroke was being completed, and thus speed up the process. In the absence of evidence, ancient or more recent, this is no more than a supposition.

The *f. veruculata* is not an isolated example of improvement in the design of this class of implement. The Naples museum contains two excellent specimens of extremely large sickles of the open shape, both very well balanced and easy to handle. In addition, we have Pliny's reference (*HN* 18. 261) to large two-handed implements used on the Gallic *latifundia*. These may well be the type represented on the Porte de Mars at Reims (for the classification of these implements see pp. 209 f.).

3. THE GREAT CHESTERFORD SCYTHE-BLADES

These remarkable scythe-blades have attracted no serious attention since their original publication by Neville more than a century ago. The common opinion is that they are so large and heavy that they would be extremely difficult to handle; yet all twelve specimens show signs of considerable wear. Nor are they unique; in his recent excavations on the site of the Roman villa at Barnsley Park,

Dorset, Dr Graham Webster unearthed two badly worn blades of the same size, with the same type of heavy flange, and the same type of long tang and small, upturned point.

The chief questions posed by these implements are: (1) what kind of handle was used, and how was it attached to the blade? (2) what purpose would be served by such very long and weighty scythes? In order to fit them into the pattern of the agrarian economy of late Roman Britain, both exhaustive laboratory tests of the blades, and detailed study of the economy of the two estates will be necessary. In the meantime, the following tentative suggestions are offered. On the question of the handle and its attachment it should be pointed out that the scythe normally has its tang sharply angled from the line of the blade, so that the angle between handle and blade is approximately a right angle, the plane of the handle being offset towards the operator. Now the tangs of these scythes are peculiar in three ways: they are unusually long, run in the same plane as the blades, and terminate in a small, upturned point. This means that the handle or snead will have been almost horizontal. Various shapes of snead are possible. Experiments have already shown that they will work moderately well with straight sneads; but the hand-grip for the right hand must be set much higher than any possible point on a straight handle; this then demands an extension to carry it to the snead. The hafting problem thus raises fundamental questions concerning the evolution of the implement (see pp. 99 ff.). Attachment of snead to tang was probably by lashing, the small upturned point serving as an end-stop. One of the Barnsley Park blades shows signs of riveting. Concerning the second problem, that of the purpose served by these extremely long scythes, only tentative conjectures can be made at this stage, pending further study both of the implements themselves and of the areas in which they were found. The Great Chesterford estate is on the chalk, and therefore on land with a good potential for grass; if hay was being cut on a large scale very large implements of this type will have effected a considerable saving in labour (see e.g. Pliny, *HN* 18. 261 on the large two-handed scythes used on the Gallic *latifundia*). The time factor is also important in these northern regions; in Italy in Pliny's time haymaking started at the beginning of June, the driest month of the year. In Britain, however, the hay is, and presumably was then, cut much later than this, at a time when summer storms can seriously damage or even ruin the crop, giving rise to the well-known proverb about making hay while the sun shines. The problems posed by these scythes are complex, and much essential information is lacking, but with increasing knowledge of the economic conditions of late Roman Britain it may be possible to place these remarkable implements in a socio-economic pattern which is at present known to us only in vague outline.

4. THE GALLIC SCYTHES FROM THE PORTE DE MARS

A. de Laborde, *Les monuments de la France* (Paris 1816), pl. CXIII (reproducing the drawings made by H. Bence). H. Stern, *Le calendrier de 354: étude sur son texte et ses illustrations* (Paris, 1953), p. 208 and pl. XXXVIII, fig. 4. Idem, 'Le cycle des mois de la Porte de Mars à Reims' in Hommages à Albert Grenier, t. 3, *Coll. Latomus* (1962), pp. 1441–6 and pl. CCLXXXIX.

The July Tableau (shown on Plate 13)

Three labourers are represented in varying attitudes. To left, a labourer, his head turned to the left, leaning on the shaft of a sickle-shaped implement, which

is standing upside down. Centre, a labourer sharpening a similar implement with a honing stone. The implement is held in his right hand, the handle resting on a stone block so as to raise the blade of the implement to eye level. His right foot is on the ground, his left on the block, supporting the handle with his thigh. He is working towards the point of the blade. To his right a third labourer in action. The position of his legs indicates that he has reached the end of the back-swing, the implement being grasped by his right hand close to the butt of the blade, while the left hand is obscured by his body which faces the back wall of the panel. All three labourers wear a simple loose-fitting one-piece garment gathered in at the waist and hitched up well above the knee. They are bare-footed. The implements are of identical pattern, consisting of a large sickle-shaped blade, with a pronounced backward curvature behind the handle, the point of the blade projecting well beyond the middle of the blade. The curved blade is elliptical, approximating to circular form, and the gap between point and butt is fairly small. In shape they resemble the English brush-hook, still used for hedge-trimming and brush-cutting.

Dimensions of the implement

Stern ('Le cycle . . .', p. 1443) estimates as follows:

If the man on the right is 1 m 70 tall (= 5 ft 10 in.), then the total length will be 1 m 30 (= 4 ft 4 in.), the handle will be 0 m 90 (= 3 ft 1 in.), and the axes of the blade will be of the order of 0 m 60 and 0 m 35 (= 2 ft and 1 ft 3 in.). The dimensions are very large for this class of implement (half as large again as the open-bladed sickle from Pompeii—Fig. 52, p. 80).

Operational technique

Since the adjoining panel to the right (for August) depicts harvesting corn with a *vallus*, it is reasonable to assume that this scene depicts haymaking.[1] We are at once reminded of Pliny's reference to the longer Gallic scythes (*HN* 18. 261). The actual movements of the operator are not absolutely clear, and the implement is obviously not a conventional Roman scythe (see Figs. 76 and 77). It is, however, a two-handed implement, as may be seen not only by the position of the right hand, but by the labourer's posture; he takes a big step to the left, his body slightly bent in that direction to counterbalance the sweep of the implement to the right. It is in fact the posture of a man mowing with the full-length scythe. With such an implement it would be easy to cut the hay at middle height (Pliny, *loc. cit.*). But the curvature of the blade does present an operational problem. Possibly there is some artistic licence in the almost semicircular curvature? H. Stern ('Le cycle . . .', p. 1444) has no doubt that the implement is Pliny's Gallic *f. faenaria*. A. Steensberg (*Ancient Harvesting Implements*, pp. 190–209 and 223–32) distinguishes, alongside the sickles, a *short* and a *long* scythe. The first was spread in South Germany in the first century A.D. and the second much later. The Reims panel seems to show that at the end of the second century A.D. and the beginning of the third we have in Gaul an intermediate type which must have come into use there before the end of the first century (Pliny died in A.D. 79).

---

[1] Stern, 'Le cycle . . .', p. 1445, cites five supporting Gallo-Roman and Carolingian references for July as the haymaking month in this region.

5. ON THE VARIOUS MEANINGS OF THE TERM 'FERRAMENTVM'

The term 'ferramentum', which is used to denote iron tools as a class (e.g. in Cato's inventories, *De Agri Cultura* 10. 3 and 11. 4), is also employed occasionally to denote a specific implement, e.g. the mowing scythe (*falx faenaria*), or the vine-dresser's knife (*falx vinitoria*). The references cited below are typical, not exhaustive.

(*a*) generic use: *f.* = iron implement (see also s.vv. 'rastrum', 'ascia')

Corp. Gloss. s.v. 'bipalium'. bipalium (-llum *codd.*) ferramentum rusticum IV 25. 60.

Cato, *RR* 10. 3 (inventory of equipment for an oliveyard). 'Iron implements as follows: '8 forks, 8 hoes . . .': ferramenta: ferreas VIII, sarcula VIII . . .

(*b*) *ferramentum = falx fenaria*

Colum. 2. 17. 4 (on keeping up meadows). 'We must . . . scatter the heaps of earth which the drags usually make at the turnings, so that the *mower's scythe* may not strike against anything': grumosque, quos ad versuram plerumque tractae faciunt crates, disiciamus ita, necubi *ferramentum faenisecis* possit offendere.

(*c*) *ferramentum = falx vinitoria*

Pallad. 12. 3. 1 (on restoring an old vine). '(After close pruning) the vine should be struck with the sharp point of the *iron* . . .': vinea . . . angustius putata . . . acuto *ferramenti* mucrone feriatur . . .

The usage is quite natural, and in neither of the passages cited is there any doubt as to the identity of the implement.

APPENDIX F

SERVIUS AND SCHOL. DAN. ON VERGIL
G. 1. 170–2; 174

170   IN BVRIM in curvaturam: nam buris est curvamentum aratri, dictum quasi βοὸς οὐρά quod sit in similitudinem caudae bovis. alii burim curvaturam temonis, quae supra est, et quod est infra urvum dicunt: buris enim ut curvetur, ante igni domatur, id est amburitur; unde et quae naturaliter inveniuntur curvae, ita dicuntur. Varro ait †totum burim indici ab urbe†.

172   BINAE AVRES duae, quibus latior sulcus efficitur. DVPLICI APTANTVR DENTALIA dentale est lignum, in quo vomer inducitur. duplici autem dorso aut lato, ut [III, 87] et duplex agitur per lumbos spina: aut re vera duplici, cuius utrumque eminet latus: nam fere huiusmodi sunt vomera in Italia.

174   STIVAQVE manica aratri, qua regitur, id est gubernaculum. Cicero in Scauriana: a stiva ipsa mecum homines loquebantur. currus autem dixit propter morem provinciae suae, in quo aratra habent rotas, quibus iuvantur.

170   temonem burim dici a bubus. Thilo.

Brevis Expositio

170   IN BVRIM pars aratri, quae curvatur, buris dicta, ut videtur Modesto, a bustione: igni enim flectitur, quasi βοὸς οὐρά quod sit in similitudinem caudae bovis.

172   BINAE AVRES quibus latior sulcus efficitur.

171   TEMO aircurarathir.[1]

172   DENTALIA id est in quibus vomer inducitur: hic neutraliter, postmodum masculino genere [G. I, 261] durum procudit arator.

174   STIVA aratri gubernaculum. CVRRVS ideo 'currus' propter morem provinciae suae, in qua aratra habent rotas.
   Nonius, p. 80, 16: bura dicitur pars aratri posterior decurvata. Vergilius Georgicon lib. i 'continuo . . . in burim'.

[1] The gloss is Irish; *arathir* is gen. of *arather*, a plough.

APPENDIX G

TERMINOLOGY OF THE PLOUGH AND ITS PARTS

I. TYPES OF PLOUGH AND THE TERMS USUALLY APPLIED TO THEM

(a) *Symmetrical ploughs (ards), Latin 'aratrum'*

beam-ard	Fr. araire manche-sep
bow-ard	Fr. araire chambige
body-ard ⎱	
sole-ard ⎰	Fr. araire dental
wheeled ard	Fr. araire avant-train

(b) *Asymmetrical ploughs*

mouldboard plough ⎱	
turn-wrest plough ⎰	Fr. charrue

2. TABLE OF THE PARTS OF THE PLOUGH (see p. 214)

Notes

1. G = Gow (*JHS*, LIV, 1914, 249–75); J = Jope (*HT*, II, 81 ff.). Particular reference is made in the table (p. 214) to the terms employed in A. S. F. Gow's 'The Ancient Plough', since this work is still frequently quoted. The author uses the old popular terms 'stock', 'pole' and 'tail', and this lack of precision often makes his argument difficult to follow; thus, in a discussion of the historical evolution of the Roman plough, he writes: 'the pole, not the stock, is now the most conspicuous member in this implement'.

2. The numerous emendations of 'plaumorati' (Pliny 18. 172) fall into two groups: (a) those which assume a corruption of the two words 'plaustrum', 'a wheeled vehicle', and 'aratrum', 'a plough', e.g. 'plaustrarati' (Harduinus); (b) a much larger number, which assume a Gallic or Germanic origin of the word, e.g. 'plomerat', 'plogmetrat', deriving from older forms of the German words 'Pflug', 'a plough', and 'Rad', 'a wheel'. The most ingenious of these attempts was Baist's 'ploum Raeti'—which the Raetians call 'ploum'.[1] But the problem of the text remains unsolved.

3. THE VERGILIAN PLOUGH: R. AITKEN'S VIEW

The view put forward in the text (above, pp. 128 ff.), that Roman ploughs were commonly of the sole-ard type, has been challenged in an important paper by R. Aitken ('Virgil's Plough', *JRS*, XLVI, 1956, 97 ff.). The author proceeds from the assumption that Vergil was not writing a generalized account of the plough

G. Baist, 'Ploum-plaumarati: (Plin. XVIII. 172)', *Archiv für latein. Lexicogr. u. Gramm.* III (1886), 285–6. The most recent study is that of L. Deroy, 'La racine étrusque plau-plu et l'origine rhétique de la charrue à roues', *Studi Etruschi*, XXXI (1963), 99–121.

2. THE PARTS OF THE PLOUGH: COMPARATIVE TABLE

Latin	Latin (dial.)	Greek	English	English (dial.)	French	German	Italian
Dentale, dentalia (Vg.)	dens	ἔλυμα	Sole, share-beam	Plough-stock, stock (G, J)	Dental, sep	Sohle, Scharbaum, Pflughaupt	Il ceppo
Vomer, vomis	—	ὕνις	Ploughshare, share	—	Soc	Schar	Il vomere
Buris	Bura, urvum	γύης	Plough-beam	Draught-beam (J), pole	Chambige	Krümmel	La bure
Temo	—	ἱστοβοεύς	Yoke-beam	Draught-pole (J), pole*	Timon	Deichsel	Il timone
Stiva	—	ἐχέτλη	Stilt	Plough-tail, tail (G)	Mancheron, manche	Sterz	La stiva
Manicula, manibula (Va.)	—	—	Hand-grip	Handle (J)	—	—	La manovella
Rallum	—	—	Plough-staff	—	—	Pflugstab	—
Aures (Vg.) of aratrum auritum (Pallad.)	—	—	—	—	Orillon	—	—
Tabellae (Varr.), tabula (Plin.)	—	—	Ridging-boards	—	Versoir-planche	Streichbrett	—

* *Note:* In Gow, *art. cit.*, 'pole' refers to the single pole (= *temo* + *buris*).

at *G.* 1. 162 ff., but that he had a specific type of implement in mind; indeed he goes further and interprets Vergil's description of the making of a plough 'in the light of a visit to a craftsman's shop' (Aitken, p. 97). According to Aitken, Vergil's plough belongs to the category known as the beam-ard, in which the curved plough-beam (*bura, buris*), is pierced by a single body–handle unit (see Fig. 99, p. 127) or by a separate body and handle. The discussion is arranged in terms of the order of the parts as described by Vergil, viz. 'beam (*buris*) with pole (*temo*) as accessory; share-beam (*dentalia*); and handle (*stiva*)' (*loc. cit.*). After a brief discussion of the *bura* or *buris*, and before continuing to discuss the other parts of the plough, Aitken remarks: 'The inference is irresistible that the plough described belongs to the familiar group of SW European ploughs in which the beam, normally curved . . . is the master part on which the others depend' (p. 98). On the same page, and before the continuation of the discussion— indeed before it has got under way—the reader is presented with a drawing of a composite plough of the beam-ard type, made up from modern Spanish records, and listed as 'Fig. 13. PLOUGH OF "VIRGILIAN" TYPE'. The only argument advanced at this stage is that Vergil has clearly identified the beam (*buris*) with the plough itself, and that therefore his plough is a beam-ard; that is, the beam is conceived as 'the master part, on which the others depend'. What Aitken appears to over-look at this stage is the fact that the only point he has demonstrated so far is the *prominence* of the curved beam. Now it cannot be denied that the *buris* is a key part of the plough; but its position is equally important in the sole-ard: if the beam fails to take an unusual strain and fractures (Varro, *RR* 1. 19), the result will be equally disastrous whether the plough is a beam-ard or a sole-ard. The curved plough-beam was equally prominent in ancient Greek ploughs, which, so far as the evidence goes, were uniformly of the sole-ard type (see, for example, Hesiod, *Works and Days*, 427, 430; Gow, *art. cit.*). As for the argument that Vergil must have been describing a beam-ard because he refers to the form of the curved plough (*curvi aratri*), might one not claim on a similar line of argument that the *vomer* was the key part of the plough since the word is very frequently used to refer to the whole plough of which it is only a part, and that a detachable one? So far, no conclusive evidence in favour of the proposed identification. Aitken then proceeds to discuss the other parts in turn, with a long section on the meaning of the phrase 'duplici dentalia dorso' (*G.* 1. 172). According to Aitken, the use of the verb 'aptantur' in relation to the beam implies a beam-ard, since in this type of plough the sole (*dentalia*) is attached to the plough-beam (*buris*), not the beam to the sole, as in the sole-ard. This is surely to stretch the language of Vergil: 'dorso' is not the first, nor indeed is it the only, indirect object of the verb 'aptantur', and the precision of meaning required by Aitken's interpretation seems to be forced. Apart from this specific criticism, such precision as is required by Aitken's thesis seems out of keeping with Vergil's style and method. We have already seen (above, p. 7) that the only other reference to agricultural implements in *Georg.* 1 (apart from passing mention of familiar items such as 'falx'), viz. *vv.* 163–4, shows none of this precision: all three of the implements mentioned by Vergil are important, but no description of any of them is offered, and the poet's choice would seem to have been based primarily on the effective sound-pattern of 'tribulaque traheaeque et iniquo pondere rastri'. Discussion of the mind of an ancient poet at work is a highly subjective activity, and should be treated with the greatest caution. Thus Aitken's beam-ard theory cannot be substantiated by the evidence he adduces in its support; nor does he improve his argument by the detailed discussion of the present distribution in Italy and

elsewhere in Europe of the various types of ard, valuable though this part of the paper is to the student of the history of plough-types. Although Aitken claims to identify Vergil's plough he does in fact quite properly use a variety of supporting evidence from the Roman agronomists as well as from later commentators in support of his theory. But his use of this evidence is by no means exhaustive, nor does he cite all the Vergilian evidence that might be of use in reaching finality; in particular there are operational problems connected with the position and functioning of the *stiva* which Aitken appears to overlook; I refer to the upward and downward pressure on the handle. In the 'Virgilian' plough as conceived by Aitken (see, for example, his fig. 13, p. 98), the natural tendency for the share to dig itself into the ground must be counteracted by lifting the *stiva*, whereas the opposite is true of the horizontal sole-ard; in the latter case downward pressure is required from time to time to keep the plough from jumping out of the furrow: hence the regular phrases used both by Vergil and the agronomists, 'depresso . . . aratro' (Vergil) 'stivae inniti' (Columella); hence too the backward extension of the sole to form a platform on which the ploughman could set his foot to keep the plough from riding up. The effect of this evidence is to suggest that sole-ards were commoner than beam-ards. Aitken's treatment of the problem of the share is far from satisfactory; he admits (*art. cit.* p. 102) that the tanged share, which is necessary to his interpretation of the phrase 'duplici dorso', is not found in Italy south of Emilia or in Sardinia; yet in spite of this, he insists that 'Pliny's "genus (vomerum) . . . vulgare, rostrati vectis" (*NH* 18, 48) was undoubtedly of this form'. We have already demonstrated (above, p. 135) that Pliny's 'genus vulgare' can, on the available evidence, be equally convincingly interpreted as referring to a socketed share. He also admits the fact that in the Romance languages *vomer* never denotes a tanged share, but goes on to suggest that for Virgil, as for Pliny, *vomer* is a generic term. There is surely a grave inconsistency here: if the specific and restricted meaning of *vomer* cannot legitimately be dated back from modern to ancient Italian terminology, why should the present distribution of beam-ards in Italy be used as evidence for its distribution in Vergil's day? Finally, there is an important error on p. 102, in the discussion of ridged share-beams, where Drachmann's *R-E* article is cited in support of the statement that 'no iron share of any kind has been recorded for Italy'. This is not correct: there is a very badly worn socketed share from Pompeii in the National Museum at Naples (Cat. N. 110506; Petrie, *TW*, pl. 57, no. 34—see Fig. 110 (*a*)). Aitken's article then is an important contribution to the difficult subject of the design of Roman ploughs (especially valuable is his discussion of the terms 'aures' and 'dentalia'); his main contention, however, remains an ingenious but unproved hypothesis.

SELECT BIBLIOGRAPHY

Note. Appendix D contains a list of *R-E* articles on implements and operations. Items marked ★ were not accessible to the author.

Aitken, R. 'Vergil's plough', *JRS*, XLVI (1956), 97–106.

Angelini, F. *Indagine sugli attrezzi a mano in agricoltura.* Roma, 1939.

Applebaum, E. S. 'Some Aspects of Romano-British Land-systems of the Lowland Zone', pp. 181–206. Diss. Oxford, 1952.

Baist, G. 'Ploum-plaumarati: (Plin. XVIII. 172)', *Archiv für latein. Lexicogr. u. Gramm.* III (1886), 285–6.

Behlen, H. 'Der Pflug und das Pflügen'. Diss. Dillenburg, 1904.

Benoît, F. *Histoire de l'outillage rural et artisanale.* Paris, 1947.

Berner, U. 'Die Handhabung des Ackergerätes in ihrer Bedeutung für die Feststellung von Zusammenhängen', *Anthropos*, LV (1960).

Berner, U. 'Zur Typologie und Nomenklatur der Pflüge', *Zeitschr. für agrargesch. u. agrarsoziologie*, XI, 1 (1963), 1 ff.

Blümlein, C. *Bilder aus dem Römisch-Germanischen Kulturleben.* München–Berlin, 1926.

Braungart, R. *Die Ackerbaugeräthe in ihren praktischen Beziehungen sowie nach ihrer urgeschichtlicher und ethnographischer Bedeutung.* Heidelberg, 1881.

Brentjes, B. 'Der Pflug—ein Forschungsbericht', *Zeitschr. für agrargesch u. agrarsoziologie*, III, 1 (1955), 112 ff.

Cencelli, A. and Latrionte, G. *Macchine Agricole.* Milano, 1919.

Childe, V. G. 'The balanced sickle', *Aspects of Archaeology in Britain and Beyond.* Essays presented to O. G. S. Crawford, ed. by W. F. Grimes, pp. 39–48. London, 1951.

Corder, P. 'Some spade-irons from Verulamium', *Arch. Journ.* C (1943), 224–31.

Cou, H. F. 'Antiquities from Boscoreale', *Field Museum Publications*, 152, Anth. ser. 7, 4 (1912), 210 ff.; pls. CLXIII–CLXVI. Chicago.

Crawford, O. G. S. 'A primitive threshing-machine', *Antiquity*, IX (1935), 335–9.

Curle, J. *A Roman Frontier-post and its People.* Glasgow, 1911.

Curwen, E. C. 'Tribulum-flint from Sussex', *Antiquity*, XI (1937), 93 ff.

Curwen, E. C. 'Implements and their wooden handles', *Antiquity*, XXI (1947), 155–8.

Curwen, E. C. Review of A. W. Brøgger, *Sigd, Ljå og Snidell av det Norske Jordbruks Ophav*, Oslo, 1933, in *Antiquity*, VIII (1934), 237 f.

Del Pelo Pardi, G. 'Gli attrezzi da taglio per uso agricolo in Italia', *Nuovi Annali dell'Agricoltura*, Roma, 1933.

Denis, E. de St. 'Falx vinitoria', *Rev. arch.* XLI (1943), 163–76.

Dias, J. *Os Arados Portugueses.* Coimbra, 1948.

Dieck, A. 'Terminologie der Pflugteile, ältern Pflugarten und des Pfluges', *Zeitschr. für agrargesch. u. agrarsoziologie*, LI (1951), 160 ff.

Evans, J. 'On some iron tools and other articles formed of iron', *Arch.* LIV (1894), 139–56.

Faucher, D. *L'Homme et la machine.* Paris, 1955.

Feldhaus, F. M. *Die Säge.* Berlin, 1921.

Fenton, A. 'Early and traditional cultivating implements in Scotland', *Proc. Soc. Ant. Scot.* XCVI (1962–3), 264 ff.

Fouss, E. P. 'Le "vallus" ou moissonneuse des Trévires', *Le pays gaumais*, XIX (1958), 130 ff.

Fussell, G. E. *The Farmer's Tools, 1500–1900*. Melrose, 1952.

Fussell, G. E. and Kenny, A. 'L'équipement d'une ferme romaine', *Annales*, *(ESC)* 21. 2 (1966), 306–23.

★Glosik, J. 'Sur les faux antiques', *Z. otchtani wieków*, XXVII (1961), 78 ff. (in Polish).

Gow, A. S. F. 'The ancient plough', *JHS*, XXXIV (1914), 249–75.

Gray, A. *The Plough-wright's Assistant*. Edinburgh, 1808.

Haberey, W. *Bonn. Jahrb.* CXLIX (1949), 94 ff.

Harrison, F. 'The crooked plough', *Class. Journ.* II (1916), 323–32.

Harrison, J. E. 'Mystica vannus Iacchi', *JHS*, XXIII (1903), 292–304; XXIV (1904), 241–54.

Haudricourt, A. G. and Delamarre, M. J.-B. *L'Homme et la charrue à travers les âges*. 3rd ed. Paris, 1955.

Hawkes, C. F. C. 'The Roman villa and the heavy plough', *Antiquity*, IX (1935), 339–41.

Hopfen, H. J. *Farm Implements for Arid and Tropical Regions*. 2nd ed. Rome, 1963.

Huggard, E. R. and Owen, T. H. *Forest Tools and Instruments*. London, 1960.

Jaberg, C. and Jud, J. *Sprach- und Sachatlas Italiens und der Südschweiz*. Zürich, 1928–40.

Jacobi, L. *Das Römerkastell Saalburg*, pp. 413 ff. Homburg vor der Höhe, 1897.

Jope, E. M. 'Agricultural Implements', *A History of Technology*, ed. C. Singer, II, 81–102. Oxford, 1956.

Karslake, J. P. B. 'Plough coulters from Silchester', *Ant. J.* XIII (1933), 455–63.

★Kolendo, J. 'Techniques rurales: la moissonneuse antique en Gaule romaine', *Annales (ESC)*, XV (1960), 1009–114.

Kolendo, J. 'On harvesting techniques in Roman Gaul', *Przeg. Hist.* LI (1960) (in Czech).

Lagrange, A. 'Catalogue des Salles des travaux de la vigne et du vin et des métiers auxiliaires du Musée du Vin à Beaune', *Arts et traditions populaires*, XIII, 2 (1965), 107–80.

Lagrange, A. 'Notes sur le vocabulaire viticole', *REL*, XXV (1947), 77–80.

Lebel, P. 'La moissonneuse gallo-romaine', *REA*, X (1959), 70–4.

Le Gall, J. 'Les "falces" et la "faux"', *Ét. d'arch. class.* II à la mém. de M. Launey, *Annales de l'Est*, Mém. 22 (1959), 4, 55–72.

Leser, P. *Die Entstehung und Verbreitung des Pfluges*. Münster in Westphal., 1931.

Leser, P. *Westöstliche Landwirtschaft*, Festschr. P. W. Schmidt. *Anthropos* (1928), 416 ff.

Liger, A. *La ferronnerie ancienne et moderne*. Paris, 1873–5.

Loeschke, S. 'Denkmäler vom Weinbau aus der Zeit der Römerherrschaft am Mosel, Saar und Ruwer', *Trierer Zeitschr.* VII (1932).

Manning, W. H. 'The plough in Roman Britain', *JRS*, LIV (1964), 54–65.

Massingham, H. J. *Country Relics*. Cambridge, 1939.

Mayor, R. *As Geórgicas de Virgilio*. Lisbon, 1948.

★Meehuizen, L. S. 'De gallische maaimaschine van Buzenol', *Westerheim*, IX (1960), 24–7.

Mertens, J. 'La moissonneuse de Buzenol', *Urschweiz*, XXII (1958), 49–53.

Mertens, J. 'Sculptures romaines de Buzenol', *Le pays gaumais* (1958), 31 ff.

Nightingale, M. 'Ploughing and field shape', *Antiquity*, XXVII (1953), 20–6.

Parain, Ch. 'Das Problem der tatsächlichen Verbreitung der technischen Fortschritte in der römischen Landwirtschaft', *Z. für Geschichtswissenschaft*, Heft 2, VIII Jahrg. (1960), 357–66.

Payne, F. G. 'The plough in ancient Britain', *Arch. Journ.* CIV (1947), 82–111.

Petrie, Sir W. M. Flinders. *Tools and Weapons*. London, 1917.

Rau, L. von. 'Mähewerkzeuge', *Z. f. E.* XXII (1890). 153 ff.

Reith, A. 'Werkzeuge der Holzbearbeitung: Säge aus vier Jahrtausenden', *Saalburgjahrb.* XVII (1958), 47–60.

Renard, M. 'Technique et agriculture en pays trévire et rémois', *Latomus*, XVIII (1959), 77–108, 307–33.

Richmond, I. A. 'Trajan's army on Trajan's Column', *PBSR*, XIII (1935), 1–40.

Savastano, L. *Arboricoltura*. Napoli, 1917.

Scheuermeier, P. *Bauernwerk in Italien, der italienischen und Rätoromanischen Schweiz*. Erlenbach–Zürich, 1943.

Schmidt, L. 'Spatenforschungen. Zu einigen Arbeitsgeräten des frühen Ackerbaues', *Archiv für Völkerkunde*, VIII (Wien, 1953), 76 ff.

Steensberg, A. *Ancient Harvesting Implements*, transl. by W. E. Calvert. Copenhagen, 1943.

Steensberg, A. (ed.). *Research on Ploughing Implements*. Copenhagen, 1956.

Stern, H. 'Le cycle des mois de la Porte de Mars à Reims', *Hommages à Albert Grenier*, t. 3, *Coll. Latomus* (1962), pp. 1441–6.

Stern, H. 'Représentations gallo-romaines des mois', *Gallia*, IX (1957), 22–30.

Thielscher, P. *Des Marcus Cato Belehrung über die Landwirtschaft*. Berlin, 1963.

Timm, A. 'Zur Geschichte der Erntegeräte', *Zeitschr. für agrargesch. und agrarsoziologie*, IV (1956), 29 ff.

van Ooteghem, J. 'La moissonneuse gauloise', *Ét. classiques*, XXVII (1959), 129 ff.

Werth, E. *Grabstock, Hacke und Pflug*. Ludwigsburg, 1954.

Zryd, P. 'Ein römische Pflugwendnagel aus Augst', *Urschweiz*, XI (1947), 56–8.

GENERAL INDEX

INDEX OF GREEK WORDS

INDEX OF LATIN WORDS

This index includes Latin names of implements and Latin terms referred to in the body of the text.

LIST OF PASSAGES CITED